FINISH FORTY AND HOME

The Untold World War II Story
of B-24s in the Pacific

Phil Scearce

Number 5 in the Mayborn Literary Nonfiction Series

UNIVERSITY OF NORTH TEXAS PRESS

FRANK W. MAYBORN GRADUATE INSTITUTE OF JOURNALISM

DENTON, TEXAS

10 9 8 7 6 5 4 3 2 1

Permissions:
University of North Texas Press
1155 Union Circle #311336
Denton, TX 76203-5017

The paper used in this book meets the minimum requirements of the American National Standard for Permanence of Paper for Printed Library Materials, z39.48.1984. Binding materials have been chosen for durability.

Library of Congress Cataloging-in-Publication Data

Scearce, Phil, 1962-
 Finish forty and home : the untold World War II story of B-24s in the Pacific / Phil Scearce. -- 1st ed.
    p. cm. -- (Number 5 in the Mayborn literary nonfiction series)
  Includes bibliographical references and index.
  ISBN 978-1-57441-316-8 (cloth : alk. paper)
  1. Scearce, Herman, 1925- 2. United States. Army--Biography. 3. Soldiers--United States--Biography. 4. Radio operators--United States--Biography. 5. Radar operators--United States--Biography. 6. B-24 bomber--History. 7. World War, 1939-1945--Pacific Area--Aerial operations, American. 8. World War, 1939-1945--Campaigns--Pacific Area. 9. Pacific Area--History, Military--20th century. I. Title. II. Series: Mayborn literary nonfiction series ; no. 5.
  D767.9.S39 2011
  940.54'4973092--dc22
  [B]
                                    2011016700

Finish Forty and Home: The Untold World War II Story of B-24s in the Pacific is Number 5 in the Mayborn Literary Nonfiction Series *to Diane*

Contents

List of Illustrations (Illustrations appear after page 150)

Foreword

WE FOUGHT A SMALL WAR in the Central Pacific. Our numbers were not large but the percentage of men and planes lost was great. When I arrived in Hawaii in October of 1942, I was billeted in a barracks with the officers of four combat crews, sixteen of us in all. When I left the Pacific for home in March of 1945, there were *four* of us still alive and two of the four, Russell Phillips and Louis Zamperini, had spent two years in a Japanese prison camp. In a five-week period flying bombing missions over the Marshall and Gilbert Islands, we lost four crews and five airplanes out of eleven in the 42nd Squadron.

I finished my forty missions in January 1945. I was released as Squadron Commander and returned home on March 10, 1945, twenty-nine months after leaving.

This history brings back memories of the dear friends who gave their lives in this war and is a tribute to them and to all those, like Sergeant Herman Scearce, who laid their lives on the line and were blessed to survive. It is a comfort to know that this record has been written in remembrance of these patriots and of this part of our war in the Pacific.

Colonel Jesse E. Stay
United States Air Force, Retired

Preface

THIS BOOK IS ABOUT MY FATHER, Herman Scearce, and the men he served with during World War II, young airmen of the 11th Bombardment Group's 42nd Bomb Squadron. They fought almost anonymously in the early years of the war in the Pacific. By the time America turned its full attention to the Pacific war and 11th Group B-24 Liberator bombers reached striking distance of Japan, the glamorous new B-29 Superfortress arrived and took center stage.

My dad flew strike missions as a radio operator and gunner on a Liberator, staging from Hawaii to strike tiny Japanese-held island targets from island bases too small and poorly equipped to serve as permanent bases. These bombing missions were filled with the perils of enemy fighter interception, concentrated antiaircraft fire, and unforgiving distance. The 11th Group B-24s flew the longest missions of the war, over great expanses of featureless ocean where there was no room for the slightest navigational mistake and no alternative landing field for struggling aircraft.

My father's squadron and the rest of the 11th Group worked their way up the Central Pacific. As American forces invaded and took Japanese islands, the 11th advanced and began flying missions against the next enemy target in the chain, battling closer with each step to the Japanese home islands. The goal for American bomber crewmen was to get credit for forty strike missions, a goal that seemed impossibly out of reach in the beginning. Some, like my dad, finished forty and got home, but many men weren't so lucky.

This book was constructed from interviews and correspondence with long-lost squadron mates and other B-24 veterans, along with personal

visits with my father's former pilot and Squadron Commander Joe
Deasy in Boston, crewmate Ed Hess in Chicago, crewmate and best
buddy Jack Yankus in Tempe, and the surviving family of crewmate
Bob Lipe in Columbiana, Ohio. Interviews and correspondence were
supplemented by many hours of research at the Air Force Historical
Research Agency in Montgomery, Alabama, and the National Archives
in Washington, D.C. In some cases, names have been changed to protect
the identity of individuals.

The book includes reconstructed dialog, which is based on the memories of the men interviewed for the book. Dialog is faithful to their
recollection of events and true to the personalities of men I met and
others they remember. The clarity of their recollection was sometimes
so perfect that separate individuals remembered the same exchange of
dialog after more than sixty years.

This book is also the product of a World War II veteran's son trying to
learn all he could about his dad's war experiences, beginning when I was
a little boy riding along in the car with him, listening to his stories. I loved
riding with my father, it didn't matter where, because during those car
rides it was just me and Dad and his stories. The stories transported me
in my imagination and I never grew tired of hearing them. During those
rides Dad would say, "I'll let you be the radio operator." Looking back on
those years today, I can't say when I realized what it really meant to be the
radio operator. But I do sense the familiar feeling of wanting to ride along.

Acknowledgments

I AM GRATEFUL TO GEORGE KAY, an 11th Bomb Group B-24 veteran, who insisted on sending me his personal copy of *Grey Geese Calling*, the Group's history, after I contacted him to talk about his experiences. His generosity impressed me, and our conversation was among the first with many veterans I interviewed or corresponded with during my research. Without exception, they were patient with me and eager to share.

Jack Yankus welcomed me into his Tempe, Arizona, home and talked with me about his experiences as a B-24 flight engineer. He shared stories about my father which I could have heard from no other source. After meeting Jack Yankus, I understood why he and my dad had become such great friends.

Joe Deasy spent a day with me in his son's home in Framingham, Massachusetts, where we pored over old photographs that inspired stories, and he chatted with me for hours about the men and missions of the 42nd Bomb Squadron. I was especially honored to meet Joe Deasy, because my father held him in such high esteem.

Joe Deasy's son Jim Deasy spent a day facilitating my visit with his dad, hauling us around Boston and making the trip much easier for me. Jim also found and duplicated valuable photographs from his father's collection, published here for the first time.

Ed Hess, whom I met in Bridgeview, Illinois, also opened his home to me, and I was amused when he seemed genuinely thrilled to have me there. "I've got Herman Scearce's son in my house!" he said, and I understood more clearly why the veterans I met were so gracious: they appreciated what I was doing, but more importantly, they remembered and respected my dad.

Jesse Stay corresponded with me and answered questions about missions, especially concerning the December 1943 loss of George Smith's crew aboard *Dogpatch Express*. He contributed the foreword to this book, and in those short but profound paragraphs he helped frame the story.

Art Boone and Alf Storm corresponded with me and their input also helped shape the narrative.

Willis, Don, and Wayne Lipe and their families met with me in Don's home in Columbiana, Ohio. They shared their memories of their brother Bobby, and I revealed the story of the crash of *Naughty Nanette*, explaining why he flew with Lt. George Dechert on Dechert's next and final mission. They had wondered for years why Bobby went with Dechert on that ill fated flight, and after we talked, there was not a dry eye in the room. Don said, "You've given us closure after sixty years." My meeting with the Lipe family impressed upon me the still powerful effect of wartime losses and helped motivate me to complete this project because I hope, in a small way at least, it honors men like Bob Lipe.

Gailor Roy's niece Susan Taylor corresponded with me and shared family photos and memories from her childhood. Dave Walbeck also shared information about his great uncle, Ralph Walbeck, and sent me the 1944 letter written by George Dechert's mother to Ralph's mother. Dorothy Pratte shared memories about her cousin Charlie Pratte, and her feelings about his loss resonated with me. She still admires and looks up to Charlie.

Sydney Penczek, "Sookie," is another surviving family member of a lost airman. She corresponded with me about her brother, William Mashaw, who was lost with Charlie Pratte. Her reaction to the image of Heart Rock, at the place her brother was killed, brought home to me again how feelings of loss linger.

Ed Rosky, Bill Findle's son in law, contacted me after Sookie shared my name with him. His account of Findle's experience revealed another facet of the story, about sacrifices and casualties of war which veterans rarely discuss. Bill Findle deserved a Purple Heart.

Louis Zamperini corresponded with me and was responsible for Laura Hillenbrand's contact with me as she researched *Unbroken: A World War II Story of Survival, Resilience, and Redemption. Unbroken* is a must-read.

Laura Hillenbrand is a wonderfully talented writer whose correspondence and cooperation enriched the stories involving Louis Zamperini. She shared her research about the experiences of the crew of *Super Man*, especially on their harrowing Nauru mission, and the loss of *The Green Hornet*. Laura is an inspiration to anyone with a story to tell, and our correspondence offered me motivation and guidance. I am exceedingly grateful to her.

I am also grateful to John Donnelly and the staff of the Air Force Historical Research Agency at Maxwell Air Force Base. While I was at Maxwell, I met Dr. James Mowbray of the War College. Dr. Mowbray gave me several photographs of Pacific Island air bases and helped me appreciate and describe the challenges Air Corps units faced operating from these far-flung islands.

Doris Jackson and Sharon Culley of the National Archives and Records Administration assisted me in my research and guided me through the overwhelming volume of material housed there. They helped me accomplish in hours what would otherwise have taken weeks.

Radio station KBRD sent me a recording of Bing Crosby's "Seventh Air Force Tribute" and The Four Vagabonds' "Coming in on a Wing and a Prayer." They also guided me to John Morris of Old Homestead Records, creator of the Broadway Intermission label, which produced Bing Crosby's "Seventh Air Force Tribute" on vinyl from transcripts of an Armed Forces Radio Broadcast. John located two copies of Bing Crosby's "Seventh Air Force Tribute" for me, still in their original sealed sleeves.

Judy Schmid, Publicist with Bing Crosby Enterprises, identified the song "Seventh Air Force Tribute" from a single snippet of the song's lyrics that my dad remembered, "the Seventh Air Force, you can bet your ass!" Her input from this tiny clue led to my correspondence with KBRD, John Morris, and our copies of the record.

Shirley Powers, American Red Cross Volunteer Historian, sent me color plates of Red Cross uniforms to help with the description of the man who visited Sgt. Herman Scearce on Oahu about writing home to his worried family.

My friend and neighbor Lt. Col. Keith Allbritten, an Air National Guard navigator, provided valuable help with my understanding of navigation and the challenges crews faced in the Pacific. His knowledge and insight helped immensely.

The Collings Foundation, which maintains and operates the B-24 Liberator *The All American*, provided help with fuel consumption information on B-24 aircraft. Collings aircraft, including the Liberator, tour the United States each year and offer walk-throughs and flight experiences. I encourage anyone interested in Liberators to visit a Collings tour stop, see the plane and consider supporting this nonprofit organization.

I am indebted to Terry Price and Charlotte Rains Dixon, Directors of Middle Tennessee State University's Writer's Loft Program. This book would still be an idea if not for the structure and support The Writer's Loft provided. My writer friends, other students of the Loft, and the mentors who contribute their time and talent to the program nurture creativity, cultivate writing, and demystify the process. In addition to their responsibilities running the Writer's

Loft, Terry and Charlotte mentored me, read my material, and shared ideas and suggestions that vastly improved my efforts. Their always-positive communications buoyed me and I am forever grateful for their support.

Ron Chrisman, Director of University of North Texas Press, considered my manuscript in its earliest stages and gave me valuable editorial advice. I appreciate his guidance and commitment to my efforts. Karen DeVinney, Assistant Director/Managing Editor of UNT Press, painstakingly edited the final manuscript.

When I struggled to describe the sound of B-24 machine guns, my son, Joe, listened repeatedly to a recording of a .50 caliber machine gun and said, "It sounds like fists pounding on a steel door." He was right. My daughter Anna sacrificed her computer time so that I could work in a quiet office, and her occasional sweet and gentle requests for use of the office gave me welcome breaks from material that was sometimes hard to write. Her hugs were priceless.

Herman Scearce, my father, inspired me to begin this project years ago, a project which I originally intended to be a simple record of his wartime experiences. I wanted to capture his stories for the sake of my son and my daughter and generations to come. When I told Dad that it could become a book someday, he laughed and said, "You might have enough for a magazine article." He endured endless questions from me. My mother graciously and cheerfully chatted with me during countless phone calls, knowing that another question for Dad, or some point for clarification, was the real reason for my call.

I am especially grateful to my wife Diane for her patience, criticism, and support. It's unlikely Diane would read World War II history if I were not writing it. She is my first reader; she is the one who inspired me to complete this book.

Introduction

HERMAN SCEARCE WAS SIXTEEN when he lied about his age to join the Army. His family had disintegrated, his home town had little to offer, and Herman had nothing to lose. Many years later Herman's children laughed at stories about his impoverished early years. Enough time had passed that he thought it was funny, too, in a bittersweet way. He liked the idea that he had risen to a certain level of middle-class success, and joking about those difficult times acknowledged how far he had come. He had been so poor that he ate Corn Flakes in water because they couldn't afford milk. He had been so poor, his family moved at the end of every month because the rent came due. He said, "Well, we really did!" and his wife, Flora Ann, smiled and said, "Pshh—oh, Herman, it wasn't that bad."

But she wasn't in his life then, and at times, it really *was* that bad.

Herman's parents argued a lot when he was little. He tried to make himself small and stay out of the way when they yelled at each other, but their rented houses were cramped and the walls were thin. It was impossible for him to avoid hearing his parents hurl hurtful words against each other. Some of their fights were about his father seeing other women, but most of the time, the fights were about money. There was never enough, and Herman's mother, Pearl Pearson Scearce, wasn't above breaking the law to earn a little bit more.

1

In October 1933, when my dad, Herman Scearce Jr. was eight years old, the family lived for a short time in a rented house just over the North Carolina state line from Danville, Virginia. While living there, his mother sold homemade "pop skull" liquor from the back porch, leading to her arrest for "Violation of the Prohibition Law." It was her first arrest, and she was released on a prayer for judgment, promising to be a law-abiding citizen for the next two years. It's unlikely she kept this promise; they needed the money too badly.

Herman Sr.'s vices aggravated the family's money problems. He liked to drink, he liked to gamble, and he liked to spend money on women as if he could afford to do it. On one occasion he took advantage of his youngest son's misfortune to finance his irresponsible behavior, a con which especially incensed Pearl.

Ralph Scearce, Herman's younger brother, had to see a doctor because he had injured himself, and Herman vividly remembers how his mother reacted when she learned that the doctor's bill had been just two dollars. Herman Sr. had persuaded Pearl to endorse a loan note for fourteen dollars, and he could not account for the other twelve. Herman quietly left the house when he heard his mother start in on his father, and his father never admitted it, but the family knew he had squandered the money drinking and gambling. Twelve dollars was a huge sum of money for this family in 1937.

Each year of my father's childhood included occasions that seemed cruelly contrived to remind his family they were poor, occasions which he knew were supposed to be cheerful.

Birthdays were very simple, but birthdays were not so bad compared to Christmas. Not every kid celebrated a birthday on the same day, not every kid compared what he got for his birthday to what somebody else got on the same day as they did at Christmas. Store fronts weren't filled with special fantasies to tease poor kids on their birthdays. For my father's parents, Christmas was an annual reopening of a wound, a reminder of their low means. Pearl couldn't help but think of what might have been, if her husband hadn't been so irresponsible with their money. The token holiday decorations, chipped and fading second-hand ornaments and a wobbly card paper Santa, in their simple Danville house didn't do much to mask the melancholy.

On Christmas morning, Herman usually got a new pair of shoes, or a pair of pants, something he had needed for months. He suspected his mom found the shoes or the pants as cheaply as possible, weeks, maybe months before, and stashed them away so she would have something to put out at Christmas. Usually there was a small toy tucked up beside the shoes, maybe some chocolate drops, some nuts and an orange, all arranged around a brittle tree cut and carried in by the boys days before. Ralph, Herman, and their sister Hazel knew there was a big difference between Christmas in the better parts of Danville and Christmas where they lived.

The three siblings spent summers at their uncle's farm, setting out new tobacco plants and doing simple chores, working however children could. Their mother dropped them off for the summer and made them promise to be good and work hard for their room and board. But their efforts on the farm didn't amount to much; in truth, working at their uncle's farm was just a way for Herman Sr. and Pearl to get rid of the children for the summer.

The Scearce kids stayed in an old log boarding house squatting a stone's throw from the farm house. They ate better than they had all year, though, and the farm was more interesting than the sweltering summer streets of Danville. Farm chores in the heat and humidity of southwestern Virginia were not hard to bear because the brothers and their sister were also friends, and they had escaped, if just for the summer, from the reality of home. It was during one such summer, in July of 1938, that Herman Scearce's father left home.

Herman was thirteen. His mother had taken out a warrant against his father, a warrant for non-support, and that was the last straw. Herman Sr. went to live with his aunt on Oxford Street, only a mile away but on the opposite side of the Dan River. He stayed there just long enough to consider his options and decide where to go next.

The Juvenile Court gave custody of the children to Pearl Pearson Scearce in a hearing her husband did not bother to attend. The important thing for Pearl was support payments, and the court awarded her five dollars a week.

From Oxford Street, Herman's father moved to Roanoke Rapids, North Carolina. He rented an apartment at 411-B Madison Avenue, a dull-green, two-story frame house with asbestos siding, which had been modified into a duplex. Scearce found a job in the J. P. Stevens mill several blocks away, steady work, but he rarely paid his child support.

At fifteen, Herman went to Roanoke Rapids to live with his father. His mother was with another man and Herman sensed that the two adults didn't want him around. Without telling anyone he was leaving, Herman walked two blocks to Virginia's Route 58, the main east-west road through Danville, crossed to the eastbound side, and turned to face oncoming traffic when anyone approached, his right thumb extended. Hitchhiking the 120 miles, he was lucky to make the trip in half a day. A man in a Model A Ford picked up Herman and not long after, the Model A had a blowout of the right front tire. With no spare, the man just shrugged and drove on, shredding the blown-out tire rubber. He drove with the right wheels off the pavement and on the shoulder so the rim with no tire might not be destroyed. It was slow going and rough, but Herman was riding and he didn't care.

One night in Roanoke Rapids, Herman walked home later than his dad liked. Herman had been with a girl on her front porch, right across the street and one house over from the duplex at 411-B. Herman had lost track of time, but he didn't have a curfew, and he could have heard his dad if his dad had called for him. Herman's father beat him with a broom handle for being late, and beat him more for protesting that he'd just been across the street, and still more to drive home a point about who was in charge.

Herman quit school and went back to his mother's house on South Ridge Street in Danville the very next day. He could have gone to school in Danville, but attending school meant he would be dependent on his mother and it meant he would have no money. School was a luxury they just couldn't afford, so Herman got a job putting up roping in the Dan River Mill.

Hauling and putting up roping was one of the lowest jobs in the mill. From a steel-wheeled cart the size of a truck cab, Herman put thick bundles of roping on top of the spinning frames. The spinners then took the roping and set it up in their machines to be spun into thread. Dan River Mills paid Herman $15 per week, about the same money the sweepers made. Even doffers made more, removing spindles full of spun thread, putting them on a cart, and replacing them with empty ones. Doffers made more because "doffers were trained," Herman said later.

But Herman had some money. It wasn't much, and it didn't raise their standard of living, didn't mean they could afford "nice things," as Pearl Pearson Scearce called the luxuries in other people's houses, but it meant he wasn't such a burden on his mother. The only luxury Herman enjoyed was a membership in the Danville YMCA, but even then, someone else paid for it.

George Bendall was a lawyer and a friend of the Scearce family. Years before, when Herman's dad was a motorcycle cop on the Danville police force, the Scearce family got to know Mr. Bendall because Bendall prosecuted the cases the police investigated. More recently, Pearl Pearson Scearce went to Mr. Bendall for her divorce filing and Mr. Bendall never billed her for his services. Returning the favor, the Scearces supported Mr. Bendall when he ran for District Attorney by posting signs, distributing flyers and knocking on doors.

After winning the election, Mr. Bendall gave Herman a YMCA membership. Herman was proud to belong to the YMCA because it looked like he could afford it. The Y had board games, exercise rooms, and ball games, but Herman's favorite pastime at the YMCA was ping-pong. Once in a while, the staff of the YMCA served lemonade and cookies, real luxury items Herman never got at home.

Pearl Pearson Scearce took in boarders and worked part-time in a restaurant. She made wax flowers and sold them. The mill money Herman earned, he spent. He learned quickly that it felt good to have a dollar or two in his pocket because he knew very well how it felt to have nothing. If he wanted a bite to eat, or a cold drink, he could pay for it. He had enough to spend some of his money on girls, and more often than not, they let him, and it didn't hurt that Herman was good looking: just shy of six feet, slender, dark brown eyes and an easy smile, with blonde hair combed back from his tanned face.

Herman spent a lot of time at the Coney Island Pool Room on Craghead Street, near the restaurant where his mother worked. Craghead Street ran parallel to the Dan River, just a few blocks downhill from the house on South Ridge Street. A stout Greek man named Leo ran the Pool Room, selling beer and renting pool tables by the game. Herman helped out, racking balls for the local roughs who were Leo's regular customers. It was a small pool room, only six tables, and Herman wasn't paid. Instead, Leo let Herman shoot pool for free.

Herman shot a lot of pool, and he watched good players. Herman learned how to see the angles, how to think ahead to the next shot. He knew that the lie was as important as making the shot, so he'd have another good shot after making this one. He learned about "English," how to strike the cue ball so that it came off the object ball, or the rail, and went where he wanted it to go. A good pool player saw the whole table, the whole picture, and played with a plan.

Scearce got good at shooting pool. He learned how to hustle, how to look like he really couldn't play very well and then make a few bucks betting on his game. Herman enjoyed the walk down to the Pool Room, but he never looked forward to returning up the hill to his cheerless home.

On Thursday, May 22, 1941, the headline on the front page of *The Danville Register*, Herman Scearce's hometown daily, proclaimed "NAZI ATTACK ON CRETE IS REPULSED." Beneath the headline were articles about communists infiltrating Federal government jobs, a failed escape attempt from Alcatraz, and a murder suspect declaring that she didn't care if she got sent to the State's electric chair. Tucked among these was an article about the government's efforts to step up production of four-engined bombers:

The Danville Register
May 22, 1941
To Hike Bombing Plane Production
Allocation Made to Build New Airplane, Aluminum and Magnesium
Plants

Washington–(AP)–The government took two strides today toward the goal of vastly increased bombing plane production, which President Roosevelt recently demanded.

1. Jesse Jones, federal loan administrator, announced the allocation of $650,000,000 to build new government-owned airplane, aluminum and magnesium plants.

2. William S. Knudsen, director of the Office of Production Management, disclosed that four new contracts were being negotiated which, with existing contracts, would provide 500 long-range, four-motored heavy bombers a month.

Thursday, May 22, 1941, was also Herman Scearce's sixteenth birthday. On that spring day in Danville, however, Scearce had no interest in news about bomber production. He would have been surprised to know that he would be in the Army by the end of the year, and would have been shocked to learn that he would go to war in a new bomber at age seventeen.

His parents' divorce was final in December 1941. The divorce was just a formality, because their relationship had been over for years. Scearce's parents saw other people and it had reached the point that the kids didn't notice. Hazel was out of the house, married to Frank Cox, and she had her own household to worry about. Ralph was fourteen, not a baby any more.

Just the same, the divorce closed the door on Herman Scearce's childhood. Danville and the cotton mill didn't have much to offer, but lines were forming downtown at the Army enlistment center.

Don't give me a B-24
She's just a ground-lovin' whore.
She'll whine, moan and wheeze,
And she'll clobber the trees,
Don't give me a B-24.

From "Give Me Operations"
Army Air Corps ballad

Chapter 1

Sergeant at Seventeen

HERMAN SCEARCE WAS SIXTEEN YEARS OLD when he lied about his age and joined the Army two weeks after the Japanese attacked Pearl Harbor. Herman's mother had a little brown mantel radio, bought on credit along with everything else in her rented house, and that December when Herman switched the radio on and fine-tuned the local frequency, it buzzed with news about the attack and speculation about what the Japanese might do next.

Scearce had never heard of Pearl Harbor. He couldn't remember whether he had even heard of Hawaii. Maybe it didn't matter, because he did understand that Americans had been killed and U.S. Navy ships had been sunk. Geography certainly didn't seem to matter to the young men forming lines at the U.S. Army enlistment center at the Danville, Virginia, post office, just a half mile walk from his home.

Marvin Marshall was Herman Scearce's cousin, his mother's sister's boy. Both were sixteen, worked dead-end jobs, and they were bored. One of them, Scearce doesn't remember who, suggested they should go join the Army, that day, right then.

The cousins walked down the hill to the post office and got in line. Marvin was ahead of Herman, so he got to the recruiter first.

"Age?"

"Eighteen," Marvin lied.

"Prove it."

Marvin shrugged. He couldn't prove he was eighteen. The recruiter handed Marvin a form and told him to come back after he got his momma to sign it. Marvin grinned sheepishly at Herman, stepped out of the line, and turned to walk home. Scearce stepped up to the recruiter.

"Age?"

"Nineteen"

Without looking up, the recruiter gestured Scearce along and his enlistment began. As his cousin returned to Danville's dull routine, a doctor gave Scearce a quick physical and, on December 22, he boarded the silver Richmond-bound bus at Greyhound's Main Street terminal. Uncle Sam covered the $1.95 one-way fare. From Richmond, a waiting Army bus took him to nearby Camp Lee to be sworn in to the United States Army.

"How do you say that?" a supply clerk asked, looking at Herman's name on a clipboard on front of him.

"Scearce . . . just like the word scarce," Herman replied.

"Well, Scearce just like the word scarce, these ought to fit." And soon Scearce had all the clothing and bed linens and toilet articles the Army thought he needed.

The Army issued high-top shoes to the new soldiers and sent the men on a long hike. Soon Scearce was in the base hospital, his left ankle badly swollen from hiking in his stiff new Army shoes. While he was treated in the hospital, the men who entered Camp Lee with him shipped out to their basic training locations and a new group moved in. When Scearce was finally returned to his barracks from the hospital, he found himself feeling out of place and awkwardly self-conscious in a barracks full of experienced soldiers who had been called back to service.

If his youth was going to catch up with him, this seemed to be the most likely opportunity. His mother might think he had gone back to Roanoke Rapids to stay with his father, but she was bound to find out sooner or later that he had joined the Army. Scearce was still fairly sure the Army would discover, one way or another, how old he was and send him home, even if his mother didn't call for him.

But the experienced returning soldiers at Camp Lee weren't concerned about the raw recruit's youth and the Army's induction process resumed as soon as Scearce's ankle healed. Scearce traveled by a passenger train crowded with civilians and young soldiers to Jefferson Barracks, Missouri, for four weeks of basic training filled with marching, drill, learning how to salute, more marching, and more drill. The recruits were anxious for basic training to be over, and spirits rose as the fourth week began. Soon they would move out and get to their "real" training, training for the jobs they would do.

The high morale of the fourth week gave way to disappointment and consternation. Word was that they weren't going anywhere because there was an outbreak of meningitis, and the Army planned to keep the men contained on base until the danger of disease passed. With nothing better to do with the group, the Army put them through four more weeks of basic training filled with the same marching, drill, and saluting, spiced with salty gripes and flat jokes about having gone over this already. Scearce stayed at Jefferson Barracks a total of ten weeks.

Following basic training, Scearce assumed he would go to truck driving school, because he felt unqualified to do anything else. He had taken some tests while in basic training, and he was pleased with himself when he noticed "140" in the score box for his I.Q. Scearce felt very good about this result until he realized that the number wasn't a score after all, and the box he thought showed his I.Q. was actually a record of his weight.

Back in Danville, Scearce once worked for a man with a stovewood truck, hauling stovewood around to customers who complained about the bundles being too small or the wood burning too fast. Even then, most of Scearce's wood-hauling experience had been loading wood into the truck or sitting in the back throwing the wood off like a paper boy tossing the daily news.

When Scearce received an assignment to Radio School, he figured the Army must have plenty of truck drivers already. He would be one of 349 men in the August 1942 Radio Operator-Mechanics Class, #35. His mother had owned a radio, the little brown one on the mantel, and Scearce knew how to turn it off or on and tune in a station, but that was the extent of his expertise with radios.

Radio School at Scott Field, Illinois, was mind-numbingly boring, with row upon row and table after table of khaki-clad men quietly copying Morse code three hours a day and studying radio theory the rest of the day. As they were copying code, each student wore a headset and received coded messages that they diligently wrote into a log. When they became proficient at a rate of five words per minute, they would move up to ten, from ten to fifteen, and so on.

Scearce hated it. He wondered whether the school was specially designed to be boring, testing whether a man could stay awake enough to be a radio operator. He imagined the Army had special clocks built to move at half the speed of time. But once in a while, the monotony was broken by a visit from officers or enlisted men from one of the various organizations within the Army. Already enlisted, Scearce found himself being recruited, because the men giving these pep talks wanted the future radio operators to apply to *their* part of the Army.

On one of these special occasions a couple of Air Corps guys came into the school's assembly room.[1] They talked about flying, and how the Air Corps needed radio operators. These airmen wore crisp, pressed khaki pants with a razor's edge crease down the front, shiny black shoes, and the best looking leather jackets Herman Scearce had ever seen. The jackets were brown leather, short waisted and broken-in enough to make the men look experienced. The jackets exuded cool confidence. It said these guys were Army, but they were in a special club just the same.

An incentive for volunteering for the Army Air Forces was getting out of radio school. If Scearce got his code speed up to twenty-five words per minute, he was done, radio school was over. Freshly motivated by the visiting airmen, Scearce achieved the target speed quickly and applied for gunnery training to get on a flight crew. It was understood among radio school students that it was a good thing to get on a flight crew because the pay was better: if you were on flying status, you got your base pay plus half again. Besides, Scearce really wanted one of those leather jackets.

The physical exam for gunnery school was tough, the same physical that pilots had to pass, which didn't make a lot of sense to Army Private Herman Scearce. He knew plenty of guys who could have been good gunners, except they weren't physically fit enough to be pilots.

Scearce was assigned to gunnery school at Harlingen, Texas, and felt fortunate to get Harlingen. A lot of men went to Nellis Field, in the Nevada desert, the Army Air Forces' original flexible gunnery school.[2] Scearce liked the idea of gunnery training over the Texas coast better than gunnery training over the hot desert.

During the first few weeks of gunnery school, an Army Private's pay went from $21 a month to $50. Scearce and his single-striper buddies couldn't believe the government could afford to pay them so much.

The Army conducted flight gunnery training in AT-6 Texans, so-called because most of them were built in Dallas. Texans are single engine planes, its wing mounted forward and low on the fuselage. Texans have a wingspan of 42 feet, and are 29 feet from propeller to tail. The AT designation is for "Advanced Trainer," advanced because the AT-6 has retractable landing gear and was faster than other basic flight trainers at the time. With a nine-cylinder radial engine rated at 550 horsepower, the AT-6 Texan was a powerful plane.[3] Gunnery school Texans had a flexible .30 caliber machine gun mounted at the rear of the cockpit. The gunnery student sat behind the pilot, in tandem, except that the gunner faced rearward in a seat designed to rotate forward or aft.

Walking toward an AT-6 for the first time, Scearce eyed the plane, trying to hide his apprehension as if the aircraft might sense it, like a dog smells fear. He reassured himself that the last guy must have survived, so he'd make it too. Herman Scearce was about to fly, for the first time in his life, in a shiny silver AT-6, facing backwards, gripping a machine gun. With his slender frame strapped in place, and the pilot seated behind him, Scearce took a deep breath and waited.

The radial engine roared to life and the plane vibrated and bounced forward, until the pilot advanced the throttle and the plane accelerated on its take-off roll and soon lifted away from the white concrete runway.

There is nothing quite like facing backwards in an airplane as it climbs away from the ground. As they lifted off and the ground fell away below them, the horizon suddenly rose, the tail of the plane tilted beneath his feet, and the airfield filled Scearce's field of vision. Scearce was thrilled and terrified at the same time.

They leveled out at 2,000 feet and Scearce soon understood why it was special to be on a flight crew. The view was amazing. Below, the Texas coastline bent to the north and east, and Mexico was just across the river visible on the opposite side. As they sped across the beach and flew over the gulf, the water was first green, and then dark blue. Boats, tiny as ants, hugged the shore, white wakes marking their paths through the water. Scearce felt the cooler air of the altitude and realized he was very wet with sweat, his back cold against the padded seat cushion behind him.

In-flight gunnery training involved trying to shoot a target towed by another Texan flying off to the side. The target was a fabric sleeve about ten feet long, towed like the advertisements for restaurants and souvenir vendors towed behind planes at a crowded beach resort. The AT-6 had a sight mounted on its wingtip that lined up with the tow plane when the range was right. When the tow target was in range, the gunner started shooting at the target. There were no stops in the AT-6's .30 caliber gun, so the gunnery student could blast his own plane's tail off. But the shooting was done to the side, not toward the rear, and for the tow plane pilot's sake, his aircraft had a long lead on the sleeve target.

After Scearce fired 200 rounds on the towed target over the Gulf of Mexico, the planes turned back toward Harlingen. As he finally began to relax, take in the view, and enjoy the ride home, Scearce heard an alarming radio transmission that put his senses on edge.

"I've got an engine problem. I'm not sure I can make it back."

Scearce didn't know whether it was *his* pilot who had the engine trouble or the one towing the target. He wasn't experienced enough to know that the voice that sounded loudest in his headset was his pilot. The second pilot replied, "Set it down in that field over there and I'll get some help."

Scearce was relieved to see the other plane drop the towed target and descend, preparing to land in a farm field below. Both pilots seemed so completely casual about it, Scearce figured this sort of thing must happen all the time.

When they were finally safely parked on the flight line at Harlingen, Scearce was so eager to put his feet back on the ground that he let go of the machine gun without locking it down. As he started to climb out of the plane, the weapon swung around and smacked him hard in the head, possibly the only thing hit with the gun all day.

Gunnery school students fired rounds with bullet tips painted in lithographic ink, each student with his own color. The machine gun round left a circle of paint where it struck the target, and 5 percent hits was passing. After each flight the tow plane dropped the target at the airfield before landing, and gunnery school instructors counted the hits. In the final days of gunnery school, some students used rounds painted with another man's color in order to help him make the 5 percent grade; a poor shot could show very impressive improvement that way. Scearce assumed their superiors knew what was going on, but the practice was ignored. The Army needed gunners badly.[4]

Gunnery students learned to recognize aircraft, friend or foe, in a split second. Silhouettes of aircraft were displayed on a screen, moving across, up or down, and the gunnery student had to fire, or hold his fire, with an electronic gun after immediately determining whether the plane was American, German, or Japanese. Students had to know them all.

The school was hard work and the pressure to perform well was intense, but Scearce thought it was also interesting and, in a way, fun, especially compared to copying code and studying radio theory at Scott Field. Students fired from turrets mounted on the ground and from moving trucks, took target practice, and shot skeet.

The skeet range was run by an Army captain who was a champion shooter. He had shiny little metal badges from shooting competitions pinned all over his gun vest. He was very much "by the book" on the range, no nonsense. He insisted that every student sight down the gun with it "broken" open before the shotgun was loaded, to make sure there was nothing obstructing the barrels.

There was one shotgun for every two students. Scearce's buddy shot first and then handed him the gun. Scearce put two shells in the gun, locked it closed, and shouted "PULL!"

When the clay target flew, Scearce followed it quickly with the gun and pulled the trigger. With a deafening *BOOM!* a ten-inch piece of gun barrel flew back, barely missing Scearce's head, and imbedded itself several inches deep in the side of a little wooden shack behind the shooting position. Scearce held the sad remains of the shotgun in his hand, a little dazed but glad to be alive, and saw the skeet range captain heading toward him fast.

"What did I tell you? What did I tell you?" The captain screamed, beet red from the neck up. Scearce, smart enough not to respond, could feel the captain's spittle hitting him in the face. "Come with me!" the captain hissed through his clenched teeth.

Scearce's mischievous skeet range buddy had pushed the end of the gun barrels into the ground, driving plugs of earth into each one. He didn't admit doing it, but it didn't really matter; Scearce was supposed to check the barrels before putting shells into the gun.

Scearce followed the angry captain to his office, sure that he was going to get an ear full, stripped of rank, court martialled, or finally sent to truck-driving school. The captain cooled off, though, and went easy on his frightened student. "Ah, well. I can saw the barrel off and give it to the guards for a riot gun."

Scearce passed gunnery school on September 9, 1942. Since the Tables of Organization and Equipment, or T. O. and E's as they were called, required that radio operator/gunners hold a certain rank, Scearce was promoted from private to staff sergeant at age seventeen, still a little worried that his age might get him kicked out of the Army. For the time being, the Army thought he was twenty.

From Texas, Scearce spent ten days on troop trains comprised of clattering old converted freight cars to get to Salt Lake City. He and the other soldiers agreed that the train trips were a way for the railroads to make big money from the government. They used "least traveled routes," taking the men on a time-consuming, roundabout course to their destination. The men scoffed at the explanation they were offered: the roundabout routes would foil potential saboteurs. Making matters worse, the trains were miserable. They had wash basins but no showers, and rarely did one of the trains have a dining car. Usually the men had to work their way to a boxcar in the middle of the train where an Army mess cook was set up. The men bumped and rocked their way through other sweaty, smelly, unwashed men clutching their aluminum mess kits, and if they were lucky, they would make it back to their place with most of their food.

Whether sleeping on the train was more unpleasant than eating on the train was a matter of perspective, and it alternated according to each man's hunger or fatigue. Creaking metal beds folded out from the sides of the converted freight cars, three high, with a thin pad for a mattress, and sleep did not come easy. The joke went around that they had all been duped; they were really being trained for duty in mini-submarines.

The trains were finally met by an Army medic and a doctor in Salt Lake City. They gave the men a "short arm inspection," looking for signs of venereal disease. After days with no bath, the men figured that the poor medic pulling this duty must have drawn the short straw. The man in front of Scearce asked the medic, "Who did you piss off to get this assignment?" But the medic just shrugged and stoically replied, "There's duty worse than this."

From Salt Lake City, Scearce was sent ahead with the others who had passed the VD inspection to Davis-Monthan Field. A few guys with "leaky faucets" laughed nervously, looking forward to a clinic visit and a couple of weeks swallowing sulfa tablets.

On Davis-Monthan's flight line, the men were lined up according to their job specialty. Officers had already been organized: pilot, copilot, navigator, and bombardier. Next, flight engineers' names were called, followed by radio operators, then gunners. When Scearce's name was called, he stepped out of line and met the other men who would become his new crew.

The pilot was a big red-headed guy, a 2nd lieutenant named Richardson. Scearce thought Richardson had an arrogant air about him, and from the beginning, Scearce didn't like him. The co-pilot was 2nd Lt. Sam Catanzarite. Tanned, dark, and with an easygoing style, he looked and acted older and more experienced than the other officers. The navigator, 2nd Lt. Art Boone, had a youthful round face with a dimpled chin. Bombardier 2nd Lt. William Baber, with a strong jaw line and a handsome smile, looked like he belonged in a college fraternity house.

Technical Sergeant Herman Scearce was the second enlisted man called to the crew, following Technical Sergeant Jack Yankus. Yankus was a big man with a broad, toothy smile who seemed genuinely happy to shake Scearce's hand. Scearce wasn't sure whether Yankus was really that friendly or just glad he was no longer the only enlisted man standing with the four officers he had just met.

Next were Staff Sergeants Elmer Johnson, Ed Hess, and Bob Lipe. Scearce and Yankus had one more stripe on their sleeves than the other three enlisted men because of their specialized training as radio operator and engineer. The staff sergeants had only been through gunnery school.

Johnson, from Pasadena, California, was short, the shortest man on the crew. He had a high forehead, deep-set eyes and dark brows, giving him a very serious appearance. Broad shouldered, lanky Ed Hess from Chicago had a mischievous look, and Scearce thought Hess had a touch of vanity about him, "puttin' on airs," they called it in Danville, something in the way Hess leaned forward to shake hands and then looked away.

The last name called was Bob Lipe, and Lipe approached the rest of the men with a genuine, engaging smile. He seemed very pleased to be on this particular crew, as if somehow he knew it was better than any of the other crews forming at the same time. He had dark, wavy hair and Scearce thought Lipe looked like he could have come out of Hollywood rather than Columbiana, Ohio.

After each enlisted man joined his crew, saluted the officers, and the crew was finally assembled, the men talked about where they were from, whether they had a wife or family at home, and discussed the next steps in their training. Richardson's ideas about training, the crew quickly discovered, differed from all of the other crews.

If the training requirement called for aircrews to do something for an hour, Richardson's new crew had to go an hour and a half. If they were supposed to do it ten times, Richardson would make it fifteen. When they took low-level passes for the gunners to shoot at targets in the desert, one pass was never enough. Richardson wanted to make his crew as good as they could be, but the extra effort was tiresome. If they knew what to do, or how to do it, going over it again and again seemed like a waste of time. Scearce and his new buddy Jack Yankus and the rest of the enlisted men grew to dislike Lieutenant Richardson.

"Phase training," as it was called, was conducted at several bases, including El Paso, Pueblo, Topeka, and Alamogordo. Each base required so many flights, so many practice bombs dropped, and so many navigation legs, practice for every aspect of bomber crew operations. Sergeant Scearce and the other radio operators had to stay alert, because at some point during each flight, a practice message was sent from the ground. When the plane returned to base, the message had better be in the radio log, and it better be right.

Their four months of flight training was conducted in worn-out B-24 Liberators. The planes had a lot of problems, and Scearce wondered if the problems weren't fixed because replacement parts were sent to units already in combat or because the Army wanted the crews in training to learn to work around glitches. Some of the planes had instruments that didn't work properly. Misleading information from a faulty instrument could be worse than no information at all, because crews sometimes believed the misleading information. Problems like these might have been commonplace for skilled pilots, but these crews lacked experience. During phase training, the Army lost about one plane and crew every month.

On a training flight to Orlando, Richardson's crew landed at a Navy base fifty miles from the Army base they were supposed to reach. A Navy chief walked out to the plane and met Richardson as he leaned out of the cockpit window.

"Orlando?" the Navy chief asked.

"Yep," replied Richardson.

"About fifty miles that way," the chief said, gesturing in the direction of the Army base.

After the Navy boys got a good laugh, Richardson hopped the plane over to the Army field. A mistake like this might be funny around Orlando, but the consequences could be tragic later.

When they left Orlando, Richardson's plane was one of twelve B-24s in the flight. Someone on the ground reported that one of the bombers had hit a tree on take-off, but none of the crews thought they had hit anything, or they were not willing to admit it. As a result, the entire flight was diverted from Topeka to Tinker Field, Oklahoma, because Tinker had better runways and crash facilities.

Before they landed at Tinker, a shiny new P-51 Mustang fighter plane came up to check out each B-24. With the B-24s' landing gear down, the P-51 pilot circled around and beneath each of the big bombers, trying to see whether any of the ships had gear damage. No damage was found, and each plane landed safely. The men learned later that the P-51 inspecting their aircraft was flown by none other than famous aviator Charles Lindbergh.

Lindbergh was well qualified to inspect the incoming flight of Liberators. He was intimately familiar with B-24s from the assembly line to flight testing, serving as a consultant to Ford Motor Company as Ford built Liberators under contract from Consolidated Aircraft. Lindbergh's observations led to improvements in armor plate installation and gun placement, but perhaps most importantly, Lindbergh discovered that life rafts installed in B-24s had no break cord or sea anchor installed. When launched, the rafts would inflate automatically but might drift away before struggling crewmen could reach them.[5]

After nearly four months together, very late in the new crew's phase training, Lieutenant Richardson disappeared. He didn't say goodbye; he was simply there one day and gone the next. The enlisted men on the crew received the revelation that they were going to get a new pilot with amused interest. It was a surprise, but odds were good that the next one would be more likeable, and the men were willing to accept their chances with a new pilot. They speculated that Richardson may have had a performance problem, or maybe he had gotten sick. They never heard why Richardson left but they agreed they wouldn't miss him.

A 1st lieutenant named Joe Deasy, a Framingham, Massachusetts, native, stepped forward to take Richardson's place. The crew was happy to get him because Deasy was a B-24 instructor pilot and had flown B-17s before getting into Liberators. The crew was confident that their new pilot knew what he was doing.

Deasy was a slender man, his blue eyes piercingly sharp and level. He looked directly into the eyes of each man as he shook hands with his new crew. Deasy had an angular, intelligent face and an easy, confident manner that put his men at ease right away.

Scearce and the rest of the crew liked the status Deasy brought with him. Most of the other flight crew officers training beside them were 2nd lieutenants. Somehow a radio operator with a 1st lieutenant pilot felt a cut above a radio operator with a 2nd lieutenant, and this unofficial status touched each man on Joe Deasy's crew. Later, this little quirk of fate, the difference in their pilot's rank, would position Deasy as an operations officer and later still, squadron commander, making his crew the squadron's lead crew.

Deasy didn't humble his crew or boss them around. He expected them to do their jobs, and at the same time he respected their skills. He said, "I knew how to fly the airplane, I didn't know much else."[6]

During a driving rain in Salina, Kansas, the crew waited out the weather with orders to fly to Topeka that day. High wind and a low ceiling forced them to sit, watching the clock as hours passed. They waited for a break in the weather in a drafty squadron ready room beside the flight line while howling wind and dark squalls raced across the runways. Deasy knew that his men were tired and hungry.

Finally, Deasy decided they had had enough. "I think it's about time we got something to eat." And with that, the crew knew the wait was over and they were pleased that their new pilot was confident enough to assert his authority in spite of orders to get to Topeka. Walking out of the ready room, Yankus muttered to Scearce, "We'd have been here all night with Richardson."

The crew left the flight line to find a hot meal and get some rest. They would get over to Topeka the next day.

From their last phase training base, Topeka, they returned to Salina where their new plane was waiting. Crews making the trip to Salina to take delivery of their aircraft usually got there by air, crowded into one of the old B-24s used in training, flown by a minimal crew of pilot, co-pilot, navigator, flight engineer, and radio operator. When Deasy's crew was ready, bad Kansas weather had the planes grounded, so the men climbed into the back of Army troop trucks for the trip to Salina. In bitter cold, the trip took most of a day to cover the 150 miles. The truck wasn't designed for comfort, its stiff suspension jarring the crew as it pounded roads pot-holed and broken from winter's freezing, thawing, and refreezing. If the truck had heat, the men riding in the back could not feel it. Johnson observed that it would be a shame to die in a truck on the way to their new plane, and Catanzarite suggested that if they all got frostbite, maybe Deasy could put them in for Purple Hearts.

"My feet are like bricks," Lipe complained. "When we get to Salina, can we test fire our guns on this truck?"

Arriving beaten and tired, Deasy's crew was relieved to learn that they wouldn't have to pull guard duty on their new plane. The promise of a hot meal and a warm bunk lifted their spirits. There would be time to check out the new airplane later. They were confident, ready to go to Europe, finish their missions, and come home heroes with medals pinned to their chests.

The next morning, Lt. Joe Deasy signed a shipping ticket, just as if he was signing for a parcel:

Item	Quantity	Name
1	1	AIRPLANE, Complete, B-24-D
2	1	KIT, B-24-D, per one airplane
3	1	KIT, B-24-D per 5 airplanes
4	2	KIT, Overwater
5	2	LIFERAFTS, Complete
6	1	KIT, Mechanics, armorer
7	1	KIT, Mechanics, crewchief
8	1	KIT, Operators, radio
9	2	CANS, For water
10	11	MICROPHONES, Type T-30
11	11	HEADSETS, Type H S 23
12	5	CANS, Foot powder (3 1/2 oz. each)
13	5	TAPE, Adhesive (1" x 5 yds. roll)
14	2	BAG, Drop message
15	1	PAPER, Toilet (1000 sheets)
16	1	BRUSH, Standard, counter dusting
17	1	GUN, Hand spray and insecticide
18	1	BUCKET, Gov. Issue, Galv.
19	1	TABLETS, Sodium chloride, 1500pk.
20	1	SOAP, Gov. Issue
21	100	CUPS, Paper, drinking
22	1	KIT, Medical
23	4	KIT, Medical, aeronautic
24	10	E-RATION, In ship (loose)
		A. C. FORMS & KEYS
25	1	KEYS, For airplane
26	1	A. C. Form, 60-A
27	4	A. C. Form, 60-B
28	4	A. C. Form, 61

ORDNANCE

29	2	SIGNAL, Aircraft, D/S AM-M28 R/R
30	2	SIGNAL, Aircraft, D/S AM-M29 Y/Y
31	2	SIGNAL, Aircraft, D/S AM-M30 G/G
32	2	SIGNAL, Aircraft, D/S AM-M32 R/G
33	2	SIGNAL, Aircraft, D/S AM-M33 G/Y
34	2	SIGNAL, Aircraft, S/S AM-M34 R
35	2	SIGNAL, Aircraft, S/S AM-M35 Y
36	2	SIGNAL, Aircraft, S/S AM-M36 G
37	4	SIGNAL, Aircraft, D/S AM-M40 R/Y
38	12	SIGNAL, Aircraft, Parachute R/S
39	3	SIGNAL, Aircraft, Mark 1
40	3	SIGNAL, Aircraft, Mark 4
41	1000	Cart. AP & T Cal .50
42	2	PISTOLS, Pyre, H-2, 3956 & 41623
43	1	PISTOL, Pyre H-8, No. E-026821

The new plane had fewer than ten hours on it. Cost to Uncle Sam was $289,276.00.[7] As soon as he could read the B-24's tail number, Scearce had it forever etched in his mind. It would be the radio operator's call sign for the ship, 41-24214. "Two one four," he said aloud. "Two one four."

"Two one four" was a "D" model B-24 Liberator bomber, built by Consolidated Aircraft at their factory in San Diego. The contract Consolidated won from the government in 1939 called for a four-engined plane with a 3,000-mile range, top speed of 300 mph and a service ceiling of 35,000 feet. These performance specifications called for a plane that would out-perform the older B-17 Flying Fortress.[8]

Consolidated was best known for making flying boats, and B-24s look a lot like Consolidated's earlier Model 31 flying boat. In fact, the B-24 was built around the wing designed for the Model 31.[9] The wing had a high aspect ratio, meaning that the ratio of its length to average width was high. The result was a long, tapering wing that contributed to the B-24's long range and high performance ceiling. It was a lighter wing structure than the B-17's, benefiting fuel and bomb load but at the cost of strength and the airframe's ability to absorb damage.

The first experimental B-24 flew at Consolidated's San Diego plant on December 29, 1939.[10] It was 64 feet long and had a 110-foot wingspan. With twin rudders connected by a horizontal elevator, the plane looked different from most aircraft. Its tricycle landing gear, with a nose wheel in front and main wheels under each of its high-mounted wings, added to the plane's unconventional look.

By contrast, the B-17 Flying Fortress had a single vertical rudder and a tail wheel. A parked B-17, its nose pointed high, tail down, with broad, muscular-looking wings mounted low, has a proud and graceful look, as if it is eager to leap skyward. A parked B-24 looks squat, tail up, as if it is about to pounce on a bug.

Consolidated engineers designed the B-24 using mathematical models. There wasn't much thought to the plane's appearance, except for a last minute change made by Consolidated President Reuben Fleet. Fleet added three feet of length ahead of the plane's cockpit, improving the snub-nosed look of the prototype.[11] Still, B-17 crews derided the slab-sided Liberator, calling it "the box ours came in."

On February 7, 1943, Lt. Joe Deasy and his crew received orders to report to Hickam Field, Territory of Hawaii.[12] The crew was disappointed to be ordered to Hawaii rather than England, because it was understood that aircrews flying against Germany were racking up mission credits in a hurry, and the crew would get to return home only after completing the thirty combat missions required by the Air Corps for bomber crews. But instead of east toward England, they aimed west from Salina for Hamilton Field, California, their last stop before the long flight over water to Hawaii.

Navigator Lt. Art Boone was too sick to make the trip to Hamilton Field. That frigid truck ride to Salina had left him with bad cold symptoms that were finally diagnosed as pneumonia. The crew was upset by the news, because this meant they might get a brand-new and unproven replacement navigator, someone they didn't know, someone who had not yet earned their confidence. It also meant they would have to wait, bored, for who knew how long, until the replacement arrived.

The crew was anxious to get going, but it would be a few days before they could leave. Other planes and crews arrived bound for Hawaii and ground crews inspected the aircraft, preparing them for the long flight. As they waited, each man on the crew checked out his position in their brand-new plane. Pilots Joe Deasy and Sam Catanzarite made a discovery, which they promptly shared with the rest of the crew: women who had worked on the plane left notes under the buttons in the center of the two pilot's yokes with their names and addresses and well wishes, and the crew was delighted. They thought it would have been helpful if the women had also left their pictures with the plane.

Deasy went to the Air Transport Command's office at Hamilton Field with a request: loan us one of your navigators for the flight to Hawaii, and we'll be out of your way. Deasy didn't tell the crew he was making this request, because he expected to be turned down. If the crew knew what he was doing, they might get their hopes up, and a rejection could hurt the crew's morale.

Lieutenant Deasy was pleased when the ATC commander agreed. This meant that the crew would have an experienced navigator for the long over-water trip, a risky proposition in 1943, especially for crews fresh out of training. A navigational error of just one degree on a flight of 2200 miles would mean missing Hickam by nearly forty miles. With an ATC navigator the crew would be on its way without worry.

Deasy was second in line as seven B-24 Liberators queued for take-off. When the lead plane developed an engine problem, Deasy asked the tower if he could go ahead. He got permission, pulled out of line, and was first to take off. The rest of the flight followed him, taking off into a gentle breeze coming in from the San Pablo Bay. Passing over the blue water of the bay, Scearce remembered gunnery school flights over the Texas coast. Turning south and west over the Golden Gate, they were on their way to Hickam Field, Territory of Hawaii, where the men expected to gas up and take off again for the combat zone.

Chapter 2

Hawaii

SIX B-24 LIBERATORS approached Hickam Field on the morning of February 9, 1943, arriving from Hamilton Field, California. Aboard aircraft number 41-24214, Sergeant Herman Scearce got up from the radio operator's table for a better view.

From the southwest, Hickam Field lay directly ahead. The dark green mountains of the Koolau Range rose in the distance, wispy clouds hanging close to the ridge line. To the left, beside the air base, were dozens of fat, round, fuel storage tanks, and beyond those, Pearl Harbor's aquamarine water seemed to glow.

"There's the *Arizona*," Deasy said.

On final approach, Scearce and the crew had just a moment to put eyes on the battleship, resting beside Ford Island, its gray structure rising above a shining, luminescent pool of oil.

"Sons o' bitches," Sgt. Jack Yankus muttered, from his fold-down jump seat on the flight deck between Deasy, in the left seat, and Catanzarite on the right. Yankus was ready to call out the aircraft's speed, the flight engineer's job during landings. His comment resonated for a moment, hanging there, profound. "Okay . . . 130," he said next.

On the ground at Hickam, Scearce and the rest of the enlisted men got directions to the mess hall, looking forward to a hot meal. They gawked at the pale yellow buildings and palm trees, and pointed out Diamond Head to one another. Lipe said he wanted to stay on Oahu long enough to see Waikiki, smiling and nodding knowingly, as if there would be girls there waiting just for him. For his part, Ed Hess hung back a few paces from the other enlisted men, like a tolerant school master in charge of four silly boys on a field trip.

There would be plenty of time for Waikiki. The crew was ordered to Kahuku, on the opposite side of the island at Oahu's northern tip. They made the hop over from Hickam on the same day they arrived from California. It dawned on them that they weren't going to gas up and head to the combat zone, and it didn't look like they were going to get thirty missions in a hurry.

Quonset huts housed the aircrews on Kahuku. Corrugated metal buildings on a concrete slab, Quonset huts were prefabricated, sectional units that could be set up quickly. They served as barracks, offices, hospitals, warehouses, and assembly rooms, and met countless other needs during the war. With long, rounded sides, they looked like a short section of half-buried tube. The arch shape gave them strength, but they were no barrier to a flying nemesis despised almost as much as the Japanese: mosquitoes.

Each man was issued a mosquito net for his protection while sleeping. The nets worked well enough to keep the insects off, but there were so many swarming around every net, trying to find some opening, that the noise kept men awake. It was unnerving, and Scearce never got used to the sound.

Flying out of Kahuku, Deasy's crew flew submarine patrol. They looked for periscopes, which they had been told would leave a little tell-tale wake on the water's surface, were they ever to see one. They looked for planes that were supposed to have landed but had missed their Estimated Time of Arrival and were presumed crashed in the ocean. They practiced bomb runs and navigation legs. None of it was combat, and the crewmen were keenly aware that they weren't making progress toward the magic number of thirty combat missions needed before they could go home. They didn't consider that every hour they spent flying around Hawaii sharpened their skills, increased their experience, and improved their odds of surviving the war.

Military bases of every description dotted Oahu. Another B-24 base was at Kualoa, on the northeast side of Oahu on Kaneohe Bay, built on the site of an old sugar mill. The runway at Kualoa took up most of the available land, with mountains on the west side and the bay on the other three sides. Enlisted men's quarters were little wooden and tarpaper shacks snugged up against the foot of the mountains, perched there, precarious, as if by moving in the men might throw the shacks out of balance and tumble with them right down into the ocean.

On their first hop to Kualoa, Flight Engineer Jack Yankus took his usual position between the pilots in order to call out airspeed on approach to the landing strip. The approach to Kualoa took them to the east side of the island, over Kaneohe Bay, with "Chinaman's Hat" an unmistakable point of reference. Mokolii, called Chinaman's Hat because of its shape, is a small island in Kaneohe Bay just offshore near the airfield. The air strip began and ended within rock-throwing distance of the water. The coast road crossed the runway with warning lights on each side, like a railroad crossing, and guards stopped traffic when planes were taking off or landing.

Deasy banked his plane around Chinaman's Hat on approach to the base. The plane descended on final approach and the large main landing gear wheels under the wings touched down first, and then the nose wheel came down, as usual. When the nose wheel touched, there was a sudden deafening roar. Yankus grabbed the pilot's seats on either side of him for dear life and shouted, "What the HELL?"

It was their first time landing on an all-metal strip. Made of Marston mat, the runway was built from interlocking steel grids, officially called Pierced Steel Planking.[1] Each piece was ten feet long and about fifteen inches wide. With Marston mat, a runway could appear almost overnight. Kualoa's metal runway was laid over a hard packed surface and Yankus had noticed no difference between it and more familiar concrete runways.

For weeks, Yankus' reaction to the sound was good for laughs when the crew touched down at Kualoa. The wheels would contact the runway and over the roaring sound of the tires on metal matting someone would pipe up on the interphone, "What the HELL?" and Yankus would shake his head. "I'm surrounded by a bunch of comedians."

During the first few weeks at Kahuku, "two one four" got a name. Mammy Yokum, the tough, principled upholder of law and order and decency from the cartoon *Li'l Abner,* appeared mysteriously on the right side of the aircraft's nose, below the co-pilot's windows. Clenching a corncob pipe in her mouth, she delivered a knockout punch with her left fist. In script mimicking the title of the cartoon strip were the words, "*Dogpatch Express.*" No one on the crew was sure who the artist was, but they all liked the name. Lieutenant Deasy preferred it to the scantily clad women on most of the other planes, and he made sure the art work wasn't changed.

"D" model B-24s had a rounded, Plexiglas nose. In the nose was a single, flexible .50 caliber machine gun that didn't offer a lot of protection against a frontal attack. The machine shops and repair facilities of the Hickam Air Depot solved the problem by removing the original Plexiglas nose and installing a twin .50 caliber machine gun tail turret in its place. Each of the 42nd Bomb Squadron's Liberators got a "depot turret."

The Hickam Air Depot also opened a hole in the bottom of each B-24, just aft of the waist gun positions, and installed a belly turret to protect the aircraft from attack from below.[2] These aircraft modifications impressed the new aircrews recently arrived from the States, and they began to believe that there wasn't much the Depot men couldn't do.

The belly turret was no place for anyone who couldn't handle small spaces. It was also no place for someone who couldn't handle the idea of being lowered beneath the fuselage of the aircraft, literally hanging below the plane in flight. Scearce got into it once while the plane was safely parked at Kahuku, just to see what it was like. He felt like a sardine, packed in and unable to move, and he swore he would never get into a belly turret again.

Most crewmen had similar distaste for the belly turret because it was isolated, claustrophobic, and nightmarish if its occupant became wounded. Pilots typically had to assign the belly turret to one of their crew, and among the men of *Dogpatch Express*, one gunner seemed ideally suited for the job. Elmer Johnson was short, just the right size to fold up into the spherical turret, but most importantly, he liked it, which pleased Lieutenant Deasy because it saved him from having to designate someone for the job.

Addition of the belly turret created the need for another gunner, and it was clear to the men on Joe Deasy's crew that Al Marston ought to be their man. Technical Sergeant Al Marston was an Army "ground pounder" who worked guard duty at Kahuku. He had been begging to get on an aircrew since the B-24s arrived. Marston, no relation to Marston mat steel planking, was at Schofield Barracks when the Japanese attacked fifteen months before. Following the attack, Marston spent many nights in fear of imminent Japanese invasion, his rifle always within arm's reach, carrying a supply of ammunition that he was sure wouldn't be enough. The Japanese attack created a passion in Marston to strike back.

Lieutenant Deasy had a good feeling about Al Marston, so he worked through 42nd Bomb Squadron headquarters to get Marston's orders changed.

Deasy's intuition was well founded. In the fall of 1943, Gen. Robert W. Harper, Air Staff chief of training, commented on non-flying combat veterans who volunteered to become aircrew gunners. He said, "Many of these men have been strafed, have had friends killed, and are generally 'combat-wise'. They would be of inestimable help in the gunnery schools from a morale standpoint and should become exceptionally good combat crew members."[3]

Marston became a well-motivated addition to the crew. Since Elmer Johnson was such a natural for the new belly turret, Marston took Johnson's old gun position in the tail.

The nose and belly modifications and the installation of radar receiver antennae on each side of the cockpit required some paint work. Green paint was applied around the new nose turret and on the sides where the four stubby radar antennae now protruded. The fresh green paint didn't match the original olive drab. A corner of the radar antenna panel on the right side obscured a bit of Mammy Yokum's hat. With its mismatched paint and modifications, "two one four" looked like a battle-scarred combat veteran.

On March 10, 1943, *Dogpatch Express* flew to the Naval Air Station on Johnston Island, five hours away, on a training flight. The crew was the first in the squadron to fly to Johnston. Lieutenant Deasy signed the Naval Station visitor's log, impressed to see that the previous signature on the log was Frank Knox, Secretary of War, visiting weeks before on an inspection tour of the island.[4]

Johnston Island is the largest of four coral islands in a small, isolated atoll about 700 nautical miles southwest of Oahu. It was shelled by the

Japanese after the Pearl Harbor attack, but aside from occasional gun fire by Japanese submarines, Johnston was out of the way of the fighting.

The Johnston Island mission became routine for B-24 crews, mainly for navigator training. The bomber crews also hauled the mail for the Navy garrison there. Johnston's forlorn sailors liked to see the Liberators coming and always wanted to hop a ride back to Hawaii.

Scearce felt sorry for the guys who were stationed on Johnston Island because they seemed to have nothing to do. The poor guys stationed there couldn't even enjoy a smoke outside at night because of the submarine threat; any light visible outside was forbidden. Scearce and his friends stationed at Kualoa realized they didn't have it so bad, after all. Their biggest off-duty problem was figuring out how to get across Oahu to Honolulu and how to get back to their base on time. Getting into town and back took creativity, especially with an 8:00 "lights out," because none of the men had a car. The regularly scheduled mail truck could get them into town, but it was a one-way ride. The men had to catch a ride with someone or hitchhike back to base.

Every couple of months, the crew got a three-day pass. Scearce and his buddies rented a cheap room a few blocks off Waikiki and then went to unwind in the elegant lobby of the famous waterfront Moana Hotel or relax on the beach right outside and pretend they were staying there.

There were lots of card games, and worldly Ed Hess liked to play for money. Hess had a friend on the island, Eddie Howard, who ran a drive-in restaurant called Kau Kau Korner. The local boys, many of them sons of wealthy business families, played cards at Howard's apartment. They kept it reasonable when Hess was in the game, but as soon as Hess backed out, the stakes would jump. On his Army Air Forces pay, Hess just didn't have as much to lose.

Scearce and his crew mates dated the civil service girls who worked at the base. Sometimes they went out with local girls, some the daughters of the women who worked the little roadside produce stands and sundries stores dotting the coast road. With the 8:00 curfew, most dates started at about two or three o'clock in the afternoon. Car lights were prohibited after curfew. Other men didn't care about playing the game of courting girls, trying to get dates, or fretting about the curfew. Honolulu had lots of prostitutes, and the prostitutes had plenty of business.

There was a redhead named Maxine with a smooth business operation in an upstairs Honolulu flat. She had three rooms, working them assembly-line style. One man got ready in the first room while Maxine was with some soldier or sailor in the second, and the man in the third room dressed to leave. Maxine just moved from room to room and called her next customer into whichever room had just been vacated.

On a weekend pass, Scearce was sunning himself on Waikiki Beach one afternoon while Yankus dozed nearby. Scearce glanced up toward the Royal Hawaiian Hotel behind them and saw an officer from their squadron, Lt. Butch Austin (name changed) standing on a hotel room balcony with a redheaded woman. Scearce elbowed Yankus.

"Hey . . . isn't that. . ."

Yankus turned around to see where Scearce was looking.

"Sure is! And with *Maxine!*"

"Oh man, oh man, oh man."

"Don't he know?"

"I shoulda brought my camera!"

"Oh, man."

On their next flight together, Yankus and Scearce got on the interphone.

"Um, Lieutenant Austin, you dating a redhead?" Yankus looked over his shoulder at Scearce and winked.

"Yep. Nice girl, really nice girl."

"We saw you two in town. How'd you meet?" Scearce asked, as innocently as he could, choking back a snicker.

"We met in a club, a nice place. We really hit it off."

"What's her name?"

"Maxine."

Scearce and Yankus didn't have the heart to tell Lieutenant Austin about Maxine's booming three-room business.

Scearce became friends with Sgt. Harold Brooks at Kahuku shortly after the squadron was stationed there. Brooks, from Clarksville, Michigan, was the radio operator on *Super Man*, Lt. Russell Phillips' plane. When the two men decided to head to the Post Exchange at the same time, they went together, and on that first trip to Kahuku's PX they met Noelani, a pretty local girl who worked there. Later the same day each man promised not to go to the PX without the other while secretly plotting how to break their promise in order to see the girl alone.

Lani, as she liked to be called, had a bright smile that she couldn't hide when Scearce and Brooks were around. She enjoyed being the center of attention between the two handsome airmen as they acted out a running dispute about which of them had spotted her first. Scearce and Brooks played up a friendly competition for Lani from the beginning, and for her part, Lani was wise enough to act shy and demure when both men were around, especially if she was on the clock at the PX.

The two radio men teased Lani, asking her when she got off work, when they could pick her up, and whether she had a sister as pretty as she was. "You're going to get me in trouble," she would say. "Stop it," she would say, with a flash in her dark eyes and a sweet smile on her face. When Scearce succeeded in getting her to go out with him alone, Lani made him feel like he was her favorite, and he believed it, even though he was sure that Lani was able to make Brooks believe it, too.

Chapter 3

First Mission

THE MORNING OF APRIL 17 had a different feel, electric. The squadron's officers were still in a closed-door briefing while rumors buzzed about a bombing mission, the squadron's first. All that remained for pilots to tell their crews was when and where. When Joe Deasy met with his crew and gave them the particulars, it was the first time they had heard of Funafuti.

"Funa-who?" Yankus snorted. Twenty-three B-24 Liberators would fly to Canton Island, a porkchop-shaped atoll 1,907 miles southwest of Oahu, refuel, and continue the 737 miles to Funafuti in the Ellice Islands group, 2600 miles from Hawaii. "That's halfway to Australia," Hess muttered.

Six months before, on October 2, 1942, eleven ships of the United States Navy had entered Funafuti's lagoon and landed a Construction Battalion. The Seabees immediately began construction of an airfield and support facilities while Marines prepared defenses and set up anti-aircraft guns. To build the runway, Seabees bulldozed thousands of coconut trees and covered arable land with hard-packed coral. The airfield was completed before the end of the year.[1]

Funafuti was a forward base for the American bombers, a staging facility, not equipped for the squadron's aircraft to stay. The airmen weren't told where they were going from there; they would be briefed again on Funafuti. There was a lot of speculation, but most of the men agreed they would probably bomb Tarawa.

On the long flight to Canton, the men ate plain baloney sandwiches delivered to the flight line from Kahuku's mess hall. They used their flak jackets for pillows and stole naps in the back of the airplane. A relief tube, or "piss pipe" as crewmen called it, was built in to the side of the plane just aft of the left waist window; another one was installed behind the flight deck. There was a portable toilet, but the men avoided it unless they were desperate. It was better to wait than use the "honey bucket" and have to wash it out after landing, because if you used it, it was yours to clean. Even the piss pipe could be a nasty problem at higher altitudes where the pipe's flow could freeze and cause a messy back-up.

The Navy garrison on Canton treated their overnight guests well. The Air Corps men got a hot meal in the Navy mess hall and slept in clean barracks with fresh white bed linens. Early the next morning, *Dogpatch Express* and twenty-two more refueled B-24 Liberators took flight for the final leg of the trip to Funafuti, and on the afternoon of April 18, the wisps of land of the Ellice Islands came in to view.

The planes approached Funafuti's coral airstrip from the southeast. The island, shaped like a long, narrow boomerang, curved from the southwest to its thickest part in the middle, then arched back toward the northwest. Long and graceful, Funafuti was about fifty yards wide at each end, about 700 yards wide in the middle, and seven and a half miles long. Waves broke along the eastern side, the dark blue water of the Pacific just beyond and to the right as the aircraft approached. To the left of the island, in the middle of the boomerang, was a lagoon, its calm water a beautiful shade of light blue fading to green close to shore. Coconut trees covered the island from its lower tip, nearest the approaching planes, and ended at the airfield. The white coral runway cut straight across the leading edge of the boomerang, beginning just a few feet from the ocean, and it seemed to end in the ocean on the other side.[2]

A detachment of U.S. Marines and Navy men were stationed on the island. If it was possible to have less than the sailors on Johnston Island, these men had it. At least the Johnston Island garrison could look forward to regular visits by planes from Hawaii. Funafuti did have the advantage of a friendly, cooperative native population, and the Marines and sailors at Funafuti were amused by the pretty, dark skinned and topless girls among the island's several hundred natives. But American service men were supposed to keep their distance from native women and the novelty wore off soon enough.

There were no taxiways and very few revetments or bomb proofs on Funafuti to shelter parked aircraft, though there were plans to add them later. After landing, the aircraft were parked side by side along the runway. If something caused one of them to catch fire, the planes parked nearby would be in danger, and if one plane was hit during a Japanese air raid, the planes on either side were at risk from fire and explosion.

American planes parked wingtip to wingtip, the better to guard against saboteurs, multiplied the effectiveness of Japanese bomb hits and strafing runs during the attack on Oahu sixteen months before.[3] But the airmen on Funafuti weren't worried about a Japanese attack because Funafuti was just a staging base; they weren't going to keep the planes there long. Besides, the briefing officer back at Kahuku made it clear that the Japanese wouldn't know they were there.

Early on Monday, April 19, 1943, an officer stepped front and center on Funafuti's outdoor stage before the assembled aircrews. The men sat on felled palm logs arranged in rows like seats in a theater. Behind the officer was a map, and on the bottom right of the map was Funafuti and the rest of the Ellice Islands group, with the Gilberts to the north.

There was another island near the upper left corner, north and west of Funafuti, and beside the map was a separate, large-scale drawing of this distant island, Nauru.

The officer tapped his pointer on targets and visual references on the map of Nauru. He described anti-aircraft gun positions and the kind of fighter interception the men would face. When he was finished, a weather officer took the stage, describing the conditions expected through each part of the flight. Next, the operations officer gave the crews order of take-off and critical mission details, including engine start time. Each man mentally calculated when he needed to be at the plane in order to preflight his equipment and be ready for engine start.

After the briefing, aircrews prepared their planes for the next day's bombing mission. Ground crews fueled *Dogpatch Express* with 2,700 gallons of gas from tank trailers towed behind Cletracs, tracked vehicles similar to bulldozers. Flight Engineer Jack Yankus and Assistant Engineer Bob Lipe confirmed the fuel level and checked engine oil levels. Yankus, Lipe, Scearce, Hess, Johnson, and Marston cleaned and oiled the barrels of their machine guns and loaded them with ammunition, belts of .50 caliber rounds in a repeating sequence of two armor piercing, two incendiary, and one tracer.

Bombardier Lt. Shorty Schroeder, flying in place of Lieutenant Baber, oversaw the bomb loading of *Dogpatch Express*. Eight 500-pound General Purpose bombs were loaded in the plane's bomb bay racks from bomb trailers pulled by a truck. Most of the bombs were fused to explode on impact; some were equipped with delay fuses.

Scearce made certain that the radios were working properly and ready to go. He planned to do it again early the next morning, just to be doubly sure. Once the plane was loaded, Yankus checked the landing gear for four inches of travel in its shock-absorbing struts because less could cause the gear to fail.[4]

After a fitful few hours of sleep, the crew of *Dogpatch Express* walked to their plane. Jack Yankus checked that the ignition switches were off, then he and Bobby Lipe stepped in front of the aircraft's mighty engines and pulled the propellers through, counting six propeller blades at each engine, two full revolutions of the Liberator's three-bladed prop. Some crews shrugged off this procedure, but oil accumulation in the bottom of an engine could cause a potentially disastrous cylinder failure.

While Scearce re-checked his radio equipment, Yankus fitted the pilot and co-pilot's parachutes into the recesses of. their seats in the cockpit and reported to Lt. Joe Deasy that the plane was ready to go.

On the flight deck of *Dogpatch Express*, Lieutenants Deasy and Catanzarite completed their pre-flight checklist as pilots and co-pilots aboard twenty-two more Liberators lined up on Funafuti's runway followed the same procedure. At engine start, four fourteen-cylinder Pratt & Whitney R-1830-43 radial engines, twelve hundred horsepower each, joined the motors of the other aircraft to produce a mighty harmony unlike anything Funafuti had ever heard before.

Before his take-off roll, Deasy opened the throttles and held the brakes until engine manifold pressures reached twenty-five inches of mercury. When Deasy released the brakes, Catanzarite held the throttles to the stops so they wouldn't creep back. Yankus called out speed as *Dogpatch Express* accelerated, slowly at first with its full bomb load. At 110, Deasy began to apply gentle pressure, pulling the yoke back, and at 130, the heavy bomber lifted off Funafuti's coral runway.

In the pre-dawn darkness of April 20, twenty-three B-24s took off, each loaded with 4,000 pounds of bombs. One plane developed an engine problem and turned back to Funafuti, but the remaining bombers droned on toward a midday strike against Japanese positions on Nauru.

Nauru lies twenty-six miles below the equator, 1,000 miles northwest of Funafuti. Oval shaped with about eight square miles of territory, it was ringed by trees and a sandy beach. The interior of the island was almost solid high-grade rock phosphate, essential in metal alloys and used in bomb production. Phosphate mining, refining, and shipping facilities operated by the British on Nauru before the war were shelled by a German auxiliary cruiser in 1940 and seized by the Japanese in 1942. Far-flung Nauru, with the unusual distinction of being occupied by the British and attacked by both German and Japanese forces already during the war, was about to be bombed by Americans.[5]

Two hours into the flight, pilot Joe Deasy spoke over the interphone. "Fellows, go ahead and test fire your guns." He sounded much calmer than the skeet range captain back in Harlingen.

Scearce and Yankus moved through the airplane between racks of 500-pound General Purpose bombs in the bomb bay, along the nine-inch-wide catwalk connecting the flight deck to the rear. Bobby Lipe pulled himself up to sit in the top turret, usually the flight engineer's position because it was closest to the flight deck, but Yankus had asked Deasy if he could take a waist gun instead, claiming his legs were too long for the top turret. Besides, Lipe was an excellent mechanic, as capable as most any flight engineer, and certainly better than the assistant engineers on a lot of crews.

Lipe's mechanical inclination had revealed itself years before. He was fourteen when he opened a bicycle repair shop in his front yard with a hand-lettered sign advertising "Licensed Bicycle Repair." Barney Millen, the town marshal, took exception to Bobby's "licensed" claim, or maybe there was a zoning issue on his mind. Whatever his reason, the officer kicked Bobby's sign down.[6]

In high school, Lipe was among the few with his own car, a Model "A" Ford. Bobby maintained the car on his own with skills honed in his stepfather's auto repair shop. Bobby's stepfather raced midget cars on eastern Ohio dirt tracks and Bobby, with his brother Sox, assisted as the pit crew. Even their dog Jigs was named for a machinist's tools.

If Joe Deasy had any doubts at all about Bob Lipe's mechanical ability or qualifications as a flight engineer, he would not have agreed to let Yankus move back to a waist gun.

Hess slid into the nose turret. Johnson bent down and eased himself into the belly turret while Marston stooped to get back to the tail. Lipe fired his topside guns first, then Hess tested his guns up front in the Depot turret and Marston fired his twin .50's in the tail.

At the airplane's waist, Scearce and Yankus stood nearly back to back. They pushed a wind deflector out from the side of the plane, a panel about six inches wide running from just above the waist window to just below it. The deflectors reduced wind buffeting and made it easier for the men to handle their guns. Next, they unlocked the windows, Scearce on the right side, Yankus on the left, and they swung the windows up and inward on their hinges toward the top of the fuselage and latched them into place. Cool wind gusted through the openings and the aircraft's engines roared louder as the flight engineer and radio operator, now waist gunners, unlocked their .50 caliber machine guns and swung them out the windows. Each man charged his gun with a hard, quick pull on the handle, held the double grips, and pressed the trigger.

After a quick burst of gunfire, Scearce and Yankus reversed the test firing procedure and secured the windows into place again, because open windows created drag and burned fuel, a precious commodity on long flights over water. Johnson squeezed off a few rounds beneath the plane before climbing up and out and jacking his belly turret back into the plane.

Dogpatch Express droned on, more than halfway to the target now. Back at his position on the flight deck, Scearce monitored the mission frequency on his BC-348 radio receiver, glad that he had a job to occupy his mind while the other gunners tried to get back to their naps.

The BC-348 receiver sat on the radio operator's table, a Morse code transmitting key beside it and directly in front of a small window on the right side of the plane. The BC-348 was the ship's most powerful receiver, capable of receiving multiple bands. Its tuning dial was calibrated in six frequency ranges, but the dial was masked so that only the selected range was visible in the dial window.

On long search missions, Scearce sometimes fidgeted with the radio to pass the time. Radio operators transmitted in Morse code using a signal book that shortened the most common phrases into three-digit codes. "INTQ50," for example asked, "What is my signal strength?" "INT" indicated that a question followed, and Q50 represented signal strength. Signal strength of five was perfect. If it was much weaker, Scearce would re-tune the radio. But this was not a search mission, and radio silence was critical.

Twenty-two B-24 Liberators drew closer to Nauru, more than 220 aircrew and observers, each man wholly and irrevocably committed. There was no way to avoid whatever was to come and no place to hide. Nauru lay just beyond the horizon, the distance closing at more than three miles per minute. The American bombers would reach their target at noon, each man keenly aware that the bright, beautiful day meant Nauru's Japanese defenders would see the bombers approach with plenty of time to prepare their reception.

Scearce was at the radio operator's table behind co-pilot Sam Catanzarite when navigator Art Boone leaned toward their pilot and said, "Joe, we're one hour out." Scearce glanced at his pilot, and from the right and behind him, Scearce thought he saw Lt. Joe Deasy swallow and take a breath before speaking to the crew through the interphone. "We're sixty minutes from the target, boys. Man your guns."

Chapter 4

Nauru

SCEARCE AND YANKUS UNPLUGGED THEIR interphone headsets and moved toward the rear, as they had practiced a hundred times before. They stepped into the bomb bay, *Dogpatch Express'* four massive radial engines howling in unison, much louder than they had seemed from the flight deck. Moving along the narrow catwalk, indifferent to the thousands of pounds of high explosives just inches to their right and left, waist gunners Scearce and Yankus gripped the framework of the bomb racks as they went. The vibrating metal felt cool.

After Scearce and Yankus passed, Bob Lipe took his position in the top turret, just behind the flight deck, and rotated the turret clockwise, then back, out of habit. Ed Hess settled into the nose turret. Elmer Johnson, already in the aircraft's rear section with Al Marston, stepped back from the piss pipe and stretched himself before jacking up the belly turret with the hand pump just enough to release its safety hooks. Johnson opened a hydraulic valve and allowed the turret to slide down into the wind stream beneath the plane. He glanced back at Scearce and Yankus, smiled and made a diving motion, hands together as if he was on the high board at the YMCA, and then opened the turret's hatch door, stepped into the turret and folded himself into position. Marston moved up the sloping floor toward the twin .50's in the bomber's tail.

There was an interphone jack box at every position and each gunner plugged in, pulled on his interphone headset, and checked the jack box to make sure the switch was set to "INTER."[1]

Throat microphones around their necks, Yankus and Scearce glanced down and pushed their flak jackets flat with shuffling feet, standing on them for protection against gunfire from below. They pushed their wind deflectors out, swung open their windows and latched them overhead. Already Lipe, Hess, and Johnson had reported in, ready. Yankus and Scearce swung their machine guns into the air stream and charged their guns with an expert pull on the handle. "Right waist gun ready," Scearce said. "Left waist ready," Yankus reported, then Marston called in from the rear.

"All right, boys, keep your eyes open, keep the chatter down, and call 'em when you see 'em," Deasy said. "Hold your fire 'til they're in range."

Gunnery school had taught the men how to use the gun sight to judge whether an enemy plane was in range. Firing out of range wasted ammunition.

Hess swept the nose turret side to side. Lipe kept the top turret forward, mostly, rotating through 360 degrees, first right, then to the left, as often as his stomach could handle it. Al Marston shifted his eyes up and then straight behind the plane, scanning the sky from just below the twin rudders of his bomber, wind whistling to either side. Elmer Johnson rode below the plane, almost in his own world, the expanse of Pacific Ocean thousands of feet below.

Elsewhere in the loose formation, Scearce's buddy Harold Brooks was on the left side of *Super Man*, Lt. Russell Phillips' B-24. Brooks had traded places at the waist window with his crewmate, Clarence Douglas.[2]

Aboard *Dogpatch Express*, Scearce searched the sky. Behind him, flight engineer Jack Yankus gripped his machine gun. Back to back they shared almost identical views, a beautiful bright sky, sun directly overhead, other B-24s nearby.

Deasy's voice broke the interphone silence, clear and steady, "Eleven o'clock, got two coming in eleven o'clock high!" Scearce heard Lipe and Hess open fire from the top and front of *Dogpatch Express*. He and Yankus leaned forward, trying to see, fists gripping their guns, instinctively pointed where the men were looking.

"Two o'clock high, two o'clock high . . . coming down fast . . . coming to three o'clock, be ready, top." Lieutenant Deasy's voice was matter-of-fact, almost calming, though the words came quickly. The top turret opened up again. The first two Japanese planes, attacking head on, had broken off to one side of *Dogpatch Express*. The Zero pilots were surprised by the B-24's nose turrets; they had been taught to attack the weak glass nose of an unmodified Liberator, but the Japanese fly-ers learned quickly. They would make their subsequent attacks from other angles.[3]

Another Zero fighter came barreling almost straight down beside the American plane. Assistant Flight Engineer Bob Lipe shouted, "Out of the sun at two o'clock, high!"

Scearce's heart pounded like a jackhammer. He couldn't see the Zero yet. The nearest B-24's top turret and left waist gunner blazed away, their tracers leading Scearce's eyes above *Dogpatch Express'* right wing, when a blur of gray flashed beneath the wing. Scearce reacted instantly, pushing his machine gun barrel low, squeezing the trigger. A two-second burst and the Zero was gone before Scearce heard its fourteen-cylinder Nakajima Sakae 12 engine scream past. Elmer John-son in the belly turret then saw the Zero and squeezed off a burst.

Up top, Lipe spoke clearly, just a hint of a nervous edge in his voice: "One, two more at two o'clock high . . . out of the sun again." "Eight o'clock low, coming up! Five o'clock high! Another one at five o'clock!"

Yankus and Johnson's voices and positions on the plane were instinctively known to each man. They were parts of a whole, a working team, and part of their machine. *Dogpatch Express* was now fully engaged, every gun firing at the attacking fighters in turn. Scearce could hear Marston's .50's in the tail, distinct and staccato, and Johnson's belly turret hammering below his feet, but from where he stood, it was Yankus' gun at his back that Scearce could *feel*. The .50 caliber machine guns pounded like angry fists beating hard and fast on a steel door. Hot, spent brass and gun belt links falling to the floor clinked like glass breaking around the waist gunners' feet.

Scearce could tell from Yankus' movement behind him and the sound of the gun, where Yankus was shooting. Scearce sensed it, knew what Yankus was doing, and Yankus had the same instinct for Scearce behind him. Marston blazed away in the tail. Scearce pushed his .50 to the rear. Johnson and then Yankus fired a long burst into the Zero coming up from eight o'clock until the attacker peeled off and away.

Scearce joined Lipe, three .50 caliber machine guns blazing at a single Zero fighter, tracers spitting toward the Japanese plane in burning white lines. Lipe, in the top turret, sent a stream of gunfire into the belly of the Zero as it streaked overhead. From the left waist window, Jack Yankus saw Lipe's tracers drill the unprotected bottom of the enemy plane. He watched it pitch forward, nose down, and lost sight of it as it plummeted straight down. A few seconds of strained quiet followed, scanning the sky.

Suddenly Scearce spotted a Zero at four o'clock high and called out the position. Lipe swung around in his electrically powered turret. Scearce bent low, aiming high, ready for the range to be right. Had to be patient, had to let him come a little closer. Lipe opened up. Johnson swung left and strained to see the Zero. Scearce saw muzzle flashes through the Zero's propeller; its twin 7.7 millimeter guns seemed to be shooting straight at *him*. Squeezing the trigger, Scearce swung his gun down as the Zero passed. He saw tracers run through the Zero's cowling and remembered that a .50 caliber bullet could knock a cylinder head off a Zero's engine. Hot, spent brass clattered around Scearce's feet, smoking.

Nose gunner Ed Hess gave a quick burst from up front, swinging through ten, then nine o'clock as the fighter passed, and then it was quiet again. Scearce kicked some brass away from his feet, took a deep breath, and thought, "This is a long way from gunnery school."

As the Zeros moved off, the crew was sure the other bombers were catching hell behind them. The Zeros' twin 7.7 millimeter machine guns were supplemented by menacing 20 millimeter cannon mounted in each wing. The explosive round from the 20 millimeter gun weighed more than a quarter of a pound and hits by the Zero's cannon could be devastating.[4] But the Zero's impressive armament belied the nimble fighter's weaknesses: the Japanese plane sacrificed the added weight of self-sealing fuel tanks and armor protection in favor of speed and agility, qualities that served the Zero well in combat with other fighters.[5] As an interceptor of B-24 Liberators, however, with their armor protection, self-sealing fuel tanks, and ten .50 caliber guns, the Zero was vulnerable, even fragile. Zero pilots pressing home an attack against a Liberator needed nerves of steel.

Aboard *Dogpatch Express*, bombardier Lt. Shorty Schroeder was ready to take control of the plane for the bomb run, his bomb sight connected to the flight controls. The bombardier aimed his entire aircraft through the bomb sight.

The Japanese fighter pilots changed tactics as the bombers readied for their bomb runs and the flak batteries on the ground below began sending their shells skyward. Nine Zeros circled at a distance, chasing one another's tails in an oval, a racetrack pattern that advanced as the bombers sped forward. The Zeros fired their guns each time the circuit brought them to face the American bombers, but with his own plane's right wing and engines between him and the enemy fighters, Scearce could only watch, a white flash each time, a blink, and hope the streams of Japanese bullets missed.

Anti-aircraft gunners now took their turn. Flak bursts filled the sky ahead, inky dark puffs drifting closer as the bombers approached. In the distance a single Japanese plane idled out of range of the Liberators' guns, holding the same altitude as the American planes, reporting it to the ground batteries below. The B-24s rushed unalterably, purposefully ahead.

There was no dodging the flak. *Dogpatch Express* held 7,500 feet altitude during the bomb run, level, steady; there could be no deviation from course. This was a bomber at its most vulnerable during a strike mission, forty-five seconds that lasted forever, forty-five seconds, it seemed, before the crew could breathe again. Flak bursts, like sinister potholes in the sky, caused the plane to shake and bounce as they exploded. 2nd Lt. Shorty Schroeder's voice came through the interphone. "I've got it." Deasy and Catanzarite let go.

Anti-aircraft shells burst all around; Scearce was amazed anything flew through it. Spent flak, shards of metal blown in all directions by each explosive burst, pelted the plane like hail on a tin roof. The men wanted to be small, very small. They wanted the bomb run to end, the bombs to be away, but they also wanted the bombs to be on target. They didn't want their trip to be wasted, didn't want to have to do it again. Scearce noticed his knuckles, ghost white on the grips, and forced himself to flex his hands as he watched the sky.

Behind the flight deck of *Dogpatch Express* there suddenly was a loud thump and a metallic clang, followed immediately by an evil hissing sound behind co-pilot Sam Catanzarite. Scearce heard navigator Art Boone say, "We're hit!"

"Bombs away!" Schroeder reported as the last 500-pound bomb fell from its rack. The plane seemed to leap in the air, free of its heavy burden. Deasy pushed the control yoke forward, nosing *Dogpatch Express* over, and put the throttles to the stops, getting the hell out of there fast.

The hissing continued, but nobody was hurt and they were still in control, still together. "C'mere, Jack," Deasy commanded. As Yankus moved forward, the hissing slowed.

Yankus traced the damage. Sunlight streamed through a hole just below the leading edge of the right wing. A jagged shard of twisted metal three inches across had come through the ship just behind Bob Lipe's legs as he sat in the top turret. After cutting a compressed oxygen line, the bomb fragment had stabbed through the pilot's seat.

"Went through your seat, Joe. You okay?"

"I'm okay."

The Zeros harassed the trailing B-24s for half an hour more, and then turned away.

"How'd we do?" Deasy asked.

There was a pause, a moment's hesitation, before Yankus spoke. "Everything hit the water, sir." Scearce had seen the splashes, too. Bombardier Shorty Schroeder crushed a paper coffee cup in his right hand and muttered, "Bullshit."

Scearce and Yankus swung their guns inside, locked the windows closed, and pulled the wind deflectors in tight to the sides of the plane. Bob Lipe stepped down from his turret, wiped his face on his sleeve, and looked up at the ugly hole in his plane's skin. He hadn't heard the impact. A few feet aft, and the flak might have hit the top turret. Ed Hess unfolded himself from the nose, and from the rear, they heard Marston say, "Fellas, I'm going to sit here a minute, watch our ass a little while." Yankus steadied Johnson as he pulled himself from the belly turret and helped him jack it up and secure the turret inside the plane. Johnson stood and stretched, as he had before settling into the turret almost two hours before.

After each plane finished its bomb run, the pilot throttled up, diving and turning toward a prearranged heading for departure from the target. Once they were out of danger, the aircraft returned to a higher cruising altitude and continued toward their forward base on Funafuti. Their targets, phosphate plants, gun positions, maintenance and barracks buildings, and the runways on Nauru were so small that each plane had to make its bomb run alone and their return to Funafuti was staggered.

Since each plane had to find its own way, each crew needed a skilled navigator. There was nothing below but ocean, no point of reference except the sun. Navigators relied on dead reckoning, calculating their position based on the previous position, taking into account time, heading, and the effect of wind pushing the aircraft sideways, called drift. Errors in dead reckoning were cumulative, so each calculation increased the difference between the aircraft's plotted position and its actual location. Returning to a tiny island base hours away, burning a limited fuel supply, mistakes in navigation could be tragic. The Army Air Forces "Navigator's Information File" advised:

> In the Central Pacific celestial navigation is used in conjunction with dead reckoning on all missions. Many of the islands and atolls are plotted in error from 2 to 10 miles, usually eastward or westward. Interpretation of sun lines and fixes is important. Radio facilities are not always available in this area and you cannot always depend upon them because of local disturbances. Be careful when you use clouds for pilotage. Cumulus often builds up around islands, but shadows of clouds also look like land . . .[6]

Scearce returned to his radio operator's table and put on his headset, monitoring the frequencies assigned for the mission. Radio silence was paramount, but if a crew was in serious trouble, the radio may be their last resort, possibly to report their position before crashing into the sea. Yankus also returned to the flight deck and sat on the jump seat between the pilots. As *Dogpatch Express* cruised back to Funafuti, Yankus poured Deasy, Catanzarite, and Scearce a few swallows of tepid coffee from a dented metal Thermos.

Twelve hours after taking off, *Dogpatch Express* settled gently onto Funafuti's dusty coral strip and Deasy taxied the bomber to a stop, guided by a ground crewman's hand signals. On the ground again, the men of *Dogpatch Express* walked around their aircraft, checking it for damage. Some elevator fabric was torn away. There was the jagged flak hole behind and above the co-pilot's seat, big enough for Yankus to put his fist through. Joe Deasy found the razor-sharp metal in his parachute pack where, its energy finally spent, it had stopped less than an inch from the pilot's spine.

The flight surgeon met the crew at the flight line and offered each man a shot of whiskey. Catanzarite, Yankus, and Johnson swallowed theirs, the other men declined. The aircraft's boxy K-20 camera was removed from its mount in the rear escape hatch and taken to the photo lab, a portable darkroom in a green Army trailer where the film could be developed for analysis by intelligence officers. Each plane had a K-20, and when the bombs were released, they snapped photos automatically, looking straight down. Successive photos showed the bombs getting smaller and smaller and farther apart as they fell from the plane, until finally they could hardly be seen at all, then the last photos revealed the bomb's detonations.

Planes came into view about fifteen minutes apart, more or less. A pair lumbered in together, having found each other on the way. One struggled, number 2 engine out, its prop blades turned into the air stream to reduce drag. This was called "feathering" and was accomplished by switching settings from the flight deck. He approached first while his wingman banked, circling around to yield the runway to his stricken squadron mate.

Hess mumbled, "Too high . . . too high, man, get her down!" The left wing dipped. "Level out . . . level her out . . ."

The ship seemed almost to be flying sideways, approaching the runway like a scared cat. The pilot touched the plane down. Since he came in high he needed a lot of runway. Reaching the end of his roll, he swung the bomber around fast and tight, but he was parked. Men jumped from the aircraft and half-trotted away, looking over their shoulders like the plane might blow up at any second. It was the ground crew chief's plane now.

The next one touched down with no problem. Another followed. This one had taken some hits. He touched. Immediately Scearce saw the left wheel was flat, shot out. The plane lurched to the left, almost ground-looping into a revetment. The pilot throttled up the engines on the left side and the plane straightened and ground to a stop, perched at an angle, tire rubber shredded and wrapped around the left wheel and strut like stripes on a barber pole.

A ground crew corporal skidded up in a weapons carrier with wooden planks along its sides for seats to take the crew of *Dogpatch Express* to a thatched hut where an S-2 intelligence officer debriefed them. He gathered information about enemy fighters, how many and what tactics they used, how aggressive they were. He made notes about the anti-aircraft reception, bomb hits, fires started, what color the smoke was and how far out the smoke could still be seen.

After their debriefing and after a few bites to eat, the men walked back to the flight line. They counted twenty-two B-24s, all but one. They hoped the missing plane had landed at Nanumea, a spit of ground at the far end of the Ellice Island group where there was a landing strip and a few Marines. It was closer to the target than the base at Funafuti. If he couldn't make it here, maybe he'd made it to Nanumea. They would find out later.

Word got around about Phillips' crew. A burst from a Zero's 20 millimeter cannon had raked the side of *Super Man*, practically rolling the plane out of control. Phillips had struggled mightily to get back to Funafuti with hundreds of holes in his plane, plus the right rudder was half gone. Six men on Phillips' crew were hurt, including Harold Brooks.

A man injured on a B-24 strike mission in the south central Pacific had hours to go, perhaps longer than any soldier in any theatre of the war, before getting to a field hospital and a surgeon. There was little his crewmates could do beyond basic first aid: trying to stop the bleeding, trying to position the man correctly, giving him morphine, maybe stop the pain. Brooks had been rushed the short distance from *Super Man* to the field hospital on Funafuti, but only after the agonizingly slow flight of nearly six hours from Nauru.

Scearce returned to the tent that housed the enlisted men on his crew. He sat on his cot, untied his boots, and pulled them off. He lay down and stared straight up at the sloping canvas ceiling, turning his head when Jack Yankus stepped in. Yankus had lingered at the flight line with *Dogpatch Express* where he surveyed the severed oxygen line, checked for other damage, and got the latest news.

"Brooks, uh . . . Brooks didn't make it, Herman."

Scearce breathed in deep and exhaled. He swallowed hard and looked straight up again. "Twenty millimeter hit him in the back of the head. He never knew it."

That was the story as Scearce heard it. Brooks took a round in the back of his head and never knew what hit him; he hadn't suffered. A 20 millimeter round from a Zero entered the waist window behind Brooks and missed the plane and the other waist gunner before smashing into the back of Brooks' head. The projectile was inches from sailing incredibly but harmlessly through one open window and out the other. That was the story.

It was true that Brooks had traded places with Douglas, but Douglas was hit by the same burst, injured in the shoulder. And Brooks didn't just fall. He somehow staggered or fell forward to the bomb bay, as if going to get help, or maybe trying to return to his duty station at the radio table, no one would ever know, but he collapsed in the bomb bay. Brooks was placed sitting up in the floor of his plane, gurgling, holes in his back and head.[7] He sat for hours, he and his injured crewmates, riding in their struggling bomber back to the little field hospital on Funafuti and its waiting ambulance, an olive drab ambulance with red crosses painted on its sides.

Scearce responded weakly to Yankus, "That's bad." He sat up without looking back toward his friend, pulled his boots on again, and walked back to *Dogpatch Express*.

At the plane, Scearce climbed aboard through the open bomb bay and went to his gun position. He inspected his gun and decided against changing the gun barrel. Some gunners changed their barrels religiously, to be confident that the gun would be straight and true for the next mission. A long burst from the .50s could generate enough heat to warp the barrel, but Scearce believed that a proper inspection of the gun was more sensible than frequent barrel changes. He would install a new barrel if and when the gun needed one.

The radio man got down on his knees on the floor of *Dogpatch Express* under the right waist window. In the silent, parked bomber he knelt for a moment on his flak jacket, still flattened on the metal floor. Kneeling there he scooped up spent .50 caliber machine gun shell casings with both hands. He wondered whether Brooks had used his weapon, whether, just maybe, Brooks had gotten a burst into a Zero, possibly even the one that killed him.

Scearce dropped the spent brass into a galvanized metal bucket. After picking up the last few casings from the bottom of the airplane, he turned to check the left side and saw that Yankus had already cleaned up his area. Scearce carried the bucket forward, dropped out of the plane through the bomb bay, and set the bucket of shell casings on the ground beside a tool cart. Maybe tomorrow the crew chief would empty the casings into the island's waste dump.

The missing B-24 had landed at Nanumea, low on fuel. They gassed up and made the hop back to Funafuti, and sometime during the night of April 20, just hours after the last B-24 returned, three twin-engined Japanese aircraft took off from their base on the island of Betio in the Tarawa atoll with full bomb loads. The enemy planes turned south-southeast, headed for Funafuti.

Chapter 5

Air Raid

INTELLIGENCE INFORMATION GATHERED from each aircrew just returned from the Nauru mission was compiled and compared, and photos developed and analyzed, until an accurate accounting of the bombing results was completed. Maj. Gen. Willis Hale endorsed the final report, which was then sent to CincPac, the office of the Commander in Chief, Pacific Command.

The report described a highly successful mission:

All bombs dropped hit target except eight . . . Damage to installations and material was heavy. Personnel casualties were extremely heavy. Large fires were observed in all bombed areas . . . a group of approximately twelve buildings in the center of the runway were destroyed . . . Phosphate Plant #3 was completely demolished by at least two direct hits . . . at least three direct hits were made on Phosphate Plant #2 . . . this plant was completely destroyed. Six bombs destroyed at least three large warehouses, thirteen buildings, eleven small railroad cars, stock storage pile, two water tanks supplying plant . . . Diesel power plant, main plant elevator building, one water tank, five cisterns, seven buildings and water distillation plant badly damaged. A train of six 500-lb bombs burst in residential area. Large fires were started which were increasing in scope when last oblique photo was taken . . . most buildings in immediate area were destroyed. At least ten fragmentation bombs put out of action three machine gun positions and one heavy antiaircraft. At least fifteen motor vehicles were destroyed. Four two-engine bombers were completely destroyed, two of which burned . . . at least three one-engine fighter planes were destroyed.[1]

The report also described damage to American bombers, crediting all of it to attacking Japanese fighter aircraft, and noted that twelve airmen were wounded and one killed. All of the American aircraft made it back to Funafuti.

General Hale concluded his report, "It is believed that this operation was the first successful attack against a valuable Japanese industrial installation since the raid on Tokyo. It was probably the longest offensive air operation of the war to date—the target was in excess of 3,200 miles by air from the home base of the attacking unit."[2]

During the night, as the American bomber crews on Funafuti were debriefed, their wounded treated, and their planes inspected, back on Nauru the Japanese defenders rounded up their prisoners. These prisoners, 191 employees of the British Phosphate Commission, had been left behind when their colleagues evacuated ahead of the Japanese landing eight months before.[3] Because they feared that the aerial bombardment by the Americans was preliminary to an invasion, an invasion which would never come, and because they would not risk the prisoners' cooperation with the enemy, the Japanese executed them all.[4]

The 42nd Bombardment Squadron on Funafuti prepared for another strike mission, but *Dogpatch Express* and its crew would not be in the line-up. Ground and flight crews spent the evening fueling and "bombing-up" undamaged airplanes for a raid against Tarawa while repairs to planes damaged in the Nauru raid continued.

Repair and maintenance work on Funafuti was slow and improvised. As an advanced staging base, Funafuti was lightly equipped. Aircraft carried "72 hour kits" to the island in their bomb bays, which were adequate for three days' maintenance. Repair to some of the damaged aircraft was beyond the capabilities of the temporary base.[5] The sheet metal work to *Dogpatch Express* was completed on Funafuti, but the severed oxygen line would wait until the plane returned to Oahu.

A crew from *Life* magazine was on Funafuti, having accompanied the squadron on the flight from Hawaii via Canton. Scearce and Yankus noticed that the *Life* people spent their time talking to officers and assumed that they weren't supposed to talk to enlisted men. Yankus joked, "They might quote us griping about the food, Herman. Was your steak cooked to your liking? My filet was a little overdone. And I didn't get a mint on my pillow last night."

It didn't bother the enlisted men that the *Life* bunch kept their distance. It seemed strange having the magazine people there because the airmen weren't used to being newsworthy. But since the Nauru raid was the first strike by American heavy bombers against a Japanese industrial target, it seemed the Air Corps wanted some publicity for the mission.[6]

Besides chatting with officers, the *Life* crew toured around the island in little groups, taking pictures and writing in tiny notebooks while their officer escort pointed out Funafuti's features.

The largest building on the island was the Missionary Church, a concrete structure with a wood-framed roof thatched with pandanus, the same plant natives used to weave mats.[7] The church was built by the London Missionary Society on the west side of the island near the lagoon, almost even with the northeast end of the runway.[8] It provided an easily recognizable visual reference for pilots—American or Japanese.

About sixty native huts were on the lagoon side protected by the crescent curve of the island.[9] The huts were rectangular, with corner posts of strong coconut trunks. Roofs were similar to the church, timber framed and thatched with pandanus. The sides of the huts were also thatched and made so they could be rolled up and tied open during the day. Gentle waves in the lagoon lapped at the beach, but on the eastern side, the ocean's waves met the shore with noisy crashes and salty spray.

The natives were brown-skinned with black hair, like the locals back on Oahu. Many of them spoke English that they had learned from the London Missionary delegation. They were friendly, in fact, they had worked themselves to near exhaustion months before helping men of the 5th Marine Defense Battalion, two companies of the 3rd Marines, elements of Navy Scouting Squadron 65, and a group of Seabees unload gear and equipment from their landing vessels.[10]

Funafuti's bare-breasted women were a novelty to mischievous Air Corps men who took one another's pictures with an arm around one in particular, a beautiful teenage girl who understood very well why she garnered so much attention, but tolerated it cheerfully just the same.

A quirk of time and location had turned this place, an island paradise, into a wartime bomber base. As beautiful as it looked, like a Robinson Crusoe shipwreck setting, it was a sorry place for a military operation.

Each morning, the relentless equatorial sun heated aircraft and tools so quickly that it was difficult to work. Ground crews who serviced the several Marine F4-U Corsair fighter planes and the Navy's Kingfisher scout planes on Funafuti knew how critical it was to keep tools and equipment covered or put away, because salt and sand was everywhere. In the afternoon, it rained, cooling things a bit, but the sun quickly cooked off the rain so that humidity joined forces with the heat to make working conditions miserable.

The coral runway built by the Seabees should have been as solid as concrete, but rain prevented the live coral used to build it from curing properly. The coral packed like gravel, rutted and dusty.[11] When aircraft took off or landed, dust from the runway created storms of tiny abrasive particles. The northeast to southwest orientation of the single air strip offered no alternative if the predominantly easterly winds shifted to the southeast.[12] In those conditions, pilots met a ninety-degree cross wind, challenging enough with a heavy load on take-off, but nerve-wracking with low fuel, an engine out, or battle damage on the return.

Fresh water was provided by distillation units. The Marines and Navy men had learned to supplement the water supply by catching rain runoff in barrels placed under the drape of their tents. There was a pond, really more of a swampy bog, in the middle of the island that the Seabees had to partially fill when they built the runway, but the bog was of little practical use except to the island's mosquito and rat population.

The enlisted men of each bomber crew shared a canvas tent, which lacked a floor or electricity and was equipped with cots. Officers were also housed in tents in a separate area, but they had electricity from gasoline-powered generators.

Equipment for servicing bombers was barely adequate.[13] Ground crewmen had two Cletracs, slow, tracked vehicles, more tractor than truck, for servicing aircraft. Cletracs were excellent for towing and parking aircraft but dreadfully slow for pulling gas trailers to refuel airplanes. A mess hall and barracks were planned, but for now the men had to make do with field kitchens and tents.

The Navy finished a one-room hospital on Funafuti in November 1942. It had forty field beds and was staffed by two doctors, a dentist, and twenty-two Navy corpsmen.[14] They boasted that the famous aviator Eddie Rickenbacker was one of their first patients.

Rickenbacker was one of seven survivors of an October 1942 B-17 crash in the ocean. Crash survivors drifted for weeks in their rafts before being rescued by a small Navy Kingfisher amphibian aircraft. Rickenbacker and his men were taxied half an hour across water lashed to the aircraft's wing because the rescue made the plane overloaded for flight. The Kingfisher finally met a PT boat that took Rickenbacker the rest of the way to Funafuti.[15]

There were a few bunkers for personnel built by the Marines, but not enough for every man's protection. Supplementing the bunkers were shallow slit trenches and some holes where palm trees had been bulldozed down, but most of the island was too low for much digging. There were revetments for aircraft, but not enough to protect them all. The 42nd Squadron's best defense on Funafuti was secrecy, but the secret couldn't last.

There were only so many places from which B-24s could have attacked Nauru. The Japanese may have sent a plane to follow the Americans as they returned, or they may have reconnoitered Funafuti undetected.[16] The briefing officer on Kahuku who told the bomber crews bound for Funafuti that the Japanese wouldn't know they were there had made no promise that the secret would last.

Scearce made his way to his crew's tent before curfew. An ordnance truck, a bomb loader with a winch and lifting frame attached in the rear, was parked nearby. Scearce assumed that whoever used it last must have parked it near his own tent. Parking it in the shade of coconut trees in the crew quarters area would keep the vehicle's steering wheel and winch controls a little cooler than leaving it beside the runway.

Inside the tent, the enlisted men of *Dogpatch Express* chatted quietly. They talked about Nauru and the coming strike against Tarawa. They speculated on their next mission, and whether Lieutenant Schroeder would get his bombs on target next time. Conversation faded quickly because the men were exhausted. They hadn't slept much the night before, pumped up as they were for their first mission.

Sometime after midnight, the air raid signal sounded. A shrill, piercing siren, ten second blasts at five second intervals,[17] caused the men to stir. Marines ran from tent to tent, yelling "Air raid! Air raid!" Scearce and his heavy-eyed crewmates half-heartedly swung their legs to the ground, assuming this was someone's idea of a joke, or maybe a drill.

Then a Marine Corps anti-aircraft battery opened fire, *boom* . . . *boom* . . . *boom* . . . and the men knew immediately it was no drill. They scrambled in the dark to pull on flight suits and ran out of their tent. Now aircraft could be heard, but the direction was indistinct; there was just the sound of unsynchronized aircraft engines overhead. A familiar voice shouted, "Get in the hole! Get in the hole!"

There was a shallow hole near the crew's tent, and Scearce piled in on top of his crewmates. Falling bombs made menacing whistling sounds while explosions threw orange flashes about tree tops and tents and cast silhouettes of men running. The smell was pungent, like sulfur or a spent shotgun shell.

Forty terrified villagers huddled inside the Missionary Church, praying that its concrete walls would save them. Marine Corps Corp. Fonnie Black Ladd ran into the church, calling for the people to get out, imploring them to get away from the church, to take cover elsewhere.[18] He knew that the church was an obvious target for the Japanese.

A salvo of bombs stepped toward the hole containing the men of *Dogpatch Express*, its pattern of explosions growing louder and closer and coming straight. Scearce held the sides of his helmet with both clenched fists, trying desperately to fit under it. Knees to his chest, teeth gritted, and eyes squeezed tight, Scearce knew the next one whistling toward them would be very close.

With a terrific *whang!* the bomb hit the ordnance truck parked just a few feet away. Dirt and metal rained down. In the next second, a hissing cylinder landed in the men's tiny hole, right on top of Elmer Johnson. For a moment, the men of *Dogpatch Express* could hear nothing, then the sensation of sound returned with a high-pitched ringing, and the powerful stench of explosives filled their nostrils. Scearce's mind raced. "This is it," he thought. The metal cylinder continued to hiss, but the men didn't move, afraid they could cause it to explode. Johnson was afraid to even breathe.

While the hissing weakened, the whistling of falling bombs and their terrific explosions finally stopped. Voices were audible now, agonized screams, cries for help, shouts, people giving orders. The enemy aircraft could be heard again, leaving the island toward the north, toward Tarawa. There was crackling and popping and strange metallic groans; a Liberator was burning. In the dim light of early morning, with gray-black smoke stinging their eyes, the enlisted men of *Dogpatch Express* accounted for each other.

Yankus spoke first. "Everybody okay? Ed?"

"OK."

"Johnson?"

"I'm OK, I think."

"Scearce?"

"Yeah, OK."

"Bobby?"

"OK."

"Al?"

"OK."

"It's a fucking fire extinguisher," Johnson said. The cylinder that landed on him, the hissing object that the crew believed was a bomb, was instead the damaged pressure tank of a brass fire extinguisher blasted from the ordnance truck when the truck took a direct hit. Men had jumped under the truck for cover, Scearce thought there were four. Parts of bodies were strewn about, and one body still lay under the demolished truck. Scearce could tell the man was a staff sergeant by his stripes, but could not recognize him because his face and top of his head were gone.

Another man was slumped against a tree, a perfectly rectangular opening in the center of his forehead. The face was too splattered with blood, dirt, and oil to recognize, but the hole in the dead man's head was an image that would haunt Scearce for many years.

Nearby, men lined up for their names to be put on a list for Purple Hearts, pointing out their cuts, scrapes, and bruises. Yankus looked at Scearce and rolled his eyes, sharing the same thought: the ones who really deserved Purple Hearts weren't able to stand in the line.

Corpsmen rushed to help the injured while others fought fires. Casualties were lined up by the airstrip in the shade of planes' wings. As bulldozers cleared debris, the worst of the injured were placed aboard a plane to be sent back to the States. Others went to a hospital in Fiji, 670 miles south. Some injured men refused to be evacuated, insisting on staying with their crews.

⇛⇚

One B-24 was burned completely. Its smoking radial engines lay on the coral runway, propellers bent and folded under as if they were made of rubber. The twin rudder tail planes seemed intact although the rudder fabric was scorched away. The tail section, severed by fire, stood on the coral pitched downward as if the plane was in a steep dive.

Other aircraft were holed by shrapnel, tires blown out and Plexiglas shattered. Some of the planes could be repaired while others would be scrapped and used for parts. Bomb-loading equipment, radio gear, the mess area, and tents were damaged, burned or blown down by the concussion of bombs.

The walls of the Missionary Church stood, but its roof was gone and its interior was gutted. A bomb had crashed through the thatched roof and exploded, bringing roof timbers and flaming, dried pandanus down into the building, vacated by the villagers a moment before.

A young native man named Esau Sepetaina lay on his back as if resting, arms at his side, his chin, mouth, and left ear visible, but the rest of his head was smashed like a melon.[19] He was the only native killed in the raid, and he died beside one of the few true personnel bunkers in Funafuti's shallow earth, his feet just inches from the edge.

The Japanese air raid consisted of three medium bombers making several passes at night. The enemy planes had traversed the island back and forth, as if their crews weren't concerned in the least about the three Marine Corps anti-aircraft batteries coughing shells skyward. The Japanese seemed to take their time, taking advantage of the full moon's light on Funafuti's white coral runway. Their show of skill was sobering to the American bomber crewmen, particularly the men of *Dogpatch Express*, who had seen their own bombs explode in the water just off the sandy beach of Nauru.

On the morning after the air raid, Scearce, Lipe, Yankus, and Johnson stood with a handful of other men near the broken remains of the ordnance truck, watching helplessly as medical corpsmen lifted one of the dead men from the wreckage. They felt hollow, sick, and at the same time, relieved it wasn't them. Beside the wrecked truck lay its splattered and torn seat and the vehicle's battery, and beyond them a *Life* magazine photographer captured the scene on film.

—≡≝—

On April 21, *Dogpatch Express* took off past the still smoldering remains of its sister aircraft. The bombers in the line-up for the next mission stayed behind, scheduled to hit Tarawa the next night. The long flight back to Hawaii, with its overnight stop at Canton, lacked the sense of purpose and anticipation of success that had sustained the men on the way out. The return flight felt like retreat; the men felt beaten.

The squadron had originally planned to stay at Funafuti for several days, hitting targets in the Gilbert and Marshall Islands, but the squadron's strength was reduced significantly by the Japanese raid. The Tarawa mission would be the last one from Funafuti for now.

Deasy's crew was quiet during the flight back to Hawaii. There was a lot of time to think, and their thoughts were brooding, the mood was sullen. Scearce thought about the *Life* magazine crew. He wasn't the only one who wondered, acidly, whether the pictures and story that *Life* would print would be what the Air Corps had in mind when the mission began. His mind was troubled. *Was it always going to be like this? Will the Japs follow us home and plaster us after every mission? At least two B-24s lost, counting Phillips' shot-up plane, and seven or eight dead including Brooks, plus who knows how many more injured. We nearly bought it in the Jap raid. And for one mission credit!*

The cool confidence and pride instilled in the crew through phase training and hours of long patrols from their Hawaiian base were gone. Their hatred of the enemy, rooted in the Pearl Harbor raid, cultivated through training, and nurtured by the bravado of young fighting men, was now infused with bitter resentment.

It was easy to figure who could put bombs on a target. Ours splashed into the ocean, couldn't hit the damned island, let alone a target on the island. And they hit us with just a few planes, flying back and forth. They weren't worried about us hitting them with anything we had. And they did it at night. We're just not that good.

Feelings were mixed about the return to Hawaii. In spite of their low spirits, Scearce and his buddies were relieved to be out of danger. But it would be back to the same routine: training flights, search missions, navigational legs, and submarine patrols, but no bombing missions. The war wouldn't be over for them until they got thirty strike mission credits, and getting whipped the first time out didn't help them look forward to twenty-nine more.

During the return flight, Scearce realized that he would be the one to tell Noelani, the pretty Kahuku girl who so enjoyed the attention she got from the two airmen, that Harold Brooks was gone.

Joining the Army had been a spur-of-the-moment lark for Herman Scearce and his cousin Marvin Marshall. They laughed about it on the familiar walk down to the post office, egging each other on about how funny it would be to disappear from their mothers and from Danville. The boys saw it as an adventure, a joke, because even if they got past the recruiter, it was just a question of how long the adventure would last before the Army sent them home.

But for Sergeant Herman Scearce, it was no joke any more.

Chapter 6

Chance

CHANCE IS DEFINED AS something that happens unpredictably, without discernible human intention, a purposeless determiner of unaccountable happenings, the fortuitous or incalculable element in existence.[1] The role of chance could be depressing to a bomber crewman if he dwelt too much on it. It was better to believe that proper training and good equipment, sound strategy, and smart decisions would keep him alive. Chance played a capricious role, fickle and reckless, and whether its results were good or bad might be entirely a matter of perspective.

Any one of countless, seemingly insignificant variations might have made the difference between men living or dying. Harold Brooks was killed and Clarence Douglas badly injured, but Douglas survived. What if the two men had not traded places? Speculation on such things could go on endlessly and could drive a man to fear making the slightest misstep which might change his destiny. A turn this way or that, an extra step or a short cut? What if *Super Man's* take-off time had been a moment later, or a moment earlier?

During the Japanese raid on Funafuti, the men under the ordnance truck died, while men in a shallow hole a few feet away were shaken but unscathed. What if the Japanese bombardier had toggled his bomb release just a second or two later? The *Life* magazine photo might have captured the ordnance truck, intact, with those who had been beneath it standing among other men, in a silent semicircle, watching as corpsmen pulled the dead of *Dogpatch Express* from their hole.

Some men tried to influence fate to control the element of chance, or at least bend it toward a positive outcome. Scearce was not among the superstitious ones, but there were many. They might wear the same socks, or board the plane in a certain order before a mission. Some airmen would touch the plane in the same manner before each flight, or offer some optimistic tease to the pretty girl painted on its nose, or pat her in some bawdy way. "See you tonight, sweetheart!"

Aircrews often gave their bomber a name they hoped would bring them luck. Among Liberators flying from bases in Europe, Africa, Australia, and the Pacific there were fifty-five named "Lucky" this or that and twenty-six more named "Lady Luck." There were sixteen called "Bad Penny," since bad pennies always turn up, and eighteen named "Boomerang," because boomerangs come back every time.[2]

The type of flying required of bomber crews contributed to their intuitive sense of fate. They flew an assigned course and altitude, bombed specific targets, and had little room for deviation, especially during the bomb run. Fighter pilots, by contrast, had much more freedom to choose their course of action; they could be creative. Fighter pilots could engage or disengage, attack aggressively or more cautiously, evade and maneuver. With a fighter pilot's freedom came greater control of his fate.[3] Bomber crewmen felt as if the mission briefing officer had their plane in his hands and their fate in his words.

When ribbed about their preflight rituals, the superstitious shrugged. "Hey, it works!" And no one argued with their simple logic. If it won any measure of confidence, maybe it really did make a difference. Even those who were not superstitious often called upon the spiritual. The old saw "there are no atheists in foxholes" could have been said of bombers. Sgt.

Herman Scearce admitted, "All of us prayed, selfish prayers . . . God, just get me back on the ground again . . ."

Chance played its role in ways large and small, sometimes affecting just one man, sometimes the squadron as a whole. The circumstances of the war in the Pacific, the way the struggle developed in its first year and a half, had tremendous effect on Scearce and the bomber crews who joined that theatre of battle in 1943. Critical decisions made by leaders on both sides would ultimately change the skies over the Pacific Ocean, making them increasingly more survivable for American airmen.

The first of those critical decisions took place as Japanese planes returned to their aircraft carriers from their attacks on Pearl Harbor. Aboard the Japanese flagship, *Akagi*, flight leader Mitsuo Fuchida and his fellow pilots unanimously agreed that their aircraft should be launched for further strikes against targets on Hawaii.[4] Fuchida reported the scale of American resistance, which was lighter than the most optimistic Japanese projections. He also pointed out to his commander that the American ships that were sunk lay in shallow water, and could be salvaged. The Japanese flyers hoped to inflict additional damage and possibly locate the missing enemy aircraft carriers, or lure the American carriers into battle.

But Vice Admiral Chuichi Nagumo decided against it. His tankers were already steaming away to a safe rendezvous point, so it was not possible to change the fleet's planned route. Nagumo also felt there was a significant risk of loss to his own force, a risk he did not believe was worth the damage he might inflict on the remaining targets.[5] As a result, the American carriers were safe, and Pearl Harbor's dry docks, submarine pens, fuel and ammunition supplies, and repair facilities were relatively intact. Had Pearl's 4,500,000 barrels of oil been destroyed, the American fleet would have been forced to withdraw to the West Coast. Admiral Chester Nimitz said, "The fact that the Japanese did not return to Pearl Harbor and complete the job was the greatest help to us, for they left their principal enemy with the time to catch his breath, restore his morale, and rebuild his forces."[6]

Their unfinished work would lead ultimately to a Japanese plan to engage American carriers at Midway six months later. And the ultimate result of *that* epic battle would set the stage for Americans entering the Pacific war from that point forward, among them Sgt. Herman Scearce and the B-24 Liberator crews of the 11th Bombardment Group.

But the Japanese Midway plan did not go forward without debate. The Imperial Army wanted to focus efforts to the south, to capture Samoa, Fiji, and New Caledonia to cut off Australia from her allies.[7] But Admiral Isoroku Yamamoto favored expansion of the Japanese defensive perimeter to the east. Yamamoto believed the southern thrusts should come only after the eastern flank was secured, and he considered American-held Midway Atoll a threat. Yamamoto was persuasive because of his success at Pearl Harbor, but it was a diminutive American pilot named Jimmy Doolittle who settled the debate.[8]

To counter Japan's string of victories, pierce their rising confidence, and give Americans a much-needed morale boost, President Franklin D. Roosevelt authorized a surprise attack on Tokyo.[9] Lt. Col. James Doolittle was selected to lead the daring, high-risk venture placing Army bombers on an aircraft carrier, a tactic never before attempted.[10]

On April 18, 1942, Doolittle's twin-engined B-25 Mitchell medium bombers took off from the carrier USS *Hornet*, approaching their Japanese targets at low level to avoid detection. They bombed targets in Tokyo, Kobe, Yokohama, and Nagoya.[11] The material damage inflicted was slight but the psychological effect on Japan was dramatic. Their population had been promised that the homeland would never be bombed.[12] Religiously devoted to their emperor, they were humiliated that his safety had been compromised.

Leona Jackson was a United States Navy nurse who became a prisoner of the Japanese when Guam fell just two days after the Pearl Harbor attack.[13] She was confined in Kobe when Doolittle's B-25s struck the city, affording her the rare privilege for an American of witnessing the raid from the ground. She later observed that "The effect of this raid, whatever it might have been from a military point of view, had quite an effect on Japanese morale, because just about two weeks previous to that, one of their military spokesmen had gotten up and sounded off to the effect that Japan could not be raided by an outside power, and here was an outside power showering them that day with bombs and showing them it could be done . . . The bombing was certainly a welcome visitor as far as we were concerned."[14]

The embarrassed Japanese military command was determined that such a catastrophe must never happen again.[15] Yamamoto was convinced more than ever that it was imperative to destroy the American carriers and establish a defensive perimeter base at Midway, so Midway became Japan's objective.[16]

Yamamoto did not expect the U.S. Navy to be on the scene until Midway was in Japanese control.[17] The Japanese planned to launch air strikes against Midway, invade, and then deploy to await the Americans. Admiral Chuichi Nagumo, commander of the Pearl Harbor task force six months before, led the Japanese toward Midway.[18] The plan included a diversion in the Aleutians, intended to draw American forces toward Alaska. Nagumo's first air strike against targets on Midway took off from his carriers in the early morning of June 4, 1942.

As they returned, the leaders of the first strike advised Nagumo that a second strike was needed, because the island's defenses had not been softened enough for invasion.[19] Planes on his carriers, armed with anti-shipping bombs and torpedoes in case enemy vessels were sighted, had to be re-armed with fragmentation bombs for ground targets. As Japanese crews scurried to change the ordnance mounted to their aircraft, an airborne patrol sighted the American fleet and an initial wave of attacking American aircraft was successfully repulsed.[20]

The Japanese carriers swarmed with refueled planes, ready for take-off, now armed to bomb ground targets on Midway. Because American ships were sighted, Nagumo's aircraft were hurriedly re-armed yet again. Fragmentation bombs were left on deck where men rushed to replace them with armor-piercing shells and torpedoes needed to attack the American fleet, which had not been expected to arrive so soon.

At that moment, dive bombers from aircraft carriers *Enterprise* and *Yorktown* descended upon the Japanese ships. Nagumo's combat air patrol, its protective umbrella of fighter planes, had been brought to low altitude by the first wave of American planes.[21] They were not able to climb quickly enough to intercept. Soon the carriers *Kaga*, *Soryu* and *Akagi* were burning. The bombs left on deck and the planes full of fuel erupted in terrific explosions. *Hiryu*, last of Nagumo's four carriers that was still operational, was dive-bombed and destroyed late the same afternoon.

If Pearl was an incomplete victory, Midway was a devastating defeat for the Japanese. They would never regain the offensive in the Central Pacific, and for an American airman entering the Pacific war after these pivotal battles were decided, the loss of Japanese pilots and aircraft was nothing short of providential. The Japanese lost more than their carriers' usual number of planes and crew at Midway, because those carriers sank with additional aircraft intended to be based on the atoll after it was secured. Mitsuo Fuchida, the Japanese flight leader at Pearl

Harbor, a spectator at Midway because of an emergency appendectomy aboard *Akagi* just before the battle, estimated that 332 Japanese aircraft were lost.[22]

Even the diversionary attack by the Japanese in the Aleutians brought its own serendipitous result when a nearly perfect Zero fighter fell into American hands after crash-landing in an Alaskan bog.[23]

The captured Zero was dismantled and shipped to the U. S. Navy's air station at North Island, San Diego. There it was reassembled, repaired, studied, and flown. Tactics were designed for combat against the Zero that took advantage of its weaknesses. Every type of American fighter was flown and evaluated against the Zero. American pilots would know exactly how their machines matched up against the Japanese plane.[24]

This valuable intelligence, gathered so early in the war, contributed to the erosion of Japanese military power in the Pacific. The fearsome Zero was demystified, its quirks revealed, and American pilots became increasingly effective in combat against it.

Ill-conceived aspects of Japanese air doctrine compounded their 1942 setbacks. The consequence of their air war philosophy was a spiraling decline in air combat effectiveness that Japan would never recover.

There was no mission count for a Japanese pilot to earn a ticket home. Experienced pilots were not rotated from the front to teach student pilots. Instead, the Japanese employed a "crack man" policy, intended to keep their most skilled pilots at the cutting edge of their offensive sword.[25] Effective early on, this short-sighted policy meant that skills learned against improving American planes and tactics were lost when experienced Japanese pilots went down. Compounding this problem, the Japanese had no established system for search and rescue. Division commanders decided whether to expend resources of fuel and time and put more men and assets at risk to look for downed pilots. Many times, they made no such effort.[26]

To meet their need for combat pilots, Japanese flight school entry qualifications were relaxed and flight training graduation requirements were reduced. A Japanese fighter pilot in 1940 graduated with about 330 flight hours, progressively dropping until a graduate in the last years of the war had 100 to 120 flight hours, with no in-flight gunnery practice and only basic tactical training.[27] The "crack man" pilot deployment policy aggravated this deteriorating pilot training program.

Japan's air power was also diminished by their failure to effectively incorporate lessons learned in combat into aircraft design and production.[28] They continued to fly without protective armor and without self-sealing fuel tanks, all the worse for their increasingly less proficient pilots.[29]

In August 1942, a photograph was taken of Sgt. Herman Scearce's radio school class, 349 men assembled in front of the imposing, pillared Army Air Corps Technical School. Scearce's friends signed the back of the photograph and some added their addresses. The last signer, Louis Fallick of Chicago, Illinois, wrote, "Best of Luck."

The Pacific war had already turned in favor of aircrews who joined the conflict after 1942. The flukes and twists, choices and chances leading to their deployment at that place and at that time bent to their favor.

Chance would continue to play its arbitrary role. The May 1943, assignment of *Dogpatch Express* to the second wave of planes to bomb Japanese-held Wake Island assured its survival. During the same month, another crew's mission aboard a jinxed plane named *The Green Hornet* would be their last.

Chapter 7

May 1943

THERE WAS A DIFFERENT FEEL to Honolulu now. Oahu was the same, and familiar, but it wasn't as exciting and novel as it had been in February when the Air Transport Command navigator so capably guided the nameless B-24 number "two one four" to Hickam Field. It was strange to think that it had been just weeks since then, and the island hadn't changed, except that the men of *Dogpatch Express* saw how clean and fresh the new arrivals from the States appeared, and it dawned on them that they had looked that way just a couple of months before. New crews, giddy as tourists, stood out until they realized, self consciously, that it wasn't good to be so obviously inexperienced and untested.

After just one mission, after shooting and being shot at, witnessing death and losing friends, the men of *Dogpatch Express* were veterans. They understood that the price of a single combat mission could be quite high, and they knew firsthand that the Japanese were skilled, capable adversaries. They felt the prickling awareness of being spared in a very close brush with their own mortality, realizing that tomorrow, or next week, or next month, they could be less fortunate. Al Marston, veteran of the Japanese surprise attack on Pearl, had already been changed by such an experience.

But philosophical ideas like these weren't the kinds of things the men discussed. Jack Yankus had more to say than anyone else about the Japanese bombing of Funafuti: for weeks after the raid, he complained that he smelled cordite every time he lit a cigarette.

From this point forward, crews who had tasted combat didn't have a lot to do with green crews. It wasn't that they went out of their way to avoid the new arrivals; they just didn't have a lot in common with them. Facing adversity together forged a bond, and those who had shared the experience knew and trusted each other. The very reason some of the injured at Funafuti refused to leave their buddies was that they believed in their friends. They feared that if they were evacuated, they might be replaced and returned to duty later, reassigned to a crew who could get them killed.

On May 7, an announcement directed all Army Air Forces officers and men to return to their assigned bases immediately.[1] That evening, the officers were briefed on a possible Japanese attack on Midway. Rumors circulated that the Japanese planned to try again to take the atoll. Nine planes from the 42nd Bomb Squadron were ordered to leave the next morning for Midway, joining another group of B-24s from the 98th.

Midway Atoll, 1,373 miles west-northwest of Oahu, is comprised of two main islands, Sand Island and Eastern Island. The Navy operated a ferry service between the two islands. The smaller of the two, Eastern, was home to Midway's primary airfield. First-timers to Midway were awed by the searing white glare of the islands. They shone almost with a light of their own, and buildings and vehicles were camouflaged with white paint.[2]

Flying time to Midway from Oahu was about seven and a half hours. Scearce and each of the other airmen who made the trip understood that

Japanese bombers could make the trip in the opposite direction in about the same time, if they got control of Midway. The critical importance of Midway inspired a special red wax seal that adorned orders and flight records concerning the atoll. Inscribed in an arch across the top of the seal were the words "We'll Hold Midway" and beneath, completing the circle, "Till Hell Freezes Over."

From Scearce's point of view, every available plane had been sent to Midway. Each morning, from May 9 through May 14, bomber crews boarded their planes, pre-flighted them, and ran up the engines. Then they sat idling on Eastern Island's runway, waiting for a take-off signal from the control tower. Scearce and Yankus assumed that the Navy was scouting for a Japanese fleet, which, when sighted, they would attack, but each morning no signal came. The crews eventually shut down the engines, secured their planes, and walked back to their cramped crew area.

Midway's vast and noisy bird population was initially a source of amusement, especially when the men first caught sight of the island's awkward gooney birds. The men laughed at the big gray sea birds because the creatures needed a running start to get airborne. Marston and Yankus guffawed at Scearce mimicking radio contact with the birds as they scattered and ran, wings spread for lift off: "Midway, this is Two One Four, request permission for take off, runway Zero-Six." "Ah, Roger, Two One Four, if these other bird brains would exit the traffic pattern . . ."

But the novelty wore off quickly because the birds never seemed to quiet down, and at night, from some quarter, a sleep-deprived man could be heard shouting "Shut the fuck up!" as if the birds could understand.

Someone tried to organize afternoon ballgames, but inevitably the game would degenerate into arguments about rule interpretations, how it was done in Upper Darby or Little Rock. Bobby Lipe just wanted to play ball, and he'd try to get everyone to settle down and get on with the game. Ed Hess lost himself in the solitary pursuit of creating crossword puzzles while Scearce and Yankus played cards, refining their pinochle skills.

The Midway assignment seemed pointless because crewmen thought that bombing ships was a dim-witted idea. Boredom was tolerable if the men thought they'd eventually do something worthwhile, but they had little faith in the effectiveness of B-24s against a fleet. If enough planes dropped enough bombs, maybe they would hit something, but that was a frustrating notion, hardly a strategy at all to men who knew that the odds were greater their bombs would splash harmlessly into the water. Aircrews also knew that ships' gunners were skilled and accurate and best avoided.

B-17 Flying Fortresses from Midway, including some from the 42nd Squadron before the squadron's transition to B-24s, had flown against Nagumo's aircraft carriers as they approached the atoll back in June.[3] After the decisive Midway battle, there had been fistfights in Honolulu bars between sailors and airmen about who sank the Japanese carriers, but the truth was that the B-17s hadn't scored a single hit.[4]

After a week of this routine, the crews were briefed on a strike mission assignment. They were disgruntled to learn that the target was Wake Island, and they felt certain that the mission was make-work. The airmen being briefed for the Wake Island strike mission imagined the top brass looking over all these planes bombed-up and gassed-up, disappointed that the enemy hadn't come to the party, so now like mischievous little boys with a pack of firecrackers, they were determined to blow up something. Besides, it was quite a distance: 1185 miles one way, with no closer friendly base for a plane in trouble. Flying time would be an hour longer than the Nauru mission, and Funafuti had an alternate runway at Nanumea, forty-five minutes closer to Nauru than Funafuti. The airmen weren't convinced that there was any real tactical reason to go to Wake, but they also understood that it wasn't their decision. The mood was glum.[5]

Aversion to Wake Island missions was bred in to the 11th Bomb Group. The 11th was part of the Seventh Air Force, which had been commanded by Maj. Gen. Clarence L. Tinker in 1942. Tinker had been a strong advocate of equipping Pacific bomber squadrons with B-24 Liberators, replacing the B-17s lost early in the war. On June 6, 1942, as the decimated Japanese fleet was retiring from Midway, Tinker led four early-model B-24s on a mission from Midway to bomb Wake Island.[6] Half an hour after taking off, Tinker's aircraft flew into a gray overcast and was never seen again. The remaining three aircrews failed to find Wake and returned, solemn and subdued, to Midway.[7]

Pre-flight briefing said the May 15 mission would strike the airfield, ground installations, and beach defenses. Typically, Japanese anti-aircraft guns were placed near the beach where they could be brought to bear on surface ships as well as aircraft.[8] The aircrews were told the island was well defended, but that the Japanese would not be expecting them. The cynics among the crewmen glanced knowingly at each other at the briefing officer's words, remembering Nauru and the Japanese's proven ability to quickly prepare a reception once the American bombers came into view. The weather officer told them to expect fair skies for the mission, spotty cumulus clouds, very much like it was over Nauru a few weeks before: good flying weather, but also good for Japanese anti-aircraft battery crews and Zero pilots.

Dogpatch Express took off early on the morning of May 15, Lt. Joe Deasy at the controls. They were in the second flight, about twenty minutes behind the first. The flying time was scary: six and one-half hours out, six and one-half hours back, 2370 miles round-trip. The distance was not a problem for a Liberator unless it took hits or developed a mechanical problem. A B-24 could be a real handful if it was

damaged, and every man also understood what the distance meant for
any unfortunate soul injured during the mission.

About an hour from the target, Deasy gave the order to test fire the
guns. "Short bursts," he said. "And short bursts when it heats up." He
wanted to conserve ammunition, knowing Wake was well defended
and there could be a lot of action.

As *Dogpatch Express* approached Wake Island, the lead aircraft of
"A" flight were catching hell. Command frequency transmissions from
"A" flight Liberators were mostly garbled because of the distance, but
the simple fact that they were breaking radio silence spoke volumes.
Somebody reported casualties on board; they were turning back. The
next transmission was worse:

"... gonna go in, get Kingfisher for us."

"Got your position . . . will call Kingfisher."

"Kingfisher" was a prearranged code word for a submarine. Submarines were supposed to be in a certain position, usually fifty or seventy-
five miles from the target on a specific heading. Preflight briefing always
mentioned the submarines, but Scearce and his buddies had little faith
in the idea. They thought it was contrived to give them a shred of hope
in a hopeless situation. But somebody twenty minutes ahead of them in
"A" flight was about to ditch, and at the moment they reported *"gonna
go in,"* their hopes rested entirely on the submarine.

Lt. Thomas M. Esmond, a pilot recently transferred to the 98th Squadron, was in "A" flight when it was attacked by twenty-two Zero fighters.
Esmond was on his fifth bomb run when his number 2 engine was
knocked out and set on fire by a 20 millimeter shell. The aircraft's

automatic fire suppression system put the fire out, but on three engines the plane could not keep up with the rest of the flight. Sensing a kill, the Zeros concentrated their guns on Esmond's ship.

Esmond's crew managed to fight off attacks from the Zeros until the Japanese pilots turned back to Wake, but with one engine out and its propeller feathered, they continued to lag well behind and beneath the rest of the B-24s already droning back toward Midway.

Aboard *Dogpatch Express*, the gunners were now at their positions and less than thirty minutes out from Wake. They were anxious and wide-eyed because it sounded like a nasty fight. B-24s ahead had taken hits, already some were struggling home, and somebody, at least one crew, expected to hit the water. Scearce glanced at Yankus behind him. Yankus gave Scearce a raised-eyebrow look and exhaled through his mouth. Scearce patted Yankus on his back and turned to his window. "A" flight had poked the beehive, and a lot could happen before they faced each other again.

"A" flight moved off of Wake and it was "B" flight's turn now. The bomb run would take *Dogpatch Express* straight toward Peacock Point, the island's southernmost tip, and into a concentration of Japanese defenses. There were fires on the ground in barracks and oil storage areas that had been started by "A" flight. Flak bursts popped in front and beside them, ugly black puffs that rushed past as *Dogpatch Express* reached the initial point of its bomb run. Deasy was cool on the inter-phone: "So far they're pitching high and outside."

There were no enemy fighters. "A" flight had brought the Zeros up and the Japanese pilots had spent their fuel and ammunition. When "B" flight arrived, the Zeros were out of sight, apparently back on the ground, rearming and refueling. The effect was similar to Nagumo's combat air patrol at Midway, brought down by the first wave of American planes to attack the Japanese carriers, clearing the sky of fighters for the American planes that followed.

Dogpatch Express and the rest of "B" flight completed its bomb runs successfully, uneventfully, while "A" flight struggled home.

Meanwhile, about 140 miles short of Midway, Lieutenant Esmond's crew worried whether they had enough fuel to get home. They had already thrown everything they could from the plane to lighten the load: flak jackets, ammo boxes, even machine guns were thrown out. Esmond and his co-pilot, Lt. Richard Waters, agreed they were better off to ditch under control than to crash after the fuel supply was exhausted. The engineer broke the hinges from the emergency hatch and the waist windows and threw them out; Esmond and Waters broke the side windows out of the cockpit canopy, careful that the airstream didn't tear the fire axe from their hands. Exits had to be opened and cleared before ditching; otherwise stresses on the aircraft and pressure from rising water might trap the men inside the sinking plane.

A Navy submarine chaser, a fast surface vessel, raced to the spot where Esmond announced his intentions, and his crew braced for a crash landing in the water. They knew they would have to move fast. Even in a perfect ditching, a B-24's flight deck and fuselage were under water as soon as the plane stopped. The Emergency Procedure manual said that "leaving the airplane becomes a matter of swimming out." But the manual also said the force of ditching was sufficient to stun the crew and that the plane could only be expected to remain afloat from one to three minutes.[9]

Esmond's plane hit the water violently and it was dashed to pieces on impact. Bombardier Lt. Richard Patton was killed immediately. Two rafts burst automatically from hatches behind the top turret and the bomber sank quickly, but the rest of Lieutenant Esmond's crew got out of their broken plane and struggled into the rafts. Soon, the sub chaser's sailors rescued the survivors.[10]

Had the weather been overcast over Wake Island on May 15, "A" flight would have surprised the Japanese on the ground. The Zero pilots would have scrambled to their planes, gotten airborne and to altitude just in time to meet "B" flight, and it would have been the second wave of Liberators catching hell that day. But *Dogpatch Express* didn't take a single hit. Just the same, mission credits seemed to be coming at a steep price and Scearce had only two. He didn't think about the future a lot, though heading back to Hawaii from Midway, it occurred to Sgt. Scearce that he just might make his next birthday. One week after the Wake raid, he turned eighteen.

On May 27, twelve days after the Wake Island raid, Lt. Joe Deasy and Lt. Russell Phillips were assigned a search mission for a lost plane. A B-24 from the 530th Bomb Squadron, 380th Bomb Group, was on its way to Australia where the Group was attached to the Royal Australian Air Force.[11] The plane had not been heard from since leaving Canton and was presumed to have crashed into the ocean about 200 miles north of Palmyra Island.

Deasy was assigned aircraft #983, named *Daisy Mae*. Phillips, pilot of *Super Man* when it was shot up so badly over Nauru, had several replacements among his crew. Phillips would be flying aircraft #219, *The Green Hornet*. *The Green Hornet* had a reputation as a plane with problems; crews said that it didn't fly right, it was sluggish, a tail-dragger.[12]

Phillips and Deasy took off from Oahu at 1830, 9:00 a.m. Hawaii time, and flew side by side until they reached the search area near

Palmyra, about 800 miles below Hawaii. At that point the B-24s split up to begin five-degree search legs, flying 1000 feet above the surface of the water.

After more than ten hours in the air, and with no sign of the lost plane, Deasy brought *Daisy Mae* in for landing at the Navy base at Palmyra. There they planned to spend the night, intending to pick up the search the next day, but after midnight a sailor awakened Sergeant Scearce and took him to a Navy officer who asked to see Scearce's radio log. Phillips' B-24 was overdue and was assumed to have ditched in the ocean. Scearce asked the sailor to awaken Lieutenant Deasy while he retrieved the radio log, and with the log, the men calculated their position at the time of their last contact with Lt. Phillips' plane and decided where Phillips would most likely have ditched.

Daisy Mae took off that morning to search for Phillips' crew, all eyes straining at the windows. The men never took search missions lightly, but this was different, this was one of their own planes, a crew from their own squadron. These were friends, and there was no question whether they had gone down. It wasn't a presumed crash with a vague, best estimate position.

They searched three of the next four days, but found no trace of *The Green Hornet* or the other lost plane. Finally Lieutenant Deasy and his crew were compelled to return to Oahu because of maintenance problems with *Daisy Mae*. Other aircraft also searched, and on May 30, Lt. George Smith's crew aboard #676, *Cabin in the Sky*, spotted floating debris, yellow boxes, similar to ration boxes carried on their aircraft.[13]

The men of the 42nd typically did not mourn their losses, but this one made them think. Phillips had lost two planes in two months through no fault of his own. Making it back to Funafuti in *Super Man* was incredible as badly damaged as it was, Phillips' effort as heroic as the plane's name might suggest. And everyone agreed that *The Green Hornet's* gremlins would have brought it down regardless who was flying it. Scearce assumed darkly that if his friend Harold Brooks hadn't been killed over Nauru, he would have gone down the next month. He thought it was strange how things could turn, the lucky ones on *Super Man* were the men who got hurt and had to be replaced, and it was unsettling to consider their ill-fated replacements.

On June 6, 1943, the 42nd Bomb Squadron dropped Lt. Russell Phillips and his crew from the roll with the comment, "lost in action on May 27, 1943."[14] On the same day, Lieutenant Deasy and crew took B-24 #073, *Thumper*, from Kualoa to the bombing range at Niihau and made six practice bombing runs. The routine kept humming along.

With a three-day pass in hand, Scearce looked for a flight across Oahu to Hickam, because from there it was easy to get a ride into Honolulu. 2nd Lt. George Dechert and crew, recently arrived from the States, was scheduled to make the hop. Scearce met the crew at the plane and climbed aboard for the thirty-minute flight.

When Dechert's *Naughty Nanette* touched down at Hickam, Scearce had the unnerving sense that the nose of the plane was too high. The angle of the flight deck floor was wrong, and they were too far from the ground for the main gear to have touched down already. In the next instant, there was a sickening metallic crunch in the rear, and then Dechert braked. The front of the plane dropped fast and the nose wheel hit the concrete runway hard.

B-24s have a tail skid and bumper that extends with a hydraulic strut beneath the rear of the plane when the landing gear is lowered.[15] It's there to protect the rear of the plane in case it accidentally tilts back on its tail. Dechert landed the plane on the tail so hard that the hydraulic skid smacked the runway, driving the strut right through the bottom of the fuselage.

Dechert taxied and parked the plane. Scearce got out and took a look at the damage and left, a little shaken, but anxious to find a ride into town. He didn't want to linger and risk getting caught up in an inquisition into the botched landing.

During phase training, especially in the latter stages, Dechert would have been in hot water for such a bad landing. Maybe an instructor pilot back in the States thought about washing Dechert back, but yielded to pressure to turn out bomber crews. At Hickam, the bad landing was shrugged off.

The Air Depot would fix the plane and not much would be said about the incident.

Chapter 8

The Squadron's Objectives

WITH TWENTY-FOUR FLIGHTS in thirty days, June 1943 was the busiest flying month for Sgt. Herman Scearce since he joined the Army. He had more hours in the air during May, but May had included the long trip to Midway, the Wake mission, and the searches in the vicinity of Palmyra. June's schedule was full of activity and Scearce liked it that way. Staying busy was the best way for Scearce to shut out the image of the man with the rectangular hole in his head. It was the best way to stop thinking about his friend Harold Brooks, or the loss of *The Green Hornet* with its entire crew, or the uncertainty of a future with a thirty strike mission requirement. And as May moved into June and July, keeping busy, having something to focus on for tomorrow, and the next day and the next, was the only way to avoid dwelling on tragedy.

The squadron's primary responsibility was protection of the Hawaiian Islands. They flew patrols and search missions and conducted countless hours of training to maintain combat readiness. The 42nd sent planes into combat during the summer of 1943, occasional sorties from Funafuti to Nauru or the Gilberts, and Midway to Wake, harassing Japanese airfields and photographing their defenses, but Scearce would not fly another strike mission until September.

The 42nd's photo missions gathered intelligence information needed for America's developing war plans. It was not yet settled which
Japanese-held island would be targeted next for invasion. The Gilberts
Islands group, particularly Tarawa, was watched closely as the Japanese
strengthened defenses there, and Nauru had not been ruled out as an
invasion target.[1]

Three ships of the 42nd were scheduled to fly to Funafuti via Canton
on June 14. From Funafuti, they would conduct a nighttime photo mission of Mille Island in the Marshalls, 335 miles beyond Tarawa, a total of
1130 miles one-way from Funafuti. Mille was home to a well-defended
Japanese fighter base.[2]

Lt. Alf Storm in #073, *Thumper*, Lt. Les Scholar in #143, *Sky Demon*,
and Lt. George Smith in #216, *Thumper II*, were scheduled to take off
just before 8:00 a.m., heavily loaded with photo flash bombs and fuel.
They would need the full length of Kualoa's Marston mat runway to
get airborne.

From Transportation Officer Richard Lippman's point of view, sitting
in a jeep beside the runway, the first two bombers barely cleared the
trees beyond the airstrip.[3] Storm and Scholar piloted their B-24s into
the circular pattern above the base as Smith released the brakes on his
aircraft and began his take off roll, throttles held to the stops.

Just past halfway down the length of Kualoa's runway, Smith eased
the control column back and *Thumper II*'s nose wheel came off the
ground. As the aircraft's weight rose from the main gear tires, and they
were just about to leave the metal runway, the nose of the plane abruptly
fell. The nose wheel was unable to absorb the sudden, heavy impact
with the ground, and it collapsed under the plane's crushing weight.

Smith's B-24 gouged itself forward, wrenching its nose partially
from the airframe. It plowed ahead with speed and mass like a derail-
ing locomotive. All four engines remained at full throttle, propellers

flailing sickeningly into the prefabricated metal sections of runway. Twisted lengths of Marston mat and chunks of black earth were thrown by the bomber's out of control propeller blades as the engines continued to spin at maximum speed. The propellers from engines 1 and 2 finally ripped themselves from their mounts. Number 2 propeller wildly slashed through the left side of the aircraft and into the fuselage, leaving a fearsome vertical gash several feet down the side of the cockpit before spinning over the top of the plane. Number 1 and 2 propellers cart-wheeled crazily 60 and 120 feet into the base officer's housing area before their energy was spent. Number 3 propeller separated from its engine and jammed under the right wing. After grinding 600 feet down the runway,[4] nose down and the main wheels still rolling, *Thumper II*'s number 4 propeller still whirled at full speed. The blade tips, bent backwards from thrashing themselves into the ground and the dragging number 3 propeller forced the plane to veer to the right. The wreck careened off the runway's eastern edge where it finally stopped, nose down in the ditch that ran beside the coast road. Fires in engines 1, 2, and 3 threatened to turn the hulk, fully loaded with fuel, into an inferno while engine 4 continued to run at full throttle.

Men sped toward the ruined B-24 in crash trucks and an ambulance even before the big plane stopped sliding. Without hesitation, ground crewmen Sgt. Jacques Joos and Master Sergeant Joe Mack climbed aboard the plane and shut off its ignition switches. The crash crew extinguished fires on the three burning engines as the thirteen men aboard the plane got away, some stumbling out of the wreck on their own, others with help.

Lieutenant Smith suffered a fractured wrist; he was lucky the number 2 propeller hadn't sliced into the cockpit a few inches deeper. Lt. Charles Pangonis had an arm fracture and the eleven other men aboard *Thumper*

II escaped with cuts, bruises, and scrapes.[5] No one on the ground was hurt, and all agreed it was a miracle that no one was killed.

The photo reconnaissance mission proceeded. Lieutenants Storm and Scholar were joined by a substitute B-24 from the 26th Squadron on "detached service" with the 42nd. They took off from Funafuti on June 17 to photograph Mille, and several days later, the same three planes photographed islands in the Gilberts.[6]

For risking their lives to save Lt. George Smith's crew, Sergeant Joos was awarded the Legion of Merit and Sergeant Mack received the Soldier's Medal. Lieutenant Smith could have gone home with his injury, but he chose to stay with the squadron to fly again.

Lt. Jesse Stay joined Storm and Scholar at Canton on June 25 and Lt. Joseph Gall arrived the following day. From Canton, these planes of the 42nd flew to Funafuti to join elements of the other three squadrons of the 11th Group, the 98th, 26th, and 431st, for a raid on Nauru scheduled for June 27.

The first B-24 to take off on the June 27 mission was the 26th Bomb Squadron's newest plane, named *Knit Clipper*. *Knit Clipper* took off at 1:30 a.m. with Squadron Commander Capt. Nicholas H. Lund at the controls. Captain Lund's nose turret gunner was a newlywed, just returned to action after a thirty-day furlough in the States where he had gotten married.[7]

Lund's B-24 was barely airborne in the blackness beyond Funafuti's runway when the aircraft nosed down and fell, exploding in the surf. As the wreckage burned in the ocean, six injured men were saved by the selfless efforts of the squadron's surgeon, Capt. Dean Wallace, and an unidentified Marine who ran into the water and pulled men to shore, then went back to find more. Captain Lund was among the survivors but the nose gunner and three other men were never recovered.[8]

The mission was reorganized with Lt. Robert Holland of the 26th taking the lead. Lieutenant Stay took off behind Lieutenant Holland's ship, and four more planes got airborne behind them.

The eighth plane, #919 piloted by Lt. Richard L. Walgren of the 431st, took off and climbed to about 150 feet when it suddenly blew up. Burning debris fell into the water, and now two planes out of eight were lost. There were no survivors among the ten men on Lieutenant Walgren's crew, the first crew lost by the 431st since the Group's reorganization with B-24 Liberators.[9] Lieutenants Scholar and Gall, taxiing into position to take off, were signaled that the mission, already a disaster, was cancelled.[10]

Three aircraft returned to Funafuti. A fourth plane already airborne circled the island for several hours, landing after first light. Only Lieutenant Holland and Lieutenant Stay flew on to Nauru, unaware the mission had been called off. They arrived over Nauru at daybreak and bombed the island individually.

Stay's crew had been having trouble with their plane's bomb bay doors creeping closed. At a certain point, the closing doors were designed to trigger a limit switch, preventing bombs from being dropped. Rather than risk a release failure during the bomb run, the crew bypassed the limit switch. They dropped bombs through the partially closed bomb bay doors, damaging the doors in the process.

When five Zeros attacked Lieutenant Stay's plane, the ball turret gunner discovered he was unable to swing his guns forward because the barrels struck the torn, fluttering bomb bay doors each time he tried. Stay took his plane down to extremely low altitude, just above the surface of the ocean, to frustrate the Japanese fighter pilots who surely saw the problem with the American bomber's belly turret. Once the Zeros left, Lieutenant Stay returned to cruising altitude for the ride home.

The cause of the two devastating crashes just off Funafuti's runway would remain a mystery. The planes were heavily loaded with bombs and fuel, but that alone would not have caused them to crash. A simple but tragic mistake was the most likely explanation for Captain Lund's crash: an improper setting, inadequate air speed on take off, maybe a lost cylinder head. Heavy loads didn't cause such crashes, but they made the aircraft much less forgiving when there was a problem. Perhaps a hidden defect in the new plane caused a horrific failure. A wiring problem, a short circuit, maybe a spark claimed Lieutenant Walgren's crew.

In addition to patrolling the sea around the Hawaiian Islands and flying reconnaissance missions and harassment raids, the 42nd supplied replacement crews to the 98th, 26th, and 431st . In that role, the 42nd conducted a training program for crews arriving from the States, supplementing stateside phase training to better prepare the new arrivals for operations in the Pacific. Before assignment to forward squadrons, these crews spent six weeks practicing gunnery, bombing, and landing on unfamiliar airfields, called "strange field landings." They also flew search missions to gain navigation experience over the featureless expanse of water.

The men of the 42nd were reminded that their work was vital. They were told protection of the Hawaiian Islands was of key strategic importance. But men like Scearce, Yankus, Lipe, Marston, Hess, and Johnson would have preferred to get on with bombing missions, and they took for granted that the officers felt the same way. Pep talks on the importance of their role reminded the men that the other three squadrons were down in the combat zone flying missions, and they weren't going to go home until they had thirty strike missions to their credit. The men rarely discussed it; at this point, mission count was a sore subject. The best approach was to stay busy, work hard while on duty, and have fun off duty.

Jack Yankus was a good man to know for off-duty entertainment. On one occasion, after draining a few bottles of beer, Yankus boasted that back home in Easton, Pennsylvania, he was known to have a decent singing voice. As soon as he let this tidbit slip, he knew his buddies would never let him forget it. They became instantly, keenly interested in Yankus' vocal talents, and they asked him to go on.

"Aw, come on guys, it's no big deal. It's nothin."

"No, Jack! Honest—you can really sing, huh?"

"Really, guys, it's nothin."

Knowing he'd probably regret it, Yankus admitted that his family thought he should work the night club circuit. With Philadelphia sixty miles south of Easton and New York City seventy miles east, who knew where it could lead?

"They thought I could do good, really, maybe even . . . aw heck, guys, forget about it."

Scearce and Lipe and whoever else they could persuade to join them went with Yankus to a Honolulu bar one evening, and soon Yankus had consumed enough brew to lose his inhibitions. Sensing the moment was right, his pals encouraged him to get up and sing.

"Go ahead, Yank! Everybody wants to hear you sing!"

"Aw, come on, guys . . ."

"Really, Yank. Don't hold back."

"I don't know . . ."

"You wouldn't let your audience down would you?"

"Audience? Psssh."

"Do it for us. Do it for your pals. Please. We'll buy the beer."

"You talked me in to it, boys!"

And with that, Yankus swung his long legs from beneath the table and raised himself up, a broad grin on his face, and strolled confidently forward while his buddies self-consciously slid down in their chairs, chortling into their sleeves. Yankus said something to the man at the piano, the first notes of "Danny Boy" filled the room, and the flight engineer from Easton began his nightclub act in earnest:

Oh Danny boy, the pipes, the pipes are calling[11]

Eyes bright, Lipe glanced around at Scearce and the rest of their buddies.

From glen to glen, and down the mountain side
The summer's gone, and all the leaves are falling

The boys sat back to take it in. Yankus was feeling it now and the waitress arrived with more beer.

Tis you tis you must go and I must bide.
But come ye back when summer's in the meadow
Or when the valley's hushed and white with snow
tis I'll be there in sunshine or in shadow
Oh Danny boy, oh Danny boy, I love you so.
And when ye come, and all the flow'rs are dying
If I am dead, as dead I well may be

ye'll come and find the place where I am lying
And kneel and say an "Ave" there for me.

Yankus' flourishes, clasping his hands over his heart and kneeling, as if to address an imaginary grave, caused the boys to completely lose control. Scearce coughed, nearly choking on his drink and Lipe found out that beer burns when it's laughed through the nostrils. Yankus looked directly at his friends who doubled up, leaning into each other now as if on cue, and they sang along:

And I shall hear, tho' soft you tread above me
And oh, my grave shall warmer, sweeter be

Joe Hyson, the radio man from Charlie Pratte's crew, passed Lipe his handkerchief and Lipe sniffled and wiped make-believe tears from his eyes. Yankus nodded and smiled and sang as if the words were his very own:

For ye will bend and tell me that you love me
And I shall sleep in peace until you come to me.

And as Jack Yankus, night club performer, took his bows, his squadron mates in the Army Air Corps whistled and whooped and applauded wildly for their friend.

The trick for Scearce and Lipe was to make sure that Yankus really thought that *they* thought he was good. Yankus' crooning was a continuing source of amusement for his friends, and Yankus half-jokingly lobbied Lieutenant Deasy for all afternoon flights, preferring mornings for sleeping off the effects of his nighttime carousing and singing for free beer.[12]

Ed Hess had his own, private amusement at the expense of the thousands of young and low ranking sailors and soldiers on Oahu, many of them recently inducted. They shared a desire to avoid tongue lashings from higher ranking men, especially officers, and from the first few minutes of boot camp, they knew better than to disregard rank. Since few of them were familiar with Army Air Forces insignia, and since it was better to be safe than sorry, enlisted airmen were sometimes mistaken for officers and saluted. The leather jackets airmen wore compounded the problem, concealing the man's rank, which was worn on the shoulder of the uniform shirt sleeve. To Staff Sergeant Ed Hess, this confusion was a happy little quirk.

Most enlisted airmen smiled when they were saluted by mistake and responded to the salute by saying, "I'm not an officer," but not Ed Hess. He saluted back. Making the most of the confusion, Hess liked to wear a small, brass, winged propeller emblem on his cap. He discovered that he was frequently saluted when he wore his cap with his leather jacket hiding the golden chevrons of his staff sergeant's uniform.

His enlisted crewmates warned Hess that he'd get in trouble for this silliness sooner or later. "Hey, *they* saluted *me*," he would protest. "I'm just saluting them back!"

The crew of *Dogpatch Express* posed for a photo on Oahu in 1943, with pilot Joe Deasy sitting relaxed in the driver's seat of an olive-drab jeep, his left foot resting on the door sill, right hand lazily draped on top of the steering wheel. The jeep is parked in a muddy clearing near a recently completed landing strip, its headlights hooded to reduce their throw. The rest of Deasy's crew surround the jeep, all smiles, none of them in proper uniform. Four have no hat, and Scearce wears a sailor's cap. Co-pilot Sam Catanzarite, with his officer's hat pushed way back on his head, looks like he's leaving a bar at closing time.

In the back of the group, Ed Hess stands on top of the right rear tire, and to his left, Bob Lipe stands on the jeep's back bumper. While the other men face the photographer, Hess is glancing down his left arm, where Bob Lipe is helpfully holding Hess' sleeve with the sergeant's stripes turned directly toward the camera.

On June 29, Deasy and crew were scheduled for a search mission with a 6:15 a.m. take-off. The aircraft was #110, *Doity Goity, Big Dick* ("Dirty Gertie," in someone's idea of a New Jersey accent, with a nude blonde painted on the plane's nose, kneeling in front of two dice showing fives). Just as the plane got airborne, the cowling on number 1 engine came loose. The cowling, an oval sheet-metal engine cover, had not been secured properly after the plane's last service, and neither Lipe nor Yankus had noticed anything wrong when they pulled the propellers through during pre-flight.

A loose cowling could develop into a much more serious problem. Part of it could damage the engine, or it could be torn and thrown into another part of the plane, or a piece could interfere with the landing gear.

Deasy banked the aircraft and landed, just six minutes after take-off. Half an hour later, with the cowling secured, he lifted off again. Shortly into the second flight, Deasy and Catanzarite learned that three of the plane's generators were inoperative. At 7:30, they brought *Doity Goity* back to Kualoa, the mission was cancelled, and a piece of the Pacific near Oahu didn't get searched that day.

Doity Goity was one of the six aircraft flown to Hickam from Hamilton Field back in February, in the flight with Lieutenant Deasy's plane.[13] Its loose engine cowling was a simple mistake that could have been disastrous, but the out-of-action generators signaled a more insidious problem: many of the squadron's aircraft were already beginning to show their age.

A malfunctioning air speed indicator claimed a B-24 on July 6. Lt. Warren Sands brought #689 in for a landing at Kualoa on a wet morning. Since the airspeed indicator wasn't working, Sands could not be sure about his landing speed. He brought the plane in slightly "hot," or fast. The plane stayed straight briefly after touching down on the wet metal runway, then skidded to the right and left the runway. The nose wheel collapsed when it ran into the wet ground and the fuselage buckled like a crushed soup can. The propellers on the right side of the plane ripped free, and the right wing and main gear were damaged.

Many crashes resulted from a combination of factors, and this one was no exception: the runway was made of steel matting, which was slick because it had rained, the airspeed indicator was out, and the pilot came in hot. Eliminate any one of these factors, and Lieutenant Sands would have landed as usual. On a concrete runway like Hickam's, a wet airstrip would not have presented a problem.

Crashes related to instrumentation problems were reminiscent of phase training. If there was a silver lining, parts salvaged from wrecks like these helped keep other planes flying. Fortunately, on this occasion, no one was hurt.

It was two months before the *Life* magazine crew who had accompanied the squadron to Funafuti in April produced an article. It was published in their July 5, 1943, issue, and the magazine reached the 42nd Squadron the following week. The article included a letter written by Gen. Willis Hale, Seventh Air Force commander, to General Hap Arnold, chief of the Army Air Forces. He wrote, "On April 20 I took off at night with 22 B-24's, overloaded, each carrying approximately 4,000 pounds of various type bombs. Our targets on Nauru had been well photographed prior to arrival. We were lucky in that the weather was perfect, although it permitted the enemy to see our approach. The first elements were engaged by enemy Zero fighters and all of us received heavy antiaircraft fire. Most of our planes were damaged, and three officers and nine enlisted men were wounded. One officer is in serious condition—shot in the stomach."[14]

Reporting on the result of the mission, Hale wrote, "This mission was successful beyond my greatest hopes. I am positive that it will be many months before the Japs can restore their destroyed machinery, which was involved in the refining of phosphates."

Sergeant Scearce and his buddies joked that the phosphate refinery was probably up and running shortly after their bombing raid ended. Fueling the cynic's annoyance, the 42nd's officers led the men to believe that General Hale hadn't even gone on the mission.[15] Further, General Hale's letter understated the casualties, failing to mention that one man had been killed. But in an odd coincidence, Harold Brooks' name was included elsewhere in the July 5 issue of Life.

The magazine features a memorial to Americans killed in combat, current to the time the issue went to press.[16] The cover photo depicts a group of six soldiers carrying the flag-draped wooden coffin of a comrade, a pilot, through a wheat field. In very fine print, from page 16 to page 38, every soldier, sailor, airman, and marine killed in action was listed by name and grouped according to his state and hometown. The only soldier from Clarksville, Michigan, among the 12,987 listed is Harold V. Brooks. That the bombing mission featured later in the magazine with General Hale's proud letter was the very mission in which one of the 12,987 died was a fact which was lost to millions of Life readers, except for those who knew Harold Brooks as a son, a brother, or a friend.[17]

The 42nd participated in another mission to Wake Island on July 24, led by Lt. Jesse Stay, one of the squadron's lead pilots. Four planes from the 42nd joined one from the 98th and five from the 431st, taking off from Midway's Eastern Island between 8:00 and 8:30 a.m. Hawaii time. Weather during take-off was overcast and wet, and the planes flew directly into a cold front 250 miles out. The front was severely turbulent with visibility down to zero, forcing two aircraft to return to Midway when they lost the formation. After 100 miles of horrendous weather, the remaining eight planes emerged into beautiful, clear skies. At 2:30 p.m., the planes approached Wake Island where the ceiling and visibility were unlimited.[18]

Anti-aircraft fire from the island was heavy and accurate, and the bombers were intercepted by a swarm of Zero fighters as soon as they finished their bomb runs. Lt. Richard Thompson, pilot of #688, *Wicked Witch*, was struck in the leg by a 20 mm round. The ship's propeller pitch wiring was also damaged. As co-pilot Lt. John Lowry took control from his injured pilot, Flight Engineer T/Sgt. Clarence Sopko repaired the wiring and the plane began its long return flight to Midway.

Aboard *Wicked Witch* was Sgt. William Campbell, a Marine Corps volunteer who had taken the place of S/Sgt. Earl Nielson. Nielson was with his crew as they staged from Oahu to Midway, but was grounded there by an attack of appendicitis. Since Nielson was unable to fly, the airmen asked for a volunteer from among the Marine Corps garrison to operate one of the bomber's .50 caliber machine guns. So many Marines wanted to go on the bombing mission that names were placed in a hat for a drawing, and as soon as Sergeant Campbell's name was called, he was besieged by offers from others anxious to take *his* place. Topping them all was a Marine captain who offered Campbell $1,000 for his place on the airplane, but the sergeant refused. Over Wake

Island, Sergeant Campbell scored one of the several Zeros confirmed shot down.[19]

Lieutenant Stay's ship, *Doity Goity*, its generators repaired after the aborted search mission in June, was holed by shrapnel but no one aboard the plane was hit. Lt. Walter Schmidt lost an engine near Wake, dropped his bombs in the water, and turned back to Midway.

Daisy Mae, flown by Lt. Joseph Gall, was the last plane to complete its bomb runs. A 20 mm round from a Zero struck *Daisy Mae's* number 2 engine, which began to lose power. The Zeros concentrated their attacks on Gall's plane as it fell behind the other B-24s. Zero gunfire knocked out the interphone system and the command set radio, so the crew could not communicate with each other or the other American planes, which were now leaving them behind. As Sgt. Joseph "Pop" Evans was raising his camera, he was struck in the upper left leg by an anti-aircraft round. Flight Engineer Sgt. Arvid Ambur rushed to help Evans, but Evans motioned to Ambur to watch for Zeros instead. Bombardier Lt. Myron Jenson had moved rearward and was operating a waist gun when he was struck by Zero machine gun fire, bullets piercing his left wrist and striking his shoulder and stomach. Gall's radio operator was hit by shrapnel and the ball turret gunner was also wounded, putting the belly guns out of action. The tail gunner ran out of ammunition and came forward for more. Pieces of Jenson's watch jammed the left waist gun. With four wounded men, ammunition running low, and an engine on the verge of failure, a fire now broke out in a fuel cell in the side of the plane. Fire extinguishers could not reach the blaze, so Sergeant Ambur smothered the fire by stuffing leather flight jackets into the space.[20]

Twenty-five miles away from Wake, Lt. James Cason's ship, #676, *Cabin in the Sky*, was ambushed by Zero fighters. One of the B-24's gunners got a .50 caliber burst into an attacking plane, setting fire to the Zero, causing it to streak out of control. It flashed under Lieutenant

Cason's B-24 and struck the bomber's left rudder, tearing it away. The bomber banked to the left and fell 17,000 feet, exploding when it hit the surface of the ocean. All eleven men aboard were killed.

Aboard *Daisy Mae*, Lieutenant Gall expected to ditch because fuel was running low. With the Zeros now returning to Wake, Gall feathered number 2's propeller and gasoline was transferred from its tanks. But the effort to keep up with the rest of the flight by increasing power to the other three engines had burned a lot of fuel, and damage to the plane had caused more precious fuel to leak.

The crew threw anything loose out of the plane to lighten the load. Guns, ammunition, and spare parts went into the ocean. Lieutenant Gall coaxed his stricken Liberator toward Midway's Eastern Island. The distance was mercilessly long for *Daisy Mae's* injured crewmen, but as they recalculated their position, rate of fuel consumption, and distance, Gall began to think they might make it. "Pop" Evans, who had calmly motioned to Sergeant Ambur to watch for Zeros rather than administer first aid, died on the way.

Daisy Mae finally reached Eastern Island's airstrip. The crew cranked the landing gear down, but with the hydraulic system shot out, Gall had no brakes. The B-24 went off the end of the runway, its landing gear buckling as it lumbered awkwardly into the sand and crashed to a sliding stop on the beach. The beaten hulk hissed and groaned, its twin tail pointing toward approaching rescuers like the flukes of a great beached whale. Marines warned the airmen struggling from the plane that there were land mines buried on the beach; *Daisy Mae* had lurched to a stop between them. The injured were rushed to the Navy hospital, where Lieutenant Jenson was given 50/50 odds of surviving. He died the next day.

Jenson and Evans were given a joint funeral ceremony on Midway and were buried at sea as required by Navy regulations there.[21] Seven hundred holes in the plane were counted, and thirteen gallons of gas were drained from *Daisy Mae's* fuel cells, enough, maybe, for five more minutes' flying. The aircraft was too badly damaged to fly again.

On July 26, eight more planes of the 11th Group bombed Wake Island. They took heavy anti-aircraft fire, and Zeros rose to intercept, but the Japanese pilots did not press their attacks as they had two days before. All eight bombers returned safely to Midway from the July 26 Wake Island mission, just two days after the intensity and destruction, the losses and close calls of July 24. Navigator Lt. Elmer Jurgeson had the only close call of July 26 when a fragment from a 90 millimeter flak round struck his briefcase where it was nestled beside his seat, and the briefcase stopped the jagged metal before it could rip through the navigator's seat.[22] An airman could never be sure what to expect on any given day, over any given target.

Three B-24s flew from Kualoa to Hickam on August 6, Lt. Joseph Gall flying #073, *Thumper*, Lt. Warren Sands in #155, *Tail Wind*, and Lt. Jesse Stay with Squadron Commander Maj. Earl Cooper in #214, *Dogpatch Express*, for the purpose of parade and formation to receive decorations for the squadron's efforts during the Wake Island raids. While #073 was being towed into position, the ground crew broke the glass out of the bombardier's compartment.[23] Lieutenant Gall and his crew would have to ride back to Kualoa aboard the other two planes while the depot repaired *Thumper's* nose.

Lt. Jesse Stay received the Distinguished Flying Cross for his leadership of the July 24 mission. The citation reads, in part, "For heroism and extraordinary achievement while participating in aerial flight as leader of a squadron of heavy bombers on July 24, 1943 over the strongly held enemy base on Wake Island. In the face of heavy anti-aircraft fire and strong enemy fighter opposition, he courageously led his planes over the targets . . ."[24]

Lt. John Lowry was also awarded the Distinguished Flying Cross, for bringing *Wicked Witch* home after Lieutenant Thompson was injured. Thompson received a Purple Heart. His resourceful flight engineer, Sgt. Clarence Sopko, was awarded the Silver Star for repairing the plane's propeller wiring in flight.[25] Besides creating a risk of fire, the damaged wiring would have made it impossible to change the aircraft's propeller pitch, risking engine damage or fuel exhaustion. Of eight Distinguished Flying Crosses awarded on August 6, the 42nd won four.[26]

On July 27, Brig. Gen. Truman H. Landon wrote a letter of commendation to Major Cooper. In his letter, General Landon mentioned the storm front the squadron penetrated to reach Wake on July 24. He acknowledged the squadron's severe combat losses, and praised the unit's high morale. He stated, "one fact stands out above all else, to give the 42nd Bombardment Squadron a mission is assurance of the complete success of that mission."[27]

The July 24 Wake Island raid, the one which followed two days later, and other bombing missions flown during the summer of 1943 were intended to harass the Japanese and keep them guessing where the next American invasion would come. Sentiment in the squadron was that the cost of these missions was terribly high for objectives so hard to see.

Chapter 9

The Pacific Preferred

BACK IN FEBRUARY, HERMAN SCEARCE and his buddies had been disappointed when they found out they were headed for the Pacific. Had they known what the future held for B-24 crews going to Europe at that time, they may have been relieved.

If Lt. Joe Deasy and the crew of B-24 number 41-24214 had been ordered to Europe, they would have been assigned to one of the three Eighth Air Force groups flying Liberators. In June of 1943, these three groups, the 44th, the 93rd, and the 389th, were sent from their bases in England to North Africa.[1] From their sand-swept temporary Libyan base, they practiced extreme low-level flying for a unique mission slated for the first day of August.

Every available Liberator participated in the August 1 raid, targeting the strategically vital Romanian oil refinery complex at Ploesti. The three groups from the Eighth, joined by two from the Ninth based in Libya, took off with 178 bombers and flew in formation below 1000 feet for the seven-hour run to Ploesti. They hurtled across desert, then the Mediterranean Sea, crossed Albania's mountains, and then dropped down to treetop level across farmland toward their target.

Low altitude was critical to the plan to avoid detection by German radar. It was also critical that the bombers converge on their targets precisely as assigned, and according to a strict schedule, so that fire and smoke caused by the raid would not obscure the target for following planes, and so that Ploesti's defenses would not be alerted to late arriving bombers. Radio silence would also help maintain the element of surprise as the Liberators approached Ploesti, which was defended by cannon on rooftops, gun emplacements in water towers and church steeples, smoke generators able to conceal targets, and more flak batteries than Berlin.[2]

Operation Tidal Wave, as the Ploesti raid was code-named, was doomed from the outset. The American code had been broken by the Germans, so the coming raid was no secret to the defenders of Ploesti. To make matters worse, some of the American aircrews made navigational errors, causing their arrival over the target to be staggered and uncoordinated. Later-arriving elements of the mission flew through billowing smoke and flames that set aircraft on fire. Fully alerted, the German defenses took a dreadful toll. Gunners aboard the B-24s fired desperately at the defenders, sometimes shooting at enemy gun crews on rooftops above the level of the aircraft. Leaving the refineries, the bombers were attacked by dozens of German fighter planes. Scattered and shot-up, many of them out of ammunition, the American aircrews who hadn't already gone down faced a desperate fight to make it home.[3]

Of 1735 airmen on the raid, 310 were killed, 130 wounded, and more than 100 became prisoners of war. More airmen were killed in this raid than people on the ground, defenders and civilians combined. It was the only air battle of the war resulting in the award of five Congressional Medals of Honor, and only thirty-three of the 178 B-24s in Operation Tidal Wave were in flying condition the day after the mission.[4]

2nd Lt. Dave Gandin, a 98th Bomb Group B-24 navigator, made this entry in his diary on August 1, 1943, commenting on the aftermath of the Ploesti raid: "Our squadron is no more. Missing and probably killed in action are Dore, Finneran, Franks, Stallings, Fay, Howie, Sulflow, Schlenker, Shay, Miller, Deeds, Crump, Foster, Scarborough, Ward, Huntly, Money, Anderson, Hussey, Peterson, Dave Lewis, Jenkins, Nelson, Thomas, Nash, McCandless, plus all of their enlisted men. I hope the price was worth it. They're the finest fellows in the world."[5]

It is easy to imagine the name "Deasy" among that list. The list seems long and it is a painful sentence to read, and the phrase "plus all of their enlisted men" is a heartbreaking multiplier of the losses represented by the names. Each name listed was the pilot in command of an entire aircrew lost, and Lieutenant Gandin was writing about just his own squadron. Scearce and his crewmates read news about the Ploesti raid with keen interest, well aware that if they had gone to Europe as they had hoped, they would have flown the Ploesti mission.

The August 1, 1943, Ploesti raid reduced production capacity of the refining complex by 60 percent, but it had only been operating at half capacity. Conscripted laborers repaired the refinery quickly, and within weeks it was producing more oil for the German war effort than it had been before Operation Tidal Wave struck.[6]

The Ploesti mission was singularly devastating to the men assigned to it, but for American airmen anywhere in the skies of the European Theatre, 1943 was a dark, foreboding time. It was the worst year of the war for the Eighth Air Force's B-17 and B-24 crews, with monthly losses as high as 6.6 percent of sorties flown.[7] One thousand airmen were lost in one week in July, during the all-out massive raids known as Blitz Week.[8] During a single mission to Muenster, the 100th Bomb Group lost twelve of thirteen aircraft in twelve horrifying minutes.[9] The 384th Group, with thirty-five crews, joined the Eighth Air Force in June 1943, and during the next three months, with replacement crews shoved into the breach, they lost forty-two for a loss rate of 120 percent.[10]

As long as their missions went well, B-24 crews in the Pacific had it better than their counterparts in Europe. But the two operational areas were vastly different. Whether the Pacific or Europe was a better place to be when a bomber got into trouble depended entirely upon the specific problems the individual plane and crew faced.

Pacific Liberator crews usually flew at lower altitudes, so they did not have to worry about oxygen, cumbersome and balky masks, the lack of heat in the drafty bomber, clumsy cold weather gear or easily damaged electrically heated suits. B-24 crews in the Pacific flew in the comfort of flight suits or shirt sleeves.

Eighth Air Force flight surgeon Capt. William Sweeney studied the problem of cold-weather flying in Europe.[11] He observed that airmen who walked through rain to get to their aircraft for a mission, or got sweaty before take-off, would be wet when the mission got underway and would become casualties when they came back.[12]

Frostbite was a grave concern in Europe, especially if a bomber crewman was injured. The projectile that injured him often damaged his fragile heated suit. In his article "Frostbite in the Eighth Air Force," Captain Sweeney described a navigator whose plane took flak damage to the nose. Flak pierced the navigator's mask, cutting off adequate flow of oxygen. The man lost consciousness and lay in the freezing plane for an hour. His hands, feet, ears, and nose had to be amputated, and his frozen eyeballs had to be removed. Dead tissue fell from his cheeks, but he remained alive.[13]

The higher altitudes flown in Europe were a mixed blessing. Temperatures of forty to sixty degrees below zero were a constant danger, but altitude was safety, especially for a damaged plane. Even if a pilot could not maintain altitude, he might be able to control his aircraft's descent and reach a friendly base.

Capt. Thomas Cramer, flying a B-24 named *Captain and His Kids*, was one of twenty-one assigned to attack a German night fighter control ship that was docked at Dunkirk. Three engines were knocked out over the target, but the altitude and short distance enabled the pilot to execute a controlled descent to a crash landing on an English beach.[14] Returning home in a B-24 on one engine was miraculous, even in Europe. Losing a single engine was a grave concern for any bomber crew. In Europe, a bomber pilot might increase power on the remaining three engines and try to stay with his formation for protection. In the Pacific, an engine loss was cause to immediately jettison bombs and turn for home. Losing two in the Pacific was as stressful a situation as an airman might ever survive, and losing three was a death sentence.

The distances flown by Pacific Liberators were the longest bombing missions in the war, and the hours took their toll of injured men and damaged planes. B-24s, physically demanding to fly because their control surfaces were not power assisted, were defiant beasts when damaged. Pilots of these Liberators were sometimes helped from their planes after landing, adrenalin spent, physically and emotionally drained. Aircraft crashed into the sea because their pilots simply couldn't maintain the physical exertion.

An airman's combat tour in Europe during the latter months of 1943 was twenty-five missions. After twenty-five, he could go home, but the chance of completing twenty- five missions, at that time, was one in five,[15] and many airmen cracked under the strain. Some refused to fly; others suffered severe, sometimes debilitating stress-induced injury and never returned to combat.[16]

England's weather, or the weather over the continent, often forced missions to be scrubbed. Clear skies facilitated American and British bombing missions, and likewise signaled German defenders to be ready. Blitz Week, the tragic last week of July 1943, was possible because the clouds that had obscured German targets for the previous three months finally cleared.[17] Airmen based in Hawaii or England might debate the social aspects and nightlife qualities of London or Honolulu, but none would question the superior flying weather enjoyed by airmen in the Pacific.

Pacific Liberators did not operate alongside B-17s, so mission plans were not complicated by the B-24s greater speed. In Europe, mission planners would delay the B-24s' take-off, allowing the slower B-17s a head start, so they would arrive over the target at the same time. This arrangement put the trailing B-24s in the path of fully alerted, angry German defenses.[18]

B-17s were considered tougher to shoot down by German fighter pilots, and B-17 crews considered a nearby flight of B-24s an excellent escort, because the Germans would attack the Liberators first. German pilots knew that the wing roots of the high-mounted Davis wing of B-24s were less robust than the corresponding structure of B-17s, so that a hit that a Flying Fortress might absorb could cause the wing of a Liberator to fold up.[19]

If a crew had to land in water, a B-17 was far better than a B-24. Flying Fortresses behaved better when ditched because their broad, sturdy low-mounted wing kept the body of the plane intact and above water, often for many minutes, while Liberators with their high-mounted, thin wings tended to break into pieces and sink quickly. When Eddie Rickenbacker went down in the Pacific in a B-17 in October 1942, the plane stayed afloat long enough for each man to get out and once in their rafts, Rickenbacker's men argued about whether to go back into the plane to get provisions. Ultimately they decided not to risk it, because the plane was surely going to sink, but Rickenbacker characterized this as a mistake because "the Fortress stayed afloat nearly six minutes."[20] This in spite of seas Rickenbacker described as "twice as high as I am tall."

Many European aircrews saw salvation in their "little friends," the pilots of the Thunderbolts, Lightnings, and Mustangs that intercepted

German fighters sent to attack the bomber formations. Liberators in the 11th Bomb Group operating in the Central Pacific could not hope for friendly fighter planes for protection; they flew without escort. However, operating from islands limited the range of Japanese pilots, while the geography available to German defenders was expansive.

German flak batteries and fighter fields could be placed all along the approaches of attacking bomber formations. Bombers might be subjected to staggered attacks beginning hours from their objective. German fighters could attack, land, refuel, and re-arm their planes, and take off again to reengage the bombers. They could harass bombers all the way back to their English airfields. In the Pacific, Japanese flak guns could be placed only within the circumference of their island base, and fighters could operate only within range of the island's airfield. If a Pacific Liberator got away from the target safely and was able to defend itself from enemy planes for half an hour or so, they were past the danger of enemy action and instead faced the navigational challenge of finding their own tiny island base, hours away.

Bailing out of a damaged bomber was an airman's personal decision to make. Some airmen who bailed out over Europe were victims of atrocities committed by partisans on the ground, but such incidents were the exception. Jumping from a stricken plane over Europe an airman hoped to evade capture, but even those who became prisoners of the Germans could expect to survive the war.

Bailing out over the Pacific was a desperate act, not so much a choice as the only remaining option for an airman otherwise facing certain death. Rescue by a friendly submarine or flying boat was almost hopeless.[21] Spotting a raft in the water was extremely difficult, finding a man without one was nearly impossible, even if his position was known. If a bomber crew got into trouble, the Pacific was a very unforgiving place. There was no neutral Switzerland, no place to land a crippled plane.

Even the German countryside and almost certain capture was better than a lonely ditching in the Pacific.

There were elements of chivalry present in the air war over Europe. An airman from either side could jump from his aircraft and descend under his silk canopy without being shot by an enemy gunner. There was a tacit understanding between the Luftwaffe and the Americans and British: if German pilots who bailed out were killed by gunners on British or American planes, then American and British airmen who bailed out could expect similar treatment when they descended or were captured. Many German fighter aces were survivors of multiple jumps from stricken aircraft.[22]

A bomber over Europe could surrender to a German fighter plane. 450th Bomb Group Commander Col. "Red" McGuirk, operating B-24s from an old fighter base in Italy, taught his aircrews this procedure. "If you lose an engine or two and can't keep up, just do the best you can. No one from the group will stay with you to help. That just makes two stragglers. If you're lucky, you may pick up some fighter escort. If not, just stay with it as long as you can. If you are jumped by a German fighter, don't try to be a hero. You might take one pass from him just to make sure that he's got some ammunition, then drop your gear to indicate surrender and bail out."[23]

Lt. Col. Beirne Lay, Jr. was a co-pilot observer on a bombing mission against the Messerschmitt aircraft factory at Regensburg on August 17, 1943. He published a story about his experience in the November 6, 1943, issue of *The Saturday Evening Post*. He wrote, "I watched a crippled B-17 pull over to the curb [pull out of formation] and drop its wheels and open its bomb bay, jettisoning its bombs. Three Me-109s circled it closely, but held their fire while the crew bailed out. I remembered now that a little while back I had seen other Hun fighters hold their fire, even when being shot at by a B-17 from which the crew were bailing."[24]

There was no such chivalry in the Pacific. The Japanese shot helpless airmen in their parachutes or struggling in the water as a matter of practice.[25] There was no quarter asked by the Japanese, and none given. Since by 1943 the Japanese were on the defensive, there were fewer chances for American gunners to respond in kind, but they did when the opportunity came.

After a bombing mission against Taroa in late 1943, the 42nd Bomb Squadron's log records, "Several Jap interceptors were knocked off this mission, by Sgt. Kernyat of Sands' crew, Sgt. Brannan of Lt. Kerr's crew, and Sgt. Roth, Sgt. Ball, and Sgt. Tanner of Captain Stay's crew. These were all confirmed, having been seen to either hit the water or explode in the air. One Zeke [Zero] made a water landing, the pilot crawled out and started to swim, and was at once eliminated."[26]

News of the Eighth Air Force's appalling 1943 losses reached the men flying B-24s in the Seventh, men like Herman Scearce, and they no longer had any desire to fly over Germany. The naïve bravado they felt in February was replaced by a much more realistic appraisal of risk, and they preferred their chances in the vast and far-ranging operations of the Pacific.

Chapter 10

Softening Tarawa

IN LATE 1943, the 42nd Bomb Squadron's missions were flown against targets in the Gilbert and Marshall Islands. Strikes against these islands were intended to soften Japanese defenses. If an island was slated for invasion, air strikes would be followed by Navy ships moving in for close-range shelling, and then the Marines would go ashore. The long-range strategy was to gain control of bases close enough to reach Japan while neutralizing or minimizing threats along the flanks as American forces moved forward. Each island group in their control brought American bombers closer, and in the Gilberts, Tarawa was the primary objective.[1]

Tarawa is a triangular group of islands, altogether about twelve miles wide and eighteen miles long. The bottom of the triangle, running more or less east to west, is anchored in the west by Betio Island and in the east by Buota Island. A coral reef extends from Betio's western tip northward, enclosing a large lagoon, and ends at Buariki Island on Tarawa's northern tip. Buariki then runs south and east, with dozens of smaller islands dotting a line back down to Buota.

Betio Island was the main target of strike missions by the 42nd because Betio held Tarawa's 4400-foot airstrip, key to the island's defenses and the only completed airstrip in the Gilberts.[2] The Japanese command post was also based there.[3]

Sergeant Scearce and rest of the Deasy crew tried to hit Tarawa on September 18, 1943, but on the way to the target, Lt. Charles Delk (name changed) navigator for the flight, realized he was hopelessly lost.

Delk was one of the few navigators who were already in the service when the war started. With the influx of so many new officers, men who were already commissioned got promoted quickly, and as a result, Delk outranked the other navigators. It didn't matter that his navigation skills were rusty; the silver bar of his 1st lieutenant's rank made him the lead navigator.

Since *Dogpatch Express* was the lead ship in the formation, every plane on the mission was also lost. Squadron Commander Maj. Earl Cooper, survivor of a B-17 ditching off Hawaii back in December 1941, was in the cockpit, having joined the crew as flight commander. He reacted decisively when Delk admitted he didn't know where they were.

"Get your ass in the back of the airplane and don't come back!"[4]

Delk went to the back of the plane, crying and frustrated like a scolded schoolboy.

It was important to conserve fuel when lost, and flying with a full bomb load burned fuel faster. Besides the fuel consumption, planes usually didn't return to base with bombs aboard because it was too risky to land with a bomb load. Following the lead of *Dogpatch Express*, each crew dropped their bombs in the water and turned back, returning to base by dead reckoning and by radio contact with Funafuti.

Once the planes were on the ground, Wing Commander Colonel Holzapfel met Lieutenant Delk and led him away. Word spread quickly that Holzapfel busted Delk down to 2nd lieutenant and gave him a new job in the mess hall.

The first *successful* Tarawa mission for Sergeant Scearce and the Deasy crew was the next day, September 19, 1943. Eleven B-24s from Funafuti joined thirteen flying from Canton: seven from the 26th

Squadron, four from the 42nd, six apiece from the 98th and 431st, and one from 7th Bomber Command Headquarters.[5] Two more aircraft, *Doity Goity* and *Wicked Witch*, were unable to take off because both planes suffered tire blowouts on Funafuti's rough coral runway.[6]

Capt. James Irby of the 98th was airborne when his crew discovered a stowaway: a U.S. Marine from Funafuti's defense garrison.[7] The Marine must have concealed himself in the plane's rear fuselage hours before the raid. A very surprised airman made the discovery.

"Hey! Who . . . what the hell are you doing here?"

"I've always wanted to go on a raid and this was the only way I knew how!"

Twenty-four planes constituted a big mission in the Central Pacific. Since it was a daylight mission and weather was good, chances were high of interception by Japanese fighter planes and accurate flak from their gunners on the ground.

Four B-24s developed mechanical problems and had to return to base without completing the mission. The remaining twenty planes each dropped nine 500-pound General Purpose bombs on the targets: Betio's runway, airplanes on the runway, and the island's oil dump.[8] Anti-aircraft fire was not heavy, and much of it trailed the B-24s. Flak damaged two 42nd Bomb Squadron planes, but no one aboard was hurt. Five to ten Zeros intercepted but it was hard to count them accurately, darting in and out of view as they did and seen from so many different angles on separate aircraft. Whatever their number, angry Japanese fighters made thirty-five passes from 11:00 to 1:00 positions ahead of the bombers. The Marine aboard Captain Irby's bomber helped pass ammunition to the gunners, and according to the squadron's record, "was of great moral support in cursing the Jap pilots."[9]

On the way home, pilots of the 431st squadron chatted on the radio on frequency 6210 kilocycles. "Are you stopping at first base or going home?" "First base" referred to Nanumea, which was closer than Nu-kufetau, home of the 431st. "How are you coming, Jeff?" Transmissions carried on for nearly two hours, including aircraft positions and speed and estimated times of arrival.[10]

A frequency of 6210 kilocycles was a standard aviation frequency, and the Japanese were listening. An unfamiliar voice joined the conversation, speaking in English with a heavy accent. "Thank you, Mr. Lauber, for your information on bases at Nanumea, Nukufetau and Funafuti, and here's to many bombings!"

The transmissions between the American pilots didn't stop. Soon after the enemy voice spoke, a Liberator pilot asked, "Are you sure that's Nanumea and not Funafuti?" And another replied, "Watch your language, remember what we just heard."

The 431st Squadron pilots had committed a significant security breach. Pilots in the 98th Squadron overheard it and they must have been incredulous. The incident was reported to the 98th's intelligence officer, and surely the pilots responsible were later scolded by their squadron commander. Group records make no further mention of the incident or its aftermath, but there is also no further mention of 11th Bomb Group pilots breaking radio silence without a very good reason.

All aircraft returned safely to base, confident that they had inflicted substantial damage on the Japanese.[11] The stowaway Marine was the first man out of Captain Irby's ship, bounding out of it as soon as it was parked on Funafuti's flight line. He said, "You can have it, brother! No more for me!"[12]

The four squadrons of the 11th Bombardment Group repeatedly bombed Tarawa through October and well into November. The Group's airmen understood that the Marine Corps depended on them to take out as many Japanese as possible before the Marines went ashore. The airmen didn't know when the invasion would begin, but they figured it must be soon. Tarawa would be the first time American boys hitting the beaches were relying on the 11th to pave the way, and the airmen didn't want to let their Marine Corps buddies down.

Deasy's crew took *Dogpatch Express* over Tarawa for the last time on November 13, 1943, exactly one week before the Marines invaded. The target was Betio Island. Nine planes from the 42nd and ten from the 431st were assigned to hit Betio's runways and anti-aircraft batteries, destroy planes, materiel, and personnel while taking pictures of Japanese defenses on the island.

One of the B-24s from the 431st developed a bad oil leak in number 3 engine and didn't take off. Another 431st ship, aptly named *Tired Tessie*, flew all the way to Tarawa and back with a full bomb load, a risky and frustratingly pointless effort caused by a bomb bay door lever that was too stiff to operate.

Dogpatch Express was showing some age. Number 2 and number 4 supercharger regulators were inoperative above 12,000 feet, and number 2 and number 4 generators failed. The radio compass was erratic, and on approach to the target the ball turret gunner discovered that the left gun in his belly turret didn't work because the bolt switch had been installed improperly.

Each plane carried fragmentation cluster bombs or 500-pound General Purpose bombs. They pounded runway and taxiways. A train of 500-pounders hit a barracks area, starting a large fire, while other bombs found their marks on gun installations and defensive works. Deasy's crew also took thirty-four photographs of the island, covering it completely.

Tired Tessie's crew, with their balky bomb bay doors, sweated out the landing approach as their pilot gently set the plane down with thirty clusters of six 20-pound fragmentation bombs still in their racks.

Dogpatch Express flew home in formation with Lt. Charles Friedrich's plane, *Virginia Belle*. Friedrich's radio operator, Sgt. Neil Putnam, was a good friend of Sergeant Scearce. Another buddy, Corp. Charles Walsh, was the assistant radio operator on Friedrich's crew. An assistant radio operator, like an assistant engineer, was primarily a gunner but also an apprentice. Both Friedrich and his co-pilot, Lt. William Morrison, were married. Lieutenant Friedrich's wife was pregnant, their baby due soon, and Morrison was crestfallen if he didn't get a letter from his wife every day at mail call.[13]

Lieutenant Friedrich was flying his first mission with a crew of his own after flying as a co-pilot on Lt. Jesse Stay's crew from March 1943 until August. Lieutenant Stay and Lieutenant Friedrich had flown five bombing missions and several sea search missions together.

Virginia Belle, aircraft #645, had a shapely blonde painted on its nose. She wore high heels and a barely-there pink negligee, and she knelt on her right knee, left leg extended to the floor, as if climbing into bed. She held a letter in her left hand, and each man was left to imagine privately that the letter was for *him*. For Sergeant Scearce, *Virginia Belle* brought to mind pleasant thoughts of girls back home.

As they returned to Funafuti, Scearce watched from his right waist window as the orange ball of the sun sank into the ocean in the distance. The reassuring drone of the aircraft's engines settled his mind. It seemed strange to think that just a short while ago, the air was full of flak bursts and their interphone headsets were busy with staccato voices, all the sounds of an aircraft and crew in battle. From the right waist window of *Dogpatch Express*, Scearce watched the beautiful black silhouette of Lieutenant Friedrich's bomber against the orange glow in the west.

As the orange glow dimmed, blue flame from *Dogpatch Express'* engine superchargers became visible. Traces of fuel from the wing tanks streaked the upper surfaces of the B-24's long, thin wings, ending at the trailing edges of the flaps, because air flow tended to siphon gas from the tanks when they were full. The supercharger's flames extended past the wings from beneath. It looked dangerous and awesome and beautiful.

Nine hours and twenty-eight minutes after taking off, *Dogpatch Express* landed on the crushed coral strip at Funafuti, but Lieutenant Friedrich's plane was never seen again. Lieutenant Deasy reported the last visual contact at half an hour before midnight, 105 miles from Funafuti. Navy radar operators on Funafuti reported a plane passing within fifty miles of the island and the ground radio station tried to contact the plane, but there was no response. Fighter planes took off to intercept and lead Friedrich home, but they couldn't find him, and searches during the next several days found nothing.[14]

Virginia Belle was lost with ten men: Lt. Charles Friedrich, pilot; 2nd Lt. William D. Morrison, co-pilot; 2nd Lt. Charles P. Pangonis, Jr, bombardier; 2nd Lt. Paul R. Byers, navigator; Sgt. John Magalassi, flight engineer; Corp. William Rutherford, assistant engineer; Sgt. Neil Putnam, radio operator; Corp. Charles W. Walsh, assistant radio operator; Sgt. Charles M. Otis, armorer-gunner; and Sgt. Norbert O. Finks, gunner. There may not have been another crew with as many men who shared the same first name.

Sergeant Magalassi's mother received a letter from her son postmarked November 27, 1943. She wrote desperately to Air Adjutant General Col. John B. Cooley, pointing out the postmark date, which was two weeks after *Virginia Belle* was reported missing. The adjutant's office replied that the letter must have been written prior to her son's disappearance.[15] Some well-intentioned friend may have found the letter among Sergeant Magalassi's possessions and mailed it, or the letter's handling may have been delayed by the far-flung operations of the squadron; however it happened, the postmark date was painfully cruel to the lost airman's mother.

Lieutenant Byers' father mailed a letter to the families of the others on the crew. He wrote:

> The boys were bombing Tarawa . . . they returned after dark to Funafuti, their base, but over-shot the island, and the authorities at the base thought they had gone on to another base. Checking in the morning, they found the plane had not come in and the Navy sent out boats for two or three days to search for them, with no success. The plane came within raid-r of the island, but it was not able to establish any radio communication.
>
> Reports are that the boys received a terrible reception at Tarawa. The flak was very bad. The conclusion arrived at is that either Paul, who was the navigator, was severely injured, so that he could not do his duty . . . it is also possible that the plane was so damaged that the pilot was unable to control it.

In fact, there was no damage from flak or fighters. While the 42nd was over Tarawa, two Japanese planes were spotted at a distance of two miles. Gunners who fired at these enemy planes were scolded for wasting ammunition. The Japanese planes did not attack. On the way home, *Virginia Belle* had flown beside *Dogpatch Express* for several hours, so flight control problems would have been apparent to the *Dogpatch Express* crew.

The navigator's father didn't want to think his son had made a terrible mistake. He desperately wanted to believe that no one was to blame, but the sad truth was much crueler. *Virginia Belle* was one of many victims of rushed navigation training and inexperience, thrown into a theatre of combat where there was no landscape and no point of reference, just a great, featureless expanse of water.

Sergeant Magalassi's mother wrote again to the adjutant's office on December 29, 1943. She enclosed a photograph, taken some time after the November 13 mission against Tarawa. "I am enclosing a clipping of some of the boys in Gilbert Island," she began. "I am positive that the one kneeling down is my son. Of course, the child's arm is covering part of his face . . ."

The Army Air Forces couldn't identify anyone in Mrs. Magalassi's photograph, which had been taken by an Associated Press photographer. Had the Signal Corps taken the picture, the Adjutant General could have identified the man who looked like Sergeant Magalassi. Instead, the picture haunted Magalassi's mother. She must have clung to that photograph, praying for the man whose face was obscured by the child's arm to be her son.

The girl painted on the side of Lieutenant Friedrich's plane, the pretty blonde getting into bed clutching a letter in her left hand, once brought pleasant thoughts to the minds of the men who flew with her and beside her. But now she represents another lost crew, and the letter in her hand calls to mind pitiable letters written by grieving, anguished parents.

Bomber Command's intelligence report on the November 13, 1943, mission against Tarawa, Section V, lists the planes on the mission and records the flight duration and fuel load for each one. *Virginia Belle* #645, is listed last, with no mission data. Under "Remarks," the last column on the page, is the comment, "Failed to return." The conclusion of the report states, "The mission was successful."

Tarawa mission airmen saw themselves as heroes because they believed nothing and no one could have survived the repeated bombing. The United States Marines would walk over the island and send the Air Corps a few cases of beer in gratitude.

On Tarawa, Betio's Japanese garrison had a different assessment of the American bombing raids. Imperial Navy Petty Officer Tadao Oonuki and his comrades believed the American air force had proven itself unsuccessful, dropping bombs from high altitude and sometimes missing the island entirely. They were concerned that their garrison was losing its fighting spirit in the face of such an ineffective enemy.[16] The Japanese weren't aware that an American invasion was only one week away.

Sergeant Scearce wasn't scheduled to fly a November 15 mission against Jaluit Atoll, but he would end up going anyway. Jaluit Atoll, with more than eighty islets enclosing a large lagoon, was home to a Japanese seaplane base on Emidj Island on the atoll's eastern extreme and held support installations on Jabor Island to the southeast. The November 15 raid, a daylight bombing and reconnaissance mission, was intended to neutralize these targets in advance of the Marine invasion of Tarawa five days later.[17]

Ten B-24s from the 431st Squadron would hit the seaplane base at Emidj Island while seven from the 42nd Squadron bombed Japanese installations on Jabor. Among the 42nd Bomb Squadron crews scheduled to fly was Lt. George Dechert, pilot of #961, *Naughty Nanette*. Dechert was the inexperienced pilot who had landed a Liberator on its tail at Hickam months before, on a day Scearce happened to hop a ride.

Sergeant Scearce, like most of the more experienced men, shied away from green crews. His experience as a passenger with a weekend pass when Dechert drove the hydraulic strut through the bottom of the plane at Hickam gave Scearce a tangible reason to keep clear of this crew in particular. Squadron scuttlebutt reinforced the idea that Dechert's crew was not up to snuff.

Following a recent mission, Dechert had broken radio silence on the return trip because his crew was lost. Radio men on American-held islands triangulated Dechert's position on that flight, instructing his radio operator to hold down his Morse transmitter key while the land-based operators took bearings and compared notes to fix his position, then gave him a heading to fly and repeated the procedure until *Naughty Nanette* was securely within range of Funafuti.

Once they were on the ground, the group commander raced up in his olive drab jeep ahead of an angry, swirling cloud of coral dust to meet Dechert at the plane. Steaming hot and tugging at his collar, the commander demanded to know why they had broken radio silence and didn't they know the Japs were listening. Dechert protested, with enough "Yes, sir" and "No, sir" sprinkled in to maintain protocol, explaining that if his crew had been trained to use the new radar system recently installed on the plane, they would not have gotten lost and would not have needed to use the radio to get home.

Sergeant Scearce was skilled with the radar. And while being on the operations officer's crew had advantages, because everybody knew that the ops officer was next in line for squadron commander, there was sometimes a price to pay. It was easy for Lieutenant Deasy to solve problems by deploying the men on his own crew. Deasy instructed Scearce to fly with Dechert on Dechert's next mission, the November 15 strike on Jaluit, and use the mission as an opportunity to teach Dechert's radio operator how to use the new radar. Scearce suggested hopefully that he could show them how to use the system right there on the ground, but that argument fell on deaf ears. Deasy may have quietly assumed that Dechert wouldn't get lost again with Scearce along, and with Scearce teaching Dechert's crew how to use the radar, Dechert may never need to break radio silence again.

The mission was uneventful, even for the Japanese on Jabor Island. Each of the seven aircraft from the 42nd Bomb Squadron dropped six 500-pound General Purpose bombs, and every bomb missed. The bombs didn't simply miss their targets, they missed the island *entirely*. Six bombs fell in a line in the water to the southeast, thirty bombs exploded off shore in the lagoon, and Lt. George Dechert's bombardier placed his six bombs northeast of the island. Not one bomb hit the island, but several crews made dubious claims of hits on ships in the lagoon. Dechert's bombs hadn't even fallen in the lagoon where ships might have been anchored, but fell harmlessly instead into the ocean on the opposite side of Jabor.[18]

After the bomb run, Dechert turned #961 away from Jaluit, banked his bomber gracefully and climbed to altitude for the long flight home. Sergeant Scearce showed radio operator Sgt. Ralph Walbeck how to use the radar, how to switch between antennae, how to speed it up or slow it down, how to interpret the island signature blips that glowed yellow and them dimmed when the beam swept past.

Roughly midway on their return flight, Flight Engineer Sgt. Eugene Snodgrass tried to transfer fuel from the auxiliary tank in the bomb bay to the wing tanks, but the fuel wouldn't flow. He manipulated the switches, but still the fuel didn't flow, and the time and distance became more critical and the mood on the flight deck became increasingly tense, because the engines could only draw from the wing tanks, and there wasn't enough gas in the wing tanks to get them home.

Sergeant Scearce leaned forward, between Lieutenant Dechert and co-pilot Lt. Robert Baker, and said, "Sir, I could contact somebody and . . ." But before he could finish his statement Lieutenant Dechert replied, "Absolutely not!" Without Lieutenant Dechert's permission, the radio would not be used, not to get fuel transfer instructions from a ground base, not even to contact other planes that were also in the air returning from the mission.

Scearce sat back on his stool, dumbfounded. The bombardier, flying as a substitute for the crew's own bombardier, glanced back at Sergeant Scearce and silently shook his head, and the engineer continued to try valve and switch settings. Finally the pump began working and precious fuel flowed through the lines, up and along the wings and into the tanks for the bomber's thirsty engines, and the sense of relief on the flight deck was palpable.

For the next two hours *Naughty Nanette* cruised south in the darkness toward Funafuti. Confident they weren't lost, as they had been on their first mission, and with the fuel transfer crisis resolved, Lieutenant Dechert's crew began to relax and think about what they might find to eat once they got back to Funafuti. But in the inky blackness over Nanumea, less than an hour out from Funafuti, number 3 engine sputtered and died.

Scearce looked up from the stool he had carried along so he could sit beside Walbeck at the radio operator's table. Flight Engineer Sergeant Snodgrass confirmed that number 3 was out of gas.

"Feather 3! Shit!" growled Dechert.

Co-pilot Lt. Robert Baker feathered number 3 and Dechert pushed #961's nose down, diving fast. Scearce was astonished.

"Sir, don't we have another half hour on three?" Scearce asked from his stool. It was common knowledge that B-24 fuel gauges were woefully inaccurate, so crews routinely filled number 3's tanks fifty gallons short of the other three engines. If fuel was running low and number 3 quit, pilots knew that they had about half an hour to land somewhere, or at worst, report their position and ditch under control. A Liberator out of gas at altitude was a flying coffin.

"What the hell are you talking about?" Dechert replied furiously, and that was all Scearce needed to hear to know that Dechert's crew hadn't learned the fifty gallons short trick or had arrogantly laughed it off, and that all four engines had been gassed up equally, and now each of the remaining three engines were minutes, maybe seconds from running out of gas just like number 3. Transferring fuel had bought time, but not enough time, because throttle settings and aircraft trim hadn't been handled skillfully enough to burn the fuel efficiently.

Nanumea had a coral runway, a fuel depot, and a handful of Marines. Dechert brought *Naughty Nanette* down toward the island in a steep descent, three engines still turning, fuel hardly visible in the graduated glass gauges fixed to the side of the plane's interior.

On approach to Nanumea's runway, just as it looked like they would get on the ground okay and the landing gear was lowered, co-pilot Baker reported, "Nose wheel won't drop!"

With adequate fuel, the pilot would pull up in this situation, circle the landing strip, cycle the landing gear through again, and if the gear still wouldn't lock down, he would send a man crawling under the flight deck to the nose wheel compartment to see what was wrong. He would try to lower the wheel manually, pull or kick or pry and attempt anything he thought might work, but there wasn't time to pull up and go around again, let alone send a man to investigate. Dechert had to get his plane on the ground *now*, and with no nose wheel.

The main gear touched down, and as the Liberator slowed, the crew except for the pilots moved toward the rear from the forward bulkhead of the bomb bay, using their weight to keep the plane balanced in a see-saw game they would inevitably lose as the plane slowed and its center of gravity shifted forward.

The crew braced themselves behind the aft bomb bay bulkhead and against the stepped floor just ahead of the waist windows, and they felt the angle of the plane move under them, feeling the front of the plane dropping past where it should be and in the next instant, the plane's nose struck the coral runway.

Naughty Nanette's nose smashed into the coral with a groaning crunch, like a great wounded dragon felled from the sky, unable to hold its head up any longer and belching its final fire in protest. Plexiglas shattered and wrenched from the bombardier's nose compartment. The aircraft's metal skin, searing hot from grinding against coral, ripped and bent, the rough runway ground the nose in a shower of sparks, and the aircraft's interior lights suddenly went dark. Dechert and Baker shut down the ignition switches as the rest of the men scrambled to get the hell out.

Scearce climbed out of the top hatch, just above and behind the cockpit, second or third in the rush out of the plane's black interior. He scrambled onto the wing, which was pitched forward, engines smoking and popping as they cooled. Scearce and the rest of the men clambering up and out the top hatch crouched and scurried, left arms extended to the downward-angled wing for balance like men walking on a pitched rooftop. They felt their way onto the wing root and dropped from the plane beside the closed left forward door of the bomb bay, and ran.

From the rear, the assistant engineer chose a different route out of the plane, climbing awkwardly onto the mount of his waist gun where he jumped blindly to the coral runway. The waist window should have been a safe jumping distance from the ground, but the smashed, nose-down angle of the bomber thrust the tail up high above the runway and the waist windows were half a man's height farther from the ground than normal. In the pitch blackness, the assistant engineer could not see the ground and could not judge his fall. He struck the hard surface feet first, legs bent for impact, but he fell clumsily onto his shoulder and his collarbone snapped. He gathered himself up and trotted away from the plane, holding his arms together across his middle, hunched over in pain.

The Marines on Nanumea weren't especially hospitable to Scearce, Dechert, and the rest of Dechert's crew. They offered no food and looked unsympathetically at the assistant engineer's injury, jealous of it almost, because it was an injury sure to get the airman a ticket home, but not the kind of injury that would scar a man for life. It wasn't the kind of injury inflicted in the violent circumstances these Marines had seen before.

Scearce slept in his field jacket in the open and didn't bother to go meet the plane that came for Dechert's crew when it arrived from Funafuti the next morning. It wasn't that Scearce wanted to avoid the inevitable debriefing that Dechert and his crew would suffer through—*Naughty Nanette's* post mortem—Scearce just didn't want to fly with Dechert's crew ever again, not even as passengers. He didn't want to occupy the same space, didn't want to be associated with them at all, in any way, ever again.

When Lt. Joe Deasy got the chance, after Lieutenant Dechert emerged from his debriefing, he asked Dechert, "Where's Scearce?"

"Nanumea."

"Why is he still at Nanumea?"

"I don't know. He just didn't get on the plane."

Forty-five minutes' flying time away, on the far end of the atoll, Scearce watched as the Marines clanked a bulldozer up and under #961's tail, connected a chain to the bottom of the plane's fuselage at the tail skid, and began pulling the sad bomber off the runway. Beautiful *Naughty Nanette*, dark haired and voluptuous, on her knees with her arms crossed under her full breasts, the thin straps of her swimsuit slipped off of her shoulders, would never fly in combat again after having the aluminum canvas of her striking image torn and bent beneath her.[19] Now she suffered the final indignity of being dragged backward by uncaring leathernecks to an out of the way place on an out of the way island.

While *Naughty Nanette* sat gracelessly propped up with steel drums, several curious Marines poked and pried through the crumpled nose of the plane, investigating why the nose wheel hadn't come down. Smashed into the narrow space where one of the two nose wheel doors should have been, wedged so that the door couldn't open all the way and the wheel couldn't go down, was a metal ammo box, left there apparently by a gunner on Dechert's crew when he prepared his position for the flight.[20] An ammo box in the wrong place had destroyed a B-24 Liberator and led to a crewman's broken collarbone, but the series of events triggered by the careless placement of the ammunition box wouldn't end there.

Lieutenant Deasy, co-pilot Catanzarite and engineer Yankus, a minimal crew, made the hop from Funafuti to Nanumea later that morning to retrieve Sergeant Scearce. Scearce fully expected a thorough chewing-out for his decision to stay behind, and he had already resolved not to lie about it, not to claim he didn't know the plane was there, as if he could have missed it anyway, but to simply say he was sorry, sir, and didn't want to go anywhere with that bad news crew ever again. But no one asked Scearce for an explanation.

Assignments like the disastrous radar training mission with Dechert's crew were not routine, fortunately, but the benefits of being on the ops officer's crew accrued to Deasy's men every day. *Dogpatch Express'* men were able to move around more freely than some of the other enlisted men. As long as they didn't flaunt it, no one minded if they took liberties other enlisted men did not enjoy. Sometimes they would go into the intelligence hut to get news from the ticker tape machine or listen to the radio. On the morning of November 20, 1943, Sergeant Scearce and Sgt.

Jack Yankus listened to Funafuti's intelligence hut radio as the United States Marines hit Tarawa's beaches. Like confident but anxious football fans before a big game, they gathered with a few other men around the radio to root for the Marines. The bomber crewmen expected to hear the sounds of a decisive victory, a walkover, thanks to the thorough pre-invasion bombing by the Air Corps. After all, bomber crews returning from a mission against Tarawa on November 17, just three days before the invasion, had reported that Tarawa "looked deserted."[21]

But it didn't sound like Tarawa was deserted, not at all.

"Receiving heavy fire all along beach . . . unable to land all . . . issue in doubt."

Scearce raised his eyes and glanced at the others gathered around the radio. Yankus finally made eye contact and slowly shook his head. The air in the hut was thick, motionless. Each man leaned forward as if an encouraging intercept could somehow be pulled out of the radio, after which everyone would sit back and take a deep breath in relief.

"Boats held up on reef of right flank Red One. Troops receiving heavy fire in water."

The airmen eavesdropping on the Marines gritted their teeth and clenched their fists; it wasn't supposed to be like this. Minutes later another strained voice crackled through the radio:

"We are fifty yards inland and pinned down . . . casualties heavy . . . trying to make contact with Item Company on right . . . no contact with Easy Company on left."

Then the first voice reported, "We have nothing left to land."[22]

Sergeant Scearce's blood ran cold. He walked out of the radio hut and into the sun, squinting.

Someone asked, "What's the word on the invasion?"

Fighting back tears, Scearce said, "It ain't good . . .it ain't going too good at all."

Chapter 11

Forever Consequences

THE ARMY AIR FORCES HAD a wide range of ordnance available for bombing all kinds of targets. There were armor piercing bombs designed to penetrate the decks of ships and explode inside the hull. Fragmentation bombs of different types were designed for use against personnel and parked aircraft. Incendiary bombs would scatter over rooftops and into populated areas starting fires. But the bombs used most commonly by the 11th Bomb Group in the Central Pacific were General Purpose bombs.

General Purpose bombs were painted dull olive drab with a one-inch-wide yellow band around the nose and tail. They carried about half their total weight in high explosive and were armed in the nose and tail with vane fuses, the tiny propellers of the fuses spinning as the bomb was dropped, either unscrewing a long threaded stem to release a spring-loaded detonator in the nose, or screwing down to crush an ampoule of fluid that would dissolve a delay collar to release a detonator in the tail.[1]

General Purpose bombs carried by 11th Group B-24s were typically 500-pounders. There were 100- and 250-pound bombs as well as 1000-pounders and the biggest General Purpose bomb in the arsenal, 2000-pound bombs nicknamed Daisy Cutters. Daisy Cutters were intended to destroy reinforced concrete structures, suspension bridges, dams, battleships and cruisers.[2] When fused to detonate above ground, the concussion of Daisy Cutters with their 1061 pounds of high explosive could also be devastating to personnel. These big bombs might have made a difference to the Marines who struggled ashore at Tarawa on November 20, 1943, had they been used.

Col. David M. Shoup, leader of the Marine invasion, kept a field notebook during the planning stages of the operation. On the first page of the notebook were two entries. "Go ashore" was the first entry. The second was "Request Daisy Cutters all along Red Beach Center between airfield and north edge of island."[3]

Had these massive bombs been delivered by 11th Group Liberators on November 20, Japanese gun crews that raked and swept Americans struggling ashore would certainly have been less effective and many Marine casualties may have been avoided. But there were no B-24s over Tarawa on the twentieth , and no Daisy Cutters ever fell on Japanese defenders there.[4] The several Air Corps men like Sergeant Scearce, miles away listening to the invasion on the radio, would have been bitterly upset to learn that a request for their help had been lost somewhere in the communications network that danced from the battle front to the rear of Marine and Navy command before jumping across to the Army Air Forces and back out to its own combat units.

Instead, 11th Group B-24s flew missions against nearby Japanese-held islands, missions intended to crater runways and deny the Japanese the chance to attack the advancing Marines and ships of the United States Navy supporting the Marines on Tarawa. One of these Japanese bases was Mille in the Marshall Islands, just 295 miles north of Tarawa. The Japanese had completed an air base there in November with three runways long enough to support bombers.[5] Japanese planes flying from Mille had been harassing American forces on Tarawa since the invasion two weeks earlier, so on December 1, seven Liberators from the 42nd Bomb Squadron were scheduled to strike Mille.

Lt. George Dechert was slated to go, but his assistant engineer was recovering from the broken collarbone he suffered jumping from *Naughty Nanette* after crash-landing on Nanumea two weeks before. The assistant engineer was by now back in Hawaii, or maybe in the States, where his crewmates imagined him in all manner of fraternization with doting nurses or swooning, bored hometown honeys. Dechert needed a substitute, and it was easy for Lieutenant Deasy to draw from his own crack crew to meet such needs, and anyway, Deasy wasn't scheduled to fly on December 1. Just as Sergeant Scearce had been assigned to go along to teach Dechert's crew how to use the radar two weeks before, Sgt. Bob Lipe was detailed to go with Dechert to replace the injured assistant engineer.

Back home in Columbiana, Ohio, Bobby Lipe had worked with his stepfather in his auto repair shop, learning the trade and developing his natural mechanical ability, the same talent that made him a good assistant engineer on Joe Deasy's crew and made Deasy confident enough in him to give him the top turret, near the flight deck, so Yankus could go back to a waist gun.

The fact that Bobby maintained a car of his own in high school was a source of worry for the parents of Columbiana's teenage girls. Bobby was good looking, funny and popular, and the car made him dangerous. It was a Ford Model "A" with a metal visor mounted on the outside over the windshield, and across the visor Bobby had lettered "Mayflower." Below the name was the explanation, "Many a girl has come across in this boat." On the back of the car was the warning, "Don't laugh, your daughter may be inside."

Lipe's sense of humor made him a popular guy on his aircrew. He was the one who openly teased Hess about pretending he was an officer and amused himself by holding out Hess' sergeant's stripes for the crew photo taken back on Oahu. And Lipe was more skilled than anyone in convincing Yankus that he really should follow his family's advice and pursue a singing career, just to goad Yankus into getting up in front of everyone again to croon drunkenly to a tough crowd impressed more with the bold display of courage than the singing.

An Operations corporal awakened Lipe early on December 1, 1943, for the flight with Lieutenant Dechert. Take-off was at 0600. Lipe pulled his boots on and tucked his service-issue .45 automatic pistol under Sergeant Scearce's mattress where he lay awake, because the men never took their pistols on missions. The dark standing joke was that if they were lucky enough to bail out over land and it was enemy held, all they could hope to do with a .45 was to make the Japanese really mad, or maybe commit suicide.

Lipe said, "See ya."

"See ya," Scearce replied, but there was gravity to this simple goodbye, and Scearce would never forget it.

The seven bombers from the 42nd Squadron scheduled to bomb Mille on December 1 were piloted by Lt. Charlie Pratte, Lt. Robert Kerr, Lt. Alf Storm, Capt. Jesse Stay, Lt. Walter Schmidt, Lt. Donald Bloch in *Dogpatch Express*, and Lieutenant Dechert.

The mission didn't get off to a good start. Lieutenant Schmidt, in *Bathless*, decorated with a hobo swinging a fist, had engine trouble and aborted before take-off. *Dogpatch Express* lost power in an engine when a cylinder head failed, forcing Lieutenant Bloch to turn back to Funafuti.

Lt. Charlie Pratte got about 400 miles out when #073, *Thumper*, lost contact with the other aircraft in heavy clouds and rain squalls. Pratte dropped his six 500-pound General Purpose bombs into the ocean and headed home. Lieutenant Kerr, piloting *Sky Demon*, jettisoned his bombs near Mille because his bombardier was unable to sight the target through the clouds. Storm, Stay, and Dechert were the only pilots of the seven to get over the target that day, sighting Mille when they were right on top of it.

Lieutenant Dechert followed Captain Stay over the target to make one bombing run in formation. Just before noon, each plane peeled off to make individual runs on the target at 9,500 to 10,500 feet altitude.[6] Cumulus clouds topped out at 8500 feet and there was heavy rain from overcast.[7]

Anti-aircraft fire was light and inaccurate. The Japanese gunners had the right altitude but the flak bursts missed left and behind the bombers. Just the same, the B-24s dropped altitude to make corrections more difficult for the gunners on the ground.

As Stay turned back toward the target he saw Dechert on his bombing run. Captain Stay circled over the target, and then made his own bomb run. They saw no Zeros in the air until then, when suddenly five of them attacked Stay's aircraft. The Japanese pilots weren't very aggressive, holding back because of the weather. They seemed to want to show themselves, let the Americans know they were there, but didn't press their attacks home. None of the fighters were seen to attack Dechert's plane.

Storm and Stay returned safely to Funafuti, but there was no sign of Dechert, and murmurs became hushed speculation about the overdue plane. Somebody pointed out that Dechert's bombardier, Lt. William "Gailor" Roy, was on his first raid, a broken wrist having kept him off flying status until now, and how anxious Roy had been to get well and fly missions with his crew.[8] Someone mentioned the assistant engineer with his broken collarbone, and what tough luck this could be for his replacement, the Lipe kid from Joe Deasy's crew. Someone else suggested Dechert's crew had been damn lucky to be safe after sliding into home at Nanumea, and how Scearce had been along for that one and wouldn't even get on a plane with them after that.

Scearce kept to himself about the Marines on Nanumea finding the metal ammo box in *Naughty Nanette's* nose wheel compartment, the ammo box preventing the nose wheel door from opening so the nose wheel could drop, and there wasn't time to find it because they were out of gas. And because someone put the ammo box in the wrong place the plane crashed onto its nose so that when the assistant engineer jumped from the waist window it was much higher above ground than usual because the front of the plane was crushed, so he broke his collarbone, and Lipe had to go with Dechert on the next mission. All because somebody left a damned ammo box in the wrong place. Scearce was the only Air Corps man to know and he didn't see what there was to gain by telling anyone.

Word got to the crew area that Dechert was overdue. It gave Sergeant Scearce a sick feeling in his gut, knowing Bob was with them, and knowing the crew's history of near-disaster so well. He remembered vividly the wide-eyed panic of Dechert's crew as they brought *Naughty Nanette* down toward Nanumea, an engine out and the other three almost out of gas, and he could not help but imagine what Lipe must have felt today, flying with a crew he had no confidence in and ending up in peril. Scearce blinked away thoughts of the heartbreaking, hopeless resignation Bob Lipe must have felt, long past their estimated time of arrival, finally bracing against a bulkhead for a violent crash in the ocean.

A radio on the flight line had contact with the alternative landing sites, Nanumea and recently secured Tarawa, and radio operators at those fields confirmed Dechert wasn't there. There was no other place they could be, and soon it was obvious that the fuel supply had to be spent. The possibility that they might have landed at an alternative field grew into the more desperate hope that they'd been picked up by a ship or a submarine, but Scearce knew in his heart that they had probably made another mistake, a terrible, costly, and irreparable mistake, a mistake with forever consequences.

There was still no news about Dechert the next day, when the 42nd Squadron got word there would be a Nauru mission on December 4. There was no time to dwell on losses.

Bob Lipe's last letter home to Columbiana, dated November 23, reached his mom on December 14, 1943. A telegram arrived the same day to tell her that Bob was missing somewhere in the Central Pacific.[9] Leah Hitchcock put the telegram down and picked up Bob's letter but her hands shook too much to read it.

Bob's stepfather, Ethan Allen Hitchcock, "Hitchie," came home early that day. News traveled fast and a telegram was news, especially when it came to a house with two sons in the war. Hitchie found Leah on the sofa, Bob's letter and the War Department telegram in front of her on the floor. Hitchie said there'd be more news, that Bobby would be okay, and she shouldn't worry. She wanted to believe him, but still she felt the bottomless desperation of a mother whose helpless child was suddenly lost, except there was no place for her to look, no one to ask for help, and no use calling his name.

Each day's lack of news renewed the pain until Leah and Hitchie were numb. She continued to hope he'd be found. After all, there was no report of a crash. He'll be okay, she repeated to herself. She kept him in her prayers while Hitchie hid his belief it was hopeless.

Hitchie sometimes caught himself teasing Jigs with his foot, like Bobby used to do, and then he'd get up, leave the room, and find some mindless chore. Hitchie sold the shop in Canfield not long after Bob went missing.

Bob's mother dreamed of him. In the fog of morning, not quite awake, she would think he was there. Then she'd realize it was only a dream, blink tears away, and long for that illusion just lost when she'd been warm and content and happy he was home.

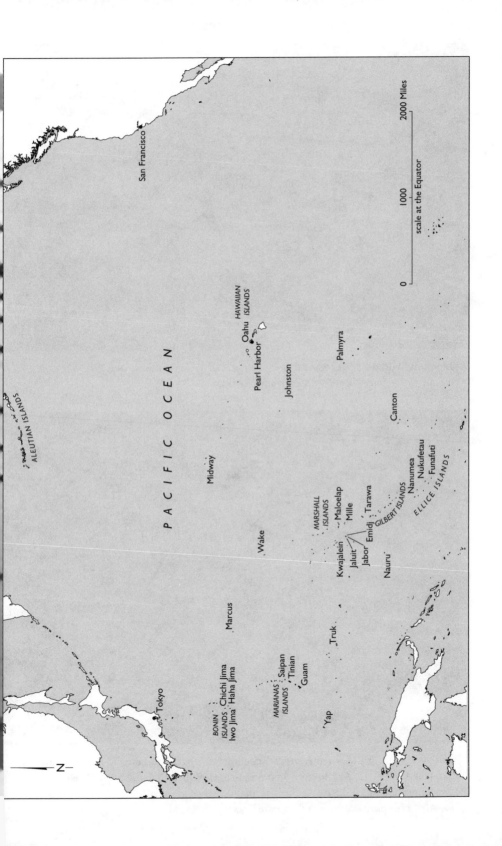

Al Marston (with dog), Herman Scearce, center, and Jack Yankus, Oahu, 1943
Army Air Corps photo courtesy of Herman Scearce

The original crew of *Dogpatch Express*. Kneeling l-r: S/Sgt. Bob Lipe, Lt. Sam Catanzarite, T/Sgt. Jack Yankus, Lt. Art Boone. Standing l-r: Lt. William Baber, Lt. Joe Deasy, S/Sgt. Elmer Johnson, S/Sgt. Ed Hess, T/Sgt. Herman Scearce
Army Air Corps photo courtesy of Herman Scearce

Dogpatch Express off Hawaii, 1943
Collection of Joe Deasy

S/Sgt. Bob Lipe of Columbiana, Ohio,
lost in action December 1, 1943
*Army Air Corps photo courtesy of
Herman Scearce*

Bombardier Lt. "Gailor" Roy, lost in
action on his first combat mission
*Reprinted by permission of
Susan Taylor*

Jack Yankus, left, and Herman Scearce at .50 caliber waist gun
Army Air Corps photo courtesy of Herman Scearce

Sam Catanzarite, left (in right seat); William Baber, center; Joe Deasy, right; Jack Yankus in hatch opening
Collection of Joe Deasy

Joe Deasy's crew, Oahu. Lipe holds Hess' sergeant stripes for the camera
Army Air Corps photo courtesy of Herman Scearce

Captain Joe Deasy
*Army Air Corps photo
courtesy of Herman Scearce*

AT-6 Texan with rear-facing gun position
National Archives and Records Administration photo 342-FH-3B-24034-39314-AC

Naughty Nanette after
crash-landing on Nanumea,
sheet metal repairs evident
at lower right
*Army Air Corps photo
courtesy of Herman Scearce*

963 unloading supplies on Funafuti. Failed to return from its December 1, 1943, mission
National Archives and Records Administration photo 342-FH-3A-42867-62905-AC

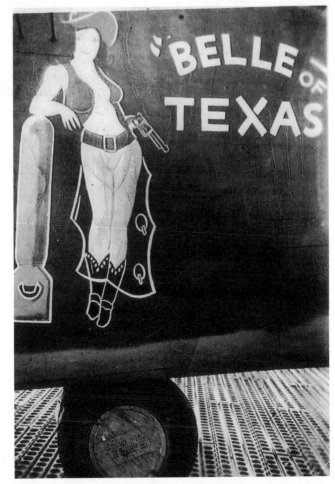

Belle of Texas on Marston
Mat steel runway
*Army Air Corps photo
courtesy of Herman Scearce*

Lt. Friedrich's plane, failed to return from its November 13, 1943, mission
Army Air Corps photo courtesy of Herman Scearce

Bombing-up for a mission, Funafuti
National Archives and Records Administration photo 342-FH-3A-42858-23791-AC

B-24 destroyed by a direct hit in Japanese raid on Funafuti
National Archives and Records Administration photo 342-FH-3A-43074-62903-AC

B-24 propeller after aircraft destroyed in Japanese raid
Army Air Corps photo courtesy of Herman Scearce

Crew quarters on Funafuti
Army Air Corps photo courtesy of Herman Scearce

Airmen with native girls on Funafuti
Army Air Corps photo courtesy of Herman Scearce

Funafuti. Runway extends from beach to ocean on the opposite side
U.S. Navy photo courtesy of Dr. James Mowbray

Lt. George Smith's crash on take-off, overloaded for a photo-reconnaissance mission. Note propeller damage to cockpit.
Collection of Joe Deasy

Daisy Mae on the beach at Midway after Wake Island raid
Collection of Joe Deasy

Dogpatch Express minutes from hitting the water, number 4 feathered, number 3 on fire,
right rudder damaged
Army Air Corps photo courtesy of Herman Scearce

Belle of Texas lands on Mullinnix Field using parachutes for brakes
National Archives and Records Administration photo 342-FH-3A-43097-51102-AC

Removing American dead from truck destroyed in Japanese raid on Funafuti. Scearce stands far right with no helmet.
Army Air Corps photo courtesy of Herman Scearce

Mess hall fire on Funafuti
Army Air Corps photo courtesy of Air Force Historical Research Agency

Engine maintenance,
Funafuti
*National Archives and
Records Administration
photo 342-FH-42940-
23788-AC*

ntelligence officer debriefs *Dogpatch Express* crew after bombing mission. l-r Deasy,
:atanzarite, Lipe, Boone
Army Air Corps photo courtesy of Herman Scearce

Chow time on Funafuti. Scearce at center, third from left
Army Air Corps photo courtesy of Herman Scearce

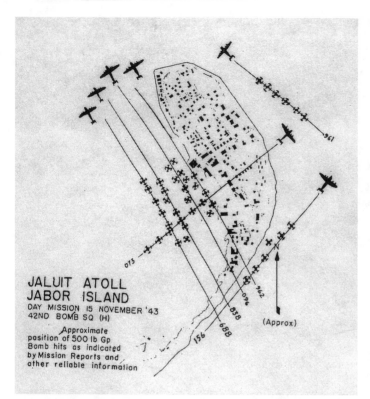

JALUIT ATOLL
JABOR ISLAND
DAY MISSION 15 NOVEMBER '43
42ND BOMB SQ (H)

Approximate
position of 500 lb Gp
Bomb hits as indicated
by Mission Reports and
other reliable information

(Approx)

Bomb plot chart from November 15, 1943 mission. *Naughty Nanette* (top right) crash-landed on Nanumea on return flight. Every bomb dropped missed the island. *Reprinted from Strike Mission Report courtesy of Air Force Historical Research Agency*

Mission briefing on Guam. Strategic bombing map of Iwo Jima on right
Army Air Corps photo courtesy of Air Force Historical Research Agency

Christmas mail call on Guam
National Archives and Records Administration photo 342-FH-3A-40101-55896-AC

42nd Squadron B-24 takes off
from Guam
*National Archives and
Records Administration photo
342-FH-3A-38625-68643-AC*

Crew quarters on Guam
Army Air Corps photo courtesy of Air Force Historical Research Agency

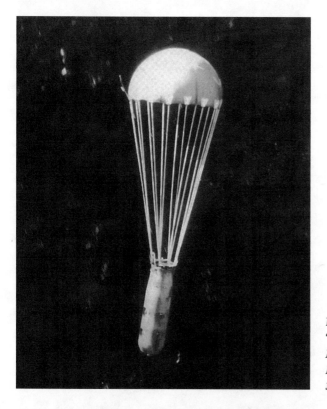

Mine released from B-24 on
"MIKE" mission
*National Archives and
Records Administration photo
342-FH-3A-42538-57609-AC*

.t. Strong's B-24 after mine crashed into fuselage over Chichi Jima
Army Air Corps photo courtesy of Air Force Historical Research Agency

431st Squadron B-24 over Iwo Jima, phosphorous bomb bursts nearby
Army Air Corps photo courtesy of Air Force Historical Research Agency

Bomb train explodes
across runways, Iwo
Jima. Island is entirely
cratered by bombs
*Army Air Corps photo
courtesy of Air Force
Historical Research
Agency*

42nd Squadron B-24 over Iwo Jima
National Archives and Records Administration photo 342-FH-3A-42209-562-AC

Chapter 12

Losing Altitude Fast

THE DIFFERENCE BETWEEN an uneventful mission and a terrifying one could be a matter of a few feet, maybe one more or one less degree of elevation or traverse by a Japanese anti-aircraft gunner as he aimed his weapon to fire. It might be just a heartbeat's difference in the gunner's hand on the aiming wheels, raising the barrel or sweeping it toward the path of incoming American bombers.

On the December 4, 1943, mission to Nauru, Lt. Robert Kerr's plane took a shell through the left stabilizer.[1] A few feet to the plane's right and the shell would have hit the tail gunner's position and would surely have exploded there and blown the tail off the plane. Instead, the round put a jagged hole through the thin vertical section just ahead of the left rudder and exploded above the aircraft, sprinkling spent shrapnel harmlessly down through the big bomber's wake.

A Navy PB4Y had joined eight B-24s for the December 4 Nauru raid. PB4Y was the Navy's designation for their version of the Liberator, Patrol Bomber 4, Y the code letter for Consolidated Aircraft, the manufacturer. The standard joke in the Air Corps was that the Navy got Liberators that didn't pass Army inspection.

The PB4Y was loaded with photographic equipment to survey the island. On approach to Nauru, the Navy crew left the bomber formation to make its own photographic runs, especially of a fighter strip believed to be under construction on the north side of the island.[2] The Navy got its photographs, and the Air Corps put every bomb on their targets: fuel tanks, phosphate refining areas, and the island's power plant. As the nine American planes left Nauru's airspace, there was an explosion in a fuel storage area on the island causing thick black oil smoke to billow skyward, rising to 10,000 feet, almost as high as the bombers flying away.

There was no Japanese fighter plane interception on December 4 over Nauru, and anti-aircraft gunnery was light and inaccurate, except for Lieutenant Kerr's close call. There were no American casualties.

In December, Lt. Dick Thompson was still off flying status. A 20 millimeter round from a Japanese anti-aircraft gun had shattered his leg on the July 24 mission to Wake, the mission that earned his co-pilot Lt. John Lowry the Distinguished Flying Cross for bringing the shot-up *Wicked Witch* back to Midway and Flight Engineer Sgt. Clarence Sopko the Silver Star for miraculously repairing the propeller pitch wiring. Thompson received a Purple Heart. Any bombing mission resulting in a pilot with a Purple Heart, the other one a DFC and the engineer earning a Silver Star and everyone gets back okay was miraculous all by itself. Lieutenant Thompson's crew had been very lucky that day.

Through December, the 11th Group continued to suppress Japanese airfields within striking distance of Tarawa. The job could never be considered complete, because coral runways cratered by bombs were quickly filled by men with trucks and bulldozers, wheelbarrows and shovels, or sometimes just wheelbarrows and shovels. Delay fuses on some General Purpose bombs were intended to slow the repair process as Japanese work details were forced to deal with the unexploded ordnance or risk dying in the explosion of a bomb dropped hours or the day before.

Taroa Island in the Maloelap Atoll of the Marshall Islands group was the target on December 20. Maloelap is a large atoll of about seventy-five islands in a jewel-like strand, a necklace of less than four square miles of land mass if all the islands are added together, surrounding an enormous lagoon of 375 square miles. If you could pick up the island strand like a string of pearls, you could drape it all the way around San Diego with room to spare. Taroa is the largest island in the atoll, and its air base was a threat to Americans at Tarawa less than 600 miles away.

Lt. George Smith flew with Lt. Dick Thompson's crew since Thompson was grounded with his leg injury. It had been only six months since Lieutenant Smith's spectacular crash while attempting to take off in B-24 *Thumper II*, overloaded for a photo reconnaissance mission leaving Kualoa, the mission in which Lieutenant Smith's left wrist was fractured when the number 2 propeller wrenched itself from its mounting bolts and smashed the cockpit right in front of Smith's face. Smith's arm injury could have been his ticket back to the States, but he had insisted on staying with his crew.

Eight planes from the 42nd were joined by a single ship from the 431st for the mission against Taroa's airfield. Lieutenant Smith, with Thompson's crew, flew *Dogpatch Express* because Deasy's crew wasn't scheduled to fly that day and there were maintenance problems on their usual aircraft. Lt. Robert Kerr flew #143, *Sky Demon*, decorated with five sinister flaming devils casting destruction upon an unseen enemy below. Also on the mission was Capt. Alf Storm in #155, *Tail Wind*, with a pretty lady in high heels clutching her sun hat with one hand and holding her skirt down with the other as a breeze reveals her mid-thigh-stockinged legs. Lt. Joseph Gall flew airplane #100, *You're Gonna Get It*, featuring the Disney dog Pluto clutching a bomb. Lt. Walter Schmidt was in #838, *Brunnhilda*, graced by a Viking warrior woman with a horned helmet and a shield, and Capt. Jesse Stay flew

#960, *Angel Face*, which had a modestly tasteful head portrait of a woman on its nose. Lt. Warren Sands piloted #073, *Thumper*, with a huge cartoon rabbit pounding the ground with a powerful hind leg and Lt. Charlie Pratte was in #156, *Belle of Texas*, adorned with a beautiful brunette, presumably from Texas, leaning on an upright bomb, holding a six-shooter and wearing a cowboy hat, a vest, boots, and not much else. Sergeant Scearce's buddy, Corp. Joe Hyson, was a gunner on Charlie Pratte's crew. Pratte and his crew were among the "old timers" who had flown to Hawaii from the mainland almost a year before.

The lone aircraft from the 431st was #007, *Little Lonnie*, decorated with a topless Hawaiian girl resting on her knees with a huge red hibiscus in her hair, flown by Lt. Thomas Perry.

The distance to Taroa made it impossible for the American bombers to have fighter escort, typical for the crews of the 11th Group. The lack of fighter support wasn't discussed much, but Scearce and Hyson had been amused by the 1943 calendar hanging in a club on Oahu, a Coca-Cola calendar depicting two olive drab B-24s flying in formation with several P-47 Thunderbolts. Hyson jabbed his finger at the P-47s and said, "That's a neat picture, but what the hell are those?"

Taroa was better defended than other targets attacked by the 42nd because Taroa had search radar.[3] Radar enabled Japanese anti-aircraft gun crews to be in position and ready well in advance, and made it easy for Japanese fighter pilots to get to altitude and hover against the sun where they became invisible, lying in wait to ambush approaching American bombers. After their comrade gun crews on the ground 10,000 feet below had done their best, the Zero pilots streamed out of the sun and plunged into the retiring bombers like angry wasps and the interphones on the bombers erupted with anxious position alerts and the American gunners swung into action.

⫸⫷

The nine American planes formed into three "V" shaped flights of three planes each for the December 20 raid, each plane carrying six 500-pound bombs. The mission would put the planes over the target at midday, also typical, because this was the best time of day for accurate bombing by sight. Pratte was in the second flight, Smith followed in the number two position of the third flight.[4] Anti-aircraft fire over the target was intense with flak bursts ahead to greet the aircrews and give them sobering notice that they weren't on a milk run.

Taroa's anti-aircraft guns were in open emplacements that American photo interpreters called "donuts."[5] The emplacements were surrounded by a circular earthen parapet that was itself surrounded by a second, larger ring of earth to form concentric circles, their entrances offset to protect against bomb blasts. The guns were grouped around sound locators and range finders, ammunition bunkers, bomb shelters, fire direction centers, and command posts connected to the search radar installation.[6]

Bombardier Lt. Ralph Ortiz, aboard *Dogpatch Express*, was on his bomb run when flak from one of the Japanese guns knocked out engine number 4 and drilled holes through the fuselage and tail of the plane. Co-pilot Lt. John Lowry looked to his right to confirm number 4 was feathered when another Japanese anti-aircraft shell tore through the aluminum skin beneath the flight deck, angling upwards to explode in the cockpit.

Twelve minutes off the target and ahead of the third flight, Captain Stay's tail gunner called him on the interphone to say that a B-24 was falling behind and was under attack from several Zeros. At that moment, Lt. Warren Sands began to turn back toward *Dogpatch Express* following a similar report from his own tail gunner, that a B-24 was smoking and losing altitude and alone. Captain Stay and his wing man Lieutenant

Pratte turned with Sands. Captain Storm, alerted by Stay's co-pilot of the straggler, also turned back, and Lieutenant Perry of the 431st turned with him. Without orders from strike commander Stay, every plane in the mission turned around, circling back to drop through the clouds where they formed up on either side of *Dogpatch Express* so that gunners on their planes could help defend the overwhelmed aircraft.

Banking past Lieutenant Smith's plane, Captain Stay saw no one in the right seat, co-pilot John Lowry's seat. The cockpit glass was splattered red with blood, and the top turret where Sergeant Sopko would have been sitting was blown out. The glass that remained in place in the top turret was also smeared with blood.[7]

Minutes after the other planes in his flight took positions just off his right and left wings, Lieutenant Smith's number 3 engine caught fire, streaming white burnt-oil smoke behind the crippled plane. The Japanese Zeros pressed their attacks harder, attacking from above and behind *Dogpatch Express*; no doubt they had also noticed the top turret. Captain Stay contacted Lieutenant Smith by VHF radio and suggested that he shut down and feather 3 and try to put out the fire with his Lux system, the fire extinguishers built in to the engine nacelle. Number 4, the outboard engine on the same side, was already feathered.

Lieutenant Smith shut down 3 and the fire went out. He responded to Captain Stay with a request that they get Dumbo service for him, because he knew he wasn't going to make it, and Captain Stay acknowledged that he would. At 3000 feet, Lieutenant Smith restarted number 3, and it began pouring white smoke again. *Dogpatch Express* dropped below the puffy white cumulous clouds at 2000 feet, number 3's white smoke intersecting the clouds at a low angle. Lieutenant Smith was losing altitude fast.

Gunners on Kerr, Sands, and Stay's crews shot down Zeros as the fighters doggedly pursued Lieutenant Smith's crippled plane. The top turret gunner and tail gunner of Lieutenant Perry's crew got credit for two Zeros out of seven shot down.[8] One Zero landed in the water, and its pilot crawled out and began to swim away. The downed Japanese pilot presented an unusual target to B-24 gunners, because B-24s would ordinarily fly too high to clearly see an enemy plane hit the water, let alone see its pilot push his cockpit canopy back, climb out, and start swimming. Sometimes Japanese fighter pilots would streak past a B-24 and quickly change their throttle setting so that the engine would cough a puff of white smoke to make it look like they had been hit, maybe get the American gunners to release their triggers and look for another target, or tempt a bomber to follow, only to end up in a fight with a perfectly intact Zero. Even the least experienced B-24 pilot would never trade the safety of altitude to follow a fighter plane down, but these pilots went to very low altitude because they were trying to defend *Dogpatch Express.*

The swimming Japanese pilot was killed by a burst from a .50 caliber machine gun as a B-24 made a low-level pass.[9]

At 1:45 in the afternoon and at a place about ninety miles east of Maloelap, *Dogpatch Express* hit the water. The plane broke in half immediately, as B-24s were known by their crews to do when they ditched, and the nose sank right away, leaving just the rear section of the bomb bay and the trailing edge of the wings above the ocean's surface. The tail section drifted just a moment, but within three or four minutes, water washed over the last visible part of the plane and the sea closed over it. The white bubble-streaked smear in the ocean where the plane had come down swirled and flattened and then resumed its gentle chop and the bubbles went away until there was no longer any difference there to see.

Lieutenant Sands brought *Thumper* down to just fifty feet above the water, where he saw one man lying across a partially inflated overturned raft, and maybe another man in the water beside it. Captain Stay saw the same raft. Lieutenant Sands ordered his crew to get another raft ready and circled around for a second pass. As Sands made his turn, his crew saw a Zero approach the crash scene and open fire, making a machine gun strafing attack on the raft. Sands' crew watched, unable to help at all, until they made their next pass and tossed their raft into the water.

Captain Stay's navigator took a sun shot to fix the position of Lieutenant Smith's water landing: 08 degrees 04 minutes north, 172 degrees 33 minutes east. Stay's radio operator called Tarawa, then Makin, then Apamama to request Dumbo service, then Stay turned toward Tarawa because they had burned too much fuel to make it all the way back to Funafuti. Ten minutes away from the crash scene, the tail gunner reported what may have been a submarine wake, so Stay banked again, turning back to see if he could help guide the submarine, if it really was a submarine, to the place where the rafts had been. Stay returned the full distance to the scene and dropped down to fifty feet where he saw two inflated rafts, one with three men in it. There may have been a fourth man in the second raft but they couldn't be sure, and there was no more evidence of a submarine in the area.[10]

Pratte, flying on Stay's wing during the strike, also took heavy fire. Pratte's radio equipment was knocked out and several oxygen tanks exploded with deafening booms when bullets pierced them. There was a hole in the left aileron from a 90 millimeter shell that struck but didn't explode. The azimuth ring for the belly gun was severed by a 20 millimeter hit, so it couldn't be turned or raised. There were several more 20 millimeter cannon hits and hundreds of shrapnel and machine gun holes. *Belle of Texas*, six-shooter in hand, had survived a terrific gun battle with her crew—incredibly—unhurt. Scearce's buddy Joe Hyson looked forward and aft from his waist gun position, awed by the holes in his ship, too many to count. From the waist he could also see leaking hydraulic fluid streaming back toward the trailing edges of the wings.

Pratte's crew in *Belle of Texas* was lucky to be alive, and just as amazing, *Belle of Texas* was still airworthy. *Dogpatch Express* had drawn the worst of the Japanese fighter pursuit as Zero pilots pounced on the B-24 in the most trouble and made sure they got the crippled plane down.

Charlie Pratte had wanted to be a pilot since his boyhood days growing up in Warren, Rhode Island. Now his resourcefulness and skill were being put to the test, piloting a badly damaged Liberator toward Tarawa.

Lieutenant Pratte knew that Seabees had just finished a fighter strip at Tarawa's Buota Island, the closest friendly runway. The fighter strip ended in a narrow stretch of beach with the Pacific Ocean beyond. Since hydraulic pressure was zero, the landing gear had to be cranked down manually and there were no brakes. The crew prepared for the brakes-out landing by buckling parachute harnesses to the waist- and tail-gun mounts, and on a signal from the flight deck, the crew planned to toss the three parachutes out of the aircraft and hope the improvised brakes would billow full and slow the plane. The men were well aware that the parachutes could just as easily be blown from their makeshift positions like chaff. Pratte began a very long, very careful landing approach. Most of the crew braced against bulkheads, their helmets strapped on, clutching the remaining parachutes for padding.

Belle of Texas had an audience. Buota's new airfield was minutes from being formally dedicated, complete with a Navy garrison at attention for a flag-raising ceremony and a speech. The airstrip was about to be officially named Mullinnix Field in memory of a Navy Rear Admiral who was killed when his ship was torpedoed and sunk by a Japanese submarine the previous month.[11] A Navy pilot was scheduled to make the first landing to christen the airfield, but a battle-damaged Army Air Forces B-24 Liberator was about to steal the show.

Three hundred feet from touchdown, number 1 engine sputtered and stalled and the plane fell out of trim for the landing approach. Pratte throttled up number 2 to even the plane's thrust and went around for another try. Flight Engineer William Mashaw stood between the pilot and co-pilot, calling out air speed as the pilots focused on the second approach. At 110 miles per hour, as slowly and as delicately as possible, the main gear touched down.[12]

Sgt. Joe Hyson and Staff Sgt. William Findle threw their air-brake parachutes from the right and left waist windows. Tail gunner Sgt. William Farrell did the same from his place at the rear, where he had knocked out the thick bullet-proof window.

Belle of Texas rumbled and bounced onto the beach and came to a stop just feet from the water's edge. Her grateful crew climbed out and surveyed their airplane, which looked like a discarded old wash tub used for target practice, shot full of holes by guns of every description. The men counted more than 300 hits in *Belle of Texas* but they also agreed she was the finest aircraft they ever saw.

The extraordinary landing was well documented by cameras intended to capture the Mullinnix Field dedication, the photographers' assignment that day turning out much more interesting than they had expected. Ground personnel quickly towed the battered plane out of the way so that the airstrip's formal dedication could go ahead as planned, and Lieutenant Pratte found a command post radio to arrange for someone from his squadron to bring a plane to pick up his crew.

Pilot Charlie Pratte became something of an Air Corps celebrity because of the inventive landing, but the part of the story Pratte enjoyed telling most concerned the reaction of some Navy men swimming just off shore. After the damaged plane touched down, and as the bomber lurched toward the beach, two startled sailors relaxing in the shallow water just beyond the runway were frightened out of their recreation.

Lieutenant Pratte later said, "Even with all the excitement, we had to laugh at a couple of sailors who were taking a leisurely bath in the ocean at the end of the runway. They looked up and saw us coming . . . those boys just lit out and tore!"[13]

"Hap" Arnold, Commanding General of the Army Air Forces, commended Pratte's crew in a letter to Maj. Gen. Willis Hale, commanding officer of the Seventh Air Force. General Arnold wrote,

The remarkable landing on Tarawa by the pilot and crew of the "Belle of Texas" has come to my attention. Photographs of the exploits are on my desk.

After distinguishing themselves in aerial combat over Maloelap, 1st Lieutenant Pratte and his crew effected a landing on a short fighter strip with a badly riddled airplane. With one engine inoperative and the brakes entirely useless, they had the skill and resourcefulness to employ three parachutes to cut the speed of the airplane and to bring it to a safe stop at the very edge of the runway.

This represents an achievement of a high order—unique, as far as I know, in operational history.[14]

Major General Willis Hale, commander of the Seventh Air Force, added his commendation to the letter from General Arnold. He called the landing a "superbly executed improvisation" saving "a valuable bomber from certain destruction."[15]

Low on fuel because of his efforts to help Lieutenant Smith, Capt. Jesse Stay brought his B-24 down on the old Japanese airstrip at Betio, another island in the Tarawa atoll, west of Pratte's chosen airstrip on Buota. The airfield, renamed Hawkins Field in memory of a Marine officer killed in action on Tarawa, had been repaired and made operational for fighter planes on December 1 and was extended for use by bombers by the middle of the month.[16] But the fuel depot at Betio was not equipped to support bomber operations, so to the dismay of his already exhausted crew, the plane had to be refueled from five-gallon cans. The men carried one thousand gallons of gas to the plane five gallons at a time, two hundred cans filled, carried, lifted, and poured into the Liberator's wing tanks.[17]

While his plane was refueled, Captain Stay surveyed it for damage. His aircraft had suffered just one hit, a 7.7 millimeter hole drilled through the bottom of his plane by a Japanese fighter pilot. Captain Stay also learned that two Navy Catalina "Dumbo" flying boats had taken off hours earlier to search for survivors from Lieutenant Smith's crash.

By the time Captain Stay finally landed at Funafuti, he and his men had been in the air seventeen of the previous twenty-four hours.[18] Stay and the rest of the flight asked for news about Lieutenant Smith and Lieutenant Thompson's crew with Smith on *Dogpatch Express*, and the news was not good. Dumbo crews searched the area but found no survivors and no trace.

On December 20, a day of extraordinary performance and tragic loss for the 42nd Squadron, the 26th Squadron on nearby Nukufetau recorded in its operational log the single entry, "Ball game and movie called on account of rain."[19] What was newsworthy for one squadron in the group on a given day could vary dramatically with what mattered to the men in another squadron.

The sad duty of going through a dead man's belongings fell to the squadron adjutant, and he usually enlisted the help of the lost crewman's friends. As they sorted through what few personal things were left behind, they talked about the ironies and the quirks of fate: Lt. George Smith, whose broken wrist back on Kualoa could have gotten him back to the States, Lt. John Lowry and his heroic flight back from the Wake mission when Lieutenant Thompson got it in the leg and Sgt. Clarence Sopko repaired the propeller wiring, and how little all that seemed to mean now, they and their crewmates all gone. The adjutant mailed Lowry's Distinguished Flying Cross and Sopko's Silver Star to their homes.

Sergeant Scearce and the rest of Joe Deasy's crew were unsettled by the loss of their plane. *Dogpatch Express* was familiar and reassuring, comfortable, even a connection to home because this was the plane they had boarded in Kansas, giddy as kids on Christmas morning, and brought overseas with them. *Dogpatch Express* was the plane that Scearce as a green radio operator had seen and touched and made his own when it was nameless and new. "Two one four," Scearce whispered the radio call sign to himself then, the first time he saw the plane's tail number, 41-24214, and he would remember it for the rest of his life. It was the plane he and his crewmates had matured into combat veterans with, proving its mettle and becoming a stronger warrior with its field modifications as the men were also hardened into something different from when they first flew to Hawaii. But now *Dogpatch Express* had touched down its last time, broken and silent, settling to its final lonely landing place ninety miles east of Maloelap in the forever bottom darkness of the Pacific.

Chapter 13

Back to Hawaii

THE 42ND BOMBARDMENT SQUADRON lost five aircrews between late May 1943 and the end of the year. A low-level search mission on May 27 claimed Lieutenant Phillips' *Green Hornet*, then in July Lieutenant Cason's plane and crew took a terrifying final plummet after colliding with a Zero on a mission against Wake Island. Lieutenant Friedrich and his *Virginia Belle* couldn't find Funafuti after a Tarawa raid in November, and Lieutenant Dechert was lost on a mission against Mille in early December. Finally, Lieutenant Smith was shot down trying to get back from Maloelap on the twentieth of the same month. Five complete B-24 crews lost, fifty men, fifty out of 110 airmen in the squadron.

Maloelap also claimed Capt. James Irby's 98th Squadron crew in December while the crew flew with a substitute pilot because Irby was hospitalized with pneumonia. Irby's men were the ones surprised by the Marine stowaway on a Tarawa mission back in September. Irby's plane, *Tuffy*, with Li'l Abner's Hairless Joe on its nose, was being flown by the 98th's Operations Officer, Capt. Gardiner Cornwell on a December 28 mission against Maloelap and was last seen near Mille, shot up and heading toward Makin.[1] Cornwell, known as "Doc" in the squadron, was a popular officer and was also considered the 98th's best pilot. His loss with Captain Irby's crew was a serious morale blow to the 98th, and Captain Irby got the sad news about his plane and crew while still confined to a hospital bed.[2]

In January, the Air Corps switched tactics against Maloelap, bombing it only under cover of darkness because too many American planes had been shot down.[3] The change came too late for the crews of *Dogpatch Express* and *Tuffy* and many more.

In addition to the 42nd Squadron's loss of five aircraft and crew during the last half of '43 was the loss of Lt. Myron Jenson and Sgt. Joseph Evans, killed in action flying with *Daisy Mae*, the plane that had barely made it back to crash land on Midway after bombing Wake. Another loss was pilot Lt. John Van Horn, killed when his A-20 Havoc went down in Kaneohe Bay just off Kualoa Point.

Van Horn was giving a thrill ride in the fast little twin-engined Havoc to bombardier Lt. Robert Becker and military police Lt. Arsenio Gansalves, and had just buzzed the Kualoa airfield at low altitude. He turned to enter the landing pattern when both engines quit.[4] Van Horn turned to approach the airfield and put his landing gear down, but the banking turn caused the plane to lose precious altitude, dropping too low to make it to the airstrip in a power-out glide. Van Horn retracted the gear for a water landing and the plane crashed into the bay 500 yards off shore.[5] It floated for a minute and a half, enough time for Becker to climb out of the plane. Gansalves was thrown clear during the crash and survived, but Van Horn never got out.

On top of the losses of planes with crew, Japanese bombers destroyed two Liberators on the ground at Funafuti during their nighttime raids. These two B-24s, *Peggy* and *Wicked Witch*, took direct hits on separate nights while parked in precisely the same revetment.[6] Further, the shot-up *Belle of Texas* sat on Tarawa's Mullinnix Field in no condition to fly since Charlie Pratte's inventive parachute-brake landing after the same December 20 mission that claimed *Dogpatch Express*.

December had been an especially tough month for the 42nd, losing Dechert and Smith, and the ground echelon of the squadron had its own problems. On the sixteenth, Sergeant Tippens and radar man Corporal Straight of the squadron's ground support were pumping fuel for their gasoline stoves from a drum beside the mess hall. A laundry was boiling nearby, and somehow suddenly the gas was ignited by the laundry fire. Flames quickly covered Sergeant Tippens and Corporal Straight's hands and arms. The injured men screamed and witnesses to the developing disaster shouted and other men grabbed fire extinguishers and ran to help, but they were reluctant to get close because the gasoline drum and stoves in the mess hall might explode at any second. Straight and Tippens were rushed to Funafuti's field hospital with terrible burns as the flames spread quickly toward the kitchen area of the mess hall.

Finally the gas drum exploded. It shot into the air in a spiral like a rocket gone wildly out of control and men bolted in every direction. By now the wooden mess hall was completely engulfed in flames. Hoses were finally dragged into position and the fire was put out, but the mess hall was gone just as completely as if a Japanese bomb had scored a direct hit. Hoses were turned on the communications building and nearby Marine Corps barracks to save them and wet blankets were thrown onto the orderly room and S-2 hut, which were also in danger.

Besides the mess hall, the squadron lost stoves, boxes of rations, all the mess equipment including tables and chairs, and a prized collection of phonograph records.[7] The stoves, rations, and mess hall equipment would be replaced, but the record collection had been pieced together from men's homes and borrowed, traded, or outright stolen from air bases on Oahu and back in the States.

Records brought from home and lost in the fire severed a connection to home, family, and friends for some men. Records lost in the fire included songs from memories of life before the war swept men far away, and it was *that* song, *that* record, and even if the record collection might be rebuilt, it could never be exactly the same. Every song, scratch, and skip had become familiar to the men who gathered in the mess hall at night, drawn there because the mess hall had food and lights and the phonograph. The mess hall was a place to sit and talk and read or write while listening to music or singing along with records, among them a recent RCA Victor release called "Comin' in on a Wing and a Prayer" by The Four Vagabonds, about an overdue bomber limping home after a mission with an engine out. The song captured the sentiment of airmen and ground crews waiting for friends to return, hoping for radio contact or scanning the sky to see the distinctive silhouette of a Liberator approaching. In the song, the overdue plane and crew returns from their mission, but in the latter half of 1943, too many crews of the 42nd hadn't been so fortunate.

The losses of men and aircraft during the last half of the year meant that the squadron's strength was severely reduced, so when it was time for the 11th Bomb Group to move out from Funafuti, and time for the other three squadrons to advance to new forward bases, the 42nd got orders to return to Hawaii for reorganization.[8] The move would leave the 431st alone on Funafuti until they moved up to Tarawa in January. Once they were relocated to Hawaii, the 42nd would provide training for new crews and then supply those new crews to the rest of the group to keep the other three squadrons at full strength. The New Year would see the 42nd on Oahu again, but one of their bombers was still sitting on Mullinnix Field at Tarawa.

Part of the Tarawa Garrison Group was a Navy outfit designated Carrier Aircraft Support Unit 16. CASU-16's job was to provide facilities and service for carrier-based planes that might stage through or be deployed there, and they were equipped to handle just about any type of repair an aircraft might need. CASUs scattered around the Pacific helped the Navy keep the planes on its carriers battle-ready.[9] CASU-16 got word to the 42nd Squadron that they could repair Pratte's *Belle of Texas*, made an inventory of parts they needed, and sent their shopping list to the Air Corps. In addition to the parts, the Air Corps would have to supply a crew to fly the plane out once CASU-16 got it ready, but before they could fill CASU-16's parts order, the men of the 42nd had a squadron to move.

The 42nd spent the days before Christmas 1943 packing for its return trip to Oahu. The weather didn't cooperate, raining steadily, and lightning was an almost constant threat. T/Sgt. Glen Cook, a crew chief with the 431st Squadron on Funafuti, was killed where he lay in bed in his tent on December 18 when lightning struck nearby and the surge ran into the tent on a wire. Cook was one of the 431st's old timers, in the Army since before the war. No one else in his tent was hurt.[10]

The news of Sergeant Cook's death contributed to a dreary resignation among the ground echelon as they packed and crated their gear in the endless rain. The work had to be done, and there was no place to go to avoid the storms, and if lightning could kill you sleeping in your tent, then it could kill you no matter where you were, so to hell with it.

On Christmas Day, the 42nd Squadron's ground support worked in four-hour shifts to truck their boxes and crates to a loading point on the Funafuti beach.[11] From there the rain-soaked gear was loaded onto a barge for the one-mile trip out to the Liberty Ship *George W. Julian* patiently riding at anchor in the lagoon, where the gear was first lifted and then lowered and stowed in the ship's hold for the voyage to Oahu. The men ate with the 431st because the 42nd's mess hall gear, what hadn't been destroyed in the fire nine days earlier, had already been packed.

Scearce was incredulous when his friend Jack Yankus opted to go back to Oahu aboard the *Julian*, but Yankus just shrugged and grinned his big, broad grin and said it might be fun. "This'll pass!" Yankus said, gesturing toward the storm clouds as if he could brush them away with the back of his hand. Yankus seemed eager to sail as if the *Julian* was a cruise boat and he was about to go on a vacation adventure. Scearce figured that Yankus expected to score big in the inevitable shipboard poker games, but Scearce shook his head. "You can have it, Yank."

The coming move and the packing and crating of the squadron's equipment resurrected stories of the ground echelon's voyage to Funafuti from Hawaii back in November aboard the ship *President Tyler* and rekindled arguments about whether the *Tyler's* destroyer escort sank a Japanese submarine.

On November 8, 1943, the day after the *Tyler* crossed the equator on its westerly trip to Funafuti, the men of the 42nd were loafing on deck or playing cards when the ship's General Quarters alarm jolted them with a surge of adrenaline. Off the *President Tyler's* port side their destroyer escort wheeled around at speed, dropping depth charges off the stern. The depth charges detonated with a muffled *whoomp* beneath the surface where a lurking Japanese submarine was surely now taking evasive action. Before the 42nd's men could get below to their General Quarters-assigned places, it was over, and whether the Navy sank a submarine, the submarine had gotten away, or there never really was a submarine at all was a point of discussion for the rest of the trip.[12]

Scearce didn't want any part of a ten-day voyage in nauseating seas worried about enemy submarines skulking about, when he could fly above the weather and be on Oahu in a couple of days.

Most of the 42nd's aircrews took off for Oahu, staging through Canton, on December 26 and the last two planes left the next day, the same day the *Julian* sailed from Funafuti's lagoon.[13] From the time it left the calm of the lagoon the *Julian* pitched and tossed and rolled, making slower progress than expected because the ship was lightly loaded and its screw came out of the water whenever the bow rode down the side of a rolling sea. Men went green and wanted to sleep, get to land, or die in the miserable sagging despair of seasickness, and the ten days they expected to be on the ship dragged into eleven and twelve and may as well have been an eternity. Others tolerated the *Julian's* eastbound labors well enough to envy the aromas from the Merchant Marine kitchen, where the ship's crew enjoyed meals far better than the simple fare provided by the Army for its men in transit.

All four squadrons of the 11th Group were on the move in January 1944. While the 42nd was on its way to new quarters on Oahu, the 98th and 431st Squadrons moved up to Tarawa from Nukufetau and Funafuti, and the 26th Squadron moved first from Canton to Nukufetau and then also to Tarawa.[14] Capt. James Irby finally recovered from pneumonia and rejoined the 98th as their new operations officer after spending more than two months in Oahu hospitals. He returned to duty the day after the landing ship transporting his squadron left the Nukufetau lagoon on its way to Tarawa.[15]

The three squadrons relocating to Tarawa occupied a former Japanese base for the first time in the war, and their awareness of very recent Japanese presence gave the airmen and their ground support a strange, prickly sensation as if they were trespassing, but it was American soil now because their Marine Corps brothers in arms had fought hard and taken it, and American bombers based there could only mean that the war was moving in the right direction.

Two crews of the 42nd Squadron were temporarily attached to the 98th at Tarawa so that weary aircrews of the 98th could fly back to Oahu for ten-day rest periods. Lt. Warren Sands and Lt. Joseph Gall, old timers of the 42nd, flew with the 98th from mid-January until early March when they rejoined the 42nd at Mokuleia.[16]

The 11th Group's three squadrons on Tarawa were impressed by the work already done by the Navy's Construction Battalion. The Seabees had repaired the runways first, benefiting aircrews like Captain Stay's on the December 20 mission when *Dogpatch Express* went down and Stay needed a refueling stop before getting back to Funafuti. Since then Tarawa's Seabees had built floored and screened tents, mess halls, headquarters buildings, and storage facilities. A new pier for supply shipments was almost ready. The Japanese occupation was evident in the battered machinery and equipment they had left behind, and while most of their dead had been buried, Air Corps men exploring the island stumbled across Japanese soldiers, putrid and decaying in defensive positions where they had died weeks before, and sometimes the sea would expose a dead man in the sandy wash of the shoreline.[17]

Ground support men of the 98th found the last Japanese survivor of the savage battle for Tarawa when a poor bedraggled mutt dog emerged from hiding and came over to their side. He was hungry and cowering and the Air Corps men could only speculate what the animal had seen and heard or how he had survived the struggle. The 98th named the dog Tojo, and Tojo entered U.S. Army Air Forces service with the 98th Bomb Squadron, joining Spoofy and Queenie, squadron dogs since before the move to Tarawa. Queenie had endured the squadron's move while pregnant, and she presented seven puppies at Tarawa.[18]

It was common for the ground echelon of the four squadrons to keep animal companions, but it wasn't practical for airmen to have pets. Aircrews moved too frequently from place to place to care for animals, and a bomber was no place for a dog or cat. Al Marston, the former foot soldier who joined Joe Deasy's crew when they needed another gunner, kept a little black dog on base, but he had to leave it behind when his aircrew assignment came through. Another dog left behind was a terrier puppy adopted by Charlie Pratte and his wife, Bernadette, before Charlie entered military service. Bernadette's parents' dog had recently given birth to seven puppies, and Pratte's in-laws named the puppies after Disney's Seven Dwarfs. The young couple took Dopey, and Dopey stayed with Charlie and Bernadette until the Air Corps required Charlie to move. Bernadette moved with her husband as he relocated during training, and Dopey went to live with Charlie's parents.[19]

The 26th had a cat at Nukufetau working under the supervision of the squadron's "bean king," the mess hall sergeant. Officially designated the Squadron Rat Exterminator, she delivered four kittens on Nukufetau just before the squadron's move to Tarawa. The 26th Squadron log indicates, "Four kittens of undetermined sexes were helped into this world by Mess Sgt. Mangrum and his assistants. Mother and kittens are doing well, the father as yet unapprehended."

The presence of animals gave the ground support men a touch of home and civility. Young men answering the war's call to service often left animal companions at home, beloved family pets who missed their owners and could not understand the separation, like Bobby Lipe's dog Jigs and Charlie Pratte's pup terrier Dopey. Animals adopted by the ground echelons of the 11th Group's bomb squadrons brought out a compassionate, humane side of the men that for many of them the war had almost taken away.

The ground echelon of the 42nd Squadron arrived at Hickam Field aboard the *George W. Julian* on January 9, 1944.[20] The voyage from Funafuti had taken thirteen days, thirteen days of queasiness for some and card games for others, sleep and wanting to die for the most nause-ated landlubbers, poker hands and fortunes won and lost for the rest. Scearce thought Yankus seemed unusually happy to see him, but Yankus wouldn't admit that he hadn't had a great time on his cruise.

The squadron's crates were waterlogged and the men's barracks bags filled with clothing and personal belongings were soggy and moldy. The *Julian's* hold wasn't weather tight, and rainwater sloshed down into it, off and on, for days. The gear was already wet when it was loaded at Funafuti because it had been exposed to a tropical downpour during the mile-long transit from the beach to the ship. The damp, moldy crates and boxes and bags were loaded onto flatcars and shipped by rail from Hickam to Mokuleia, the 42nd's home on the opposite side of Oahu, where they were unloaded on the morning of the eleventh at a rail siding next to an old rock crushing mill.[21]

With the squadron's new operational role as a training unit for re-placement crews coming from the States, the 42nd got a new com-manding officer. Captain Joe Deasy, the operations officer, was named squadron commander in Maj. Earl Cooper's place shortly after the squadron's arrival at Mokuleia. Deasy had big shoes to fill because Cooper, a former B-17 pilot, was by then an Air Corps living legend.

Earl Cooper had been a lieutenant in December 1941, and was one of the pilots in a flight of B-17s coming in from Hamilton Field, California, with the incredible timing of approaching Hickam on Sunday morning, December 7 while Japanese planes were shooting up the base.[22] Low on fuel, Cooper had no alternative except to land, so he brought his bomber in through the surrounding destruction and was lucky to survive.

Lieutenant Cooper had a second narrow escape less than three weeks after that. Cooper and his crew were overdue to return to Hickam from a routine patrol on December 26, and at midnight, his plane's gasoline supply ran out. Cooper feathered the propellers, turning the blades straight into the wind so they would not create drag, and ordered the crew to prepare to crash. The sea was calm and the ditching was perfect and all nine men in the B-17 got out, five climbed into one life raft and four in another.[23]

Once out of the plane and into their two rafts, Cooper's crew inventoried their provisions: two canteens of coffee, one damp pack of
cigarettes, and more than six hundred dollars in cash. The cash amused
the crew because it was a tidy sum but they had no place to spend it.[24]

The day after the ditching, a Navy patrol plane passed close by but
missed the airmen's signal flares. Two more Navy planes appeared on
the twenty-eighth, but they also failed to see the rafts. On December 29,
Private D. C. McCord shot a large sea bird with his .45 pistol. Incredibly, the bird landed in one of the rafts, and it was cut up and divided
among the hungry men. There was a fish in the bird's gut and it was also
eaten raw. The scraps of bird and fish were the only solid food the men
had for four days, until the thirtieth when they were finally spotted by
another Navy patrol. The Navy aircrew dropped provisions and flew
back to their base to put off crewmen who weren't essential to fly the
plane, and then returned to pick up Cooper's crew. The Navy plane,
a flying boat, landed in heavy seas and took the nine Air Corps men
aboard. Every man on Cooper's crew was safe.

Joe Deasy's assumption of command of the 42nd signaled a change
in the squadron, subtle but profound, from a seat-of-the-pants outfit
improvising a response to Japan's offensive to a more businesslike and
deliberate role in the American campaign. Cooper's legendary exploits
were a part of the Army Air Forces, which was already fading into history, and Captain Joe Deasy was well-suited to assume command from
him. The squadron's new mission as a training unit seemed tailor-made
for Deasy, an instructor pilot back in the States before his assignment
to a crew, and now a leader who was among the Liberator pilots most
experienced with the unique demands of over-water flying in the Pacific.
He could customize the training to meet the special needs of that part

of the war, helping green crews fresh from the States have a better chance of survival.

Deasy took command of the 42nd on January 17, 1944, and Capt. Jesse Stay was named operations officer in Deasy's place.[25] Cooper received a well-deserved assignment in the States, far from the front.[26]

In January there was not much flying on the schedule to keep Sergeant Scearce busy, so when he learned that a volunteer crew was needed to go to Tarawa to get Charlie Pratte's *Belle of Texas* and fly it back to Hickam, he was glad to take the assignment. Pratte's crew was buddies with Joe Deasy's crew, and Pratte's radio man Joe Hyson was a friend, so Scearce saw it as doing them a good turn. "Detached Service" (DS) it was called, when men from the squadron were separated from their outfit for some special duty. The volunteer crew going to get *Belle of Texas* left on January 26 with the parts on CASU-16's list. They expected to be DS to Tarawa no more than a day or two while the Navy men there finished the repair job.

Six officers and six enlisted men made the trip to Tarawa: two pilots, two co-pilots, and two navigators, with three enlisted crewmen for each aircraft.[27] The crews were four men short because there was no need for bombardiers or gunners on this trip. Lt. Jordan Churchill was the lead pilot on the flight, his co-pilot Lt. Frank Angel. Lt. Charlie Pratte, co-pilot Lt. Reginald Spence, and navigator Lt. Randolph Ball were along to fly *Belle of Texas* back to Hickam once it was ready.

As Churchill banked on final approach to Mullinnix Field, Lieutenant Pratte leaned into the cockpit over the flight engineer's shoulder to watch. Churchill grinned at Pratte and said, "Maybe we won't need our 'chutes this time, Charlie!" The now-famous landing with parachute brakes had ratcheted up the level of respect that other men felt for Pratte and his crew, respect which manifested itself in little deferential comments like this one and belied high esteem for a fellow warrior who had run the gauntlet and come through unscathed.

At Mullinnix Field the twelve Air Corps men walked past *Belle of Texas* on their way to Navy jeeps waiting to take them to CASU-16's mess hall. Scearce's eyes were drawn to the countless telltale spots of mismatched color on the aircraft, each one a repaired bullet hole or flak hit. There were hundreds of them and Scearce thought it was a miracle that ten men had been inside the plane and none of them suffered even a scratch. Scearce thought of the magician's trick where the pretty assistant gets in a box and he slides sword after sword through the top of the box and out the other side, and she emerges unhurt, except this time there were ten people in the box and there were hundreds of bullets rather than swords.

Lieutenant Churchill, co-pilot Lieutenant Angel, and navigator Lt. Dale Chalfant left Mullinnix Field with their three-man enlisted crew the next day as scheduled. There was no need to keep the extra crew and bomber sitting at Mullinnix Field, exposed to the risk of shelling by Japanese subs that surfaced at night or bombing by harassing Japanese planes, and the Navy men preferred to see the newly arrived B-24 leave sooner than later; no need to present the Japanese with a tempting new target on CASU-16's little piece of the atoll.

CASU-16 had completed the sheet metal work to repair the bullet and flak holes in the plane, fixed damaged wiring, and repaired punctured fuel tanks. Some of the hydraulic lines and fittings and other parts unique to B-24s weren't in CASU-16's island inventory, and these were the parts ferried to Tarawa with the Air Corps crew. The CASU men were fine mechanics, but the impression that the bomber would be fixed just a day or two after the parts arrived began to fade quickly. Yankus thought it was funny, "just like an auto repair shop," he said. "First they tell you they're waiting for the parts, then they tell you it'll be a couple days after the parts get in, then what? It's still not ready."

The day after their arrival, Scearce, Yankus, and Assistant Engineer Staff Sgt. William Findle got into a line for beer with the Navy enlisted men. They could get two bottles and then move to the back of the line again. The three Army Air Forces men were in line for just a few minutes, Findle busy bending a sailor's ear with his story of the harrowing December 20 mission, carrying on about how he had deployed a parachute from his waist gun in *Belle of Texas*, when a Navy chief petty officer saw them and walked up, tugged on Yankus and Scearce's sleeves and said, "You two come with me." The two tech sergeants turned and shrugged toward Staff Sergeant Findle and walked away with the Navy chief.

The chief took the two airmen to a tent. As they entered, Scearce and Yankus smiled and patted their new Navy friend on the back. Yankus said, "You gotta be kidding me!" Scearce scanned the room. "This is nice as the Moana."

Set before them were tables, not the tall stand-up variety like those on Funafuti, but real sit-down tables covered with spotless white tablecloths, and not benches or stools but real chairs. There were sailors with just a single stripe serving seated men with chief's stripes, pouring juice and water and coming around with more bread and coffee, taking up the plates for men who were finished eating, all this on a real wood floor.

The Navy man who'd rescued Yankus and Scearce from the beer line explained that the chiefs put up five dollars a month to staff their own mess hall. The lower-ranking sailors made extra money by serving tables and washing dishes for the chiefs. Their sponsor into the exclusive tent figured that an Army Air Forces technical sergeant was equal to a Navy chief, and poor Findle was simply one stripe short even if he was a minor celebrity for being on the parachute-landing crew, and it dawned on the two airmen that an extended stay on Buota might not be bad at all, in spite of constant threats from the Japanese.

The chief explained that the shot-up bomber had been a welcome project for CASU-16. The unit's men needed work to occupy their minds and their hands and keep their shops busy. Some of the planes CASU-16 supported went down with the escort carrier *Liscome Bay* when it was torpedoed and sunk by a Japanese submarine on November 24, and the CASU-16 men were heartbroken by the loss because they had worked on those planes and knew some of the men. The brand-new airfield being christened at the moment Charlie Pratte brought his bomber in to land, CASU-16's base on Buota, was named Mullinnix Field for the Navy Rear Admiral in command of the *Liscome Bay*, who went down with his ship after it blew up.[28] *Belle of Texas* audaciously crashing the airfield's dedication party was a great distraction on that solemn day, so the battle-damaged B-24 was a good thing from the beginning.

CASU-16's men had pushed through the loss of their comrades on the *Liscome Bay* when their own commanding officer was killed in a bizarre accident on January 2, right there on their brand-new Mullinnix Field. Naval Reserve Commander Charles Tilghman was in his jeep beside the runway, watching flight operations, when a twin-engined B-25 Mitchell bomber came in to land. The plane touched down and rolled out fine and straight and there was no cause for alarm until the bomber passed near the commander's jeep, where it suddenly ground-looped, turning sharply hard to the right in a pirouette on its right main landing gear, and the spinning propeller of the number 2 engine smashed into the commander's jeep, each blade slashing through the jeep in turn, advancing too fast for him to react as the plane continued in its horrible path until the commander was killed instantly.[29]

The chief showed Scearce and Yankus the place where the accident happened on Mullinnix Field. The smashed jeep had been towed away, loaded on a landing craft, and dumped in the lagoon. Commander Tilghman was buried on the island, and the chief showed them the grave. It was raised slightly from the ground, because the island was too low for a regular grave. Surrounding it were six posts made from large naval gun shells, three to each side, connected by a heavy chain down each side and across the foot. At the head of the grave was a wide concrete rectangular base, with "CASU 16" cast in it. Above the base was a smaller rectangle supporting a cross, also in concrete. The horizontal bar of the cross bore Commander Tilghman's name and the dates of his birth and death, and the smaller rectangle was inscribed, "IN THE SERVICE OF HIS COUNTRY."[30]

The grave was surrounded by smooth white sand and shaded by palm trees that swayed gently from the constant breeze, and it overlooked the lagoon, the lighter blue water separated from the dark ocean beyond by a white line of breakers off shore. Scearce thought it was the most beautiful grave he had ever seen, and when he had looked at it long enough, the Army Air Forces radio man brought his heels together and saluted the Navy Commander he'd never met.

The aircrew's stay on Tarawa went from days into a week. The Navy gave the airmen new clothes drawn from stacks of fatigues in a supply tent. They gave the airmen brand-new Mossberg .22 caliber rifles with a case of ammunition each, "in case the Japs drop in." "Twenty-twos'll just piss 'em off real good," Yankus said. The .22s may not have been much for island defense, but they were a lot of fun for shooting at beer bottles thrown into the lagoon.

Japanese bombers hit Tarawa almost every night. Most of the raids were against Betio on the western end of the atoll. Bombs dropped during the air raids rumbled like approaching thunder and the men on Buota, to the east of Betio, could see the bomb bursts as distant flashes of white-orange light. Rumors circulated every night about invasion and everyone on the island, including Scearce and Yankus who were none too happy about the prospect of becoming infantry, expected the Japanese to try to re-take the island at any time. At night the men were roused by air raid warnings that sent them scurrying to foxholes. They couldn't get a good night's sleep, but the Chief Petty Officer's Mess Hall made up for a lot with its all you want to eat, anything you want to drink, sit-down service. Scearce and Yankus thought they had it made.

It was the end of the first week in February when CASU-16 finally said they had *Belle of Texas* ready to fly out, and on the seventh, a Navy chief drove the crew to the plane. Scearce elbowed Yankus and pointed to the nose, where the plane had acquired a new name. On the left, the opposite side from the familiar brunette *Belle of Texas*, was the name *Patches*. Beneath the boldly lettered name was written, "Compliments CASU-16." To the right of the new name, in smaller script, was written "Repair by" and below that, a list of the crew leaders responsible for the job. CASU-16 seemed proud of their work, and to a man they believed they had themselves defeated the Japanese who had tried to bring this plane down, defeated them with their own hands and with their machine shops and metal fabrication and welding, and now this bomber would return to some Japanese-held island and would exact vengeance not only for itself but for the *Liscome Bay*, Rear Admiral Mullinnix, and Commander Tilghman.

"All you had when you got here was a toothbrush!" the Navy chief said, "And now it takes a 2½ ton truck to haul your gear to the plane!" Lieutenant Pratte stepped out of the right side of the cab and the rest of the crew hopped out of the back of the truck. The officers carried their briefcases and bags and the enlisted men carried a bundle of clothes in a new Navy duffel with their Mossberg .22 rifles and most of a case of ammunition and enough food for the return flight.

Yankus approached the side of *Belle of Texas* and opened a small access door on the right side of the plane, just ahead of the bomb bay, and pulled the auxiliary bomb door handle to raise the bomb bay doors. Pratte walked around the plane to make sure the pitot head covers for the air speed indicators were removed. He gave the plane a visual check while the bomb bay doors clattered open and the rest of the crew climbed in. Each man understood instinctively that the pre-flight checklist would be conducted by the book for this airplane, shot-up weeks before, and repaired by Navy mechanics.

Sergeant Scearce stowed his gear and his new rifle in the rear of the plane and then settled himself at the radio operator's table up front and checked settings on the radios. Yankus and Findle stuffed their own new Navy gear and rifles into the plane and Yankus switched the four fuel selector valves, mounted overhead aft of the cockpit, to "on." He checked the fuel level with the two gauges mounted on the front of the bomb bay bulkhead by switching the valves for each gauge. The outboard gauge indicated the fuel level for engines 1 and 2, the inboard gauge showed the fuel level for 3 and 4. He looked forward to make sure that the engine ignition switches were "off" so that he and Findle could pull the propellers through without worrying about an engine firing, and then the engineer and his assistant hopped out of the plane through the bomb bay to pull the props through, two complete turns, counting six blades pulled through for each engine.[31]

Scearce glanced up from the radio operator's table as the propeller blades were rotated. A group of CASU-16 men gathered beside *Belle of Texas*, *Patches* to them now, at least two dozen good-natured well wishers there to see the plane off, and the aircrew was mildly self-conscious about having an audience. Scearce assumed bets were being taken on the plane getting airborne, or maybe the Navy men were betting whether the big plane, once airborne, would bank and come right back to Mullinnix Field where the Air Corps men would walk away and find some other way home.

Lieutenants Pratte and Spence took their seats and adjusted them. Spence checked the ignition switches and saw that they were off, as Yankus had already confirmed, because the engineers were pulling the props through. The pilots surveyed their instruments and made small talk with Sergeant Scearce. Pratte pushed the parking brakes to make sure they were set and gave the Autopilot control a tug to make sure it was disengaged. Spence switched the engine instruments on and turned the altimeter setting for the barometric pressure the Navy weather officer had given him.

"We've got an audience, Charlie," Scearce said.

"I think half of them would try to stow away if they had a chance—did we check for stowaways?"

"Didn't see anybody, sir!"

"Well, that mess cook offered me a grand if I'd get him to Honolulu, and I think he was serious."

Yankus and Findle entered the plane after pulling the props through and Yankus started the auxiliary power unit under the flight deck, the putt-putt, which was used to generate power for engine start. Co-pilot Lieutenant Spence reached to his right and turned the battery switches "on" and then flipped all four ignition switches and the master switch "on." Yankus turned on the auxiliary hydraulic power then dropped back down from the plane to watch the engines start.

"Intercoolers open . . . cowl flaps open," Lieutenant Spence said. Both pilots looked left and right to confirm the cowl flaps were open, and Yankus noticed them move from his position standing in front of the plane.

Lieutenant Pratte set the propellers to high rpm. "Superchargers off," Lieutenant Spence said, then "Mix . . . set" as he confirmed the mixture controls were in the "Idle cut off" position.

The CASU-16 men standing outside seemed to be getting anxious, Sergeant Scearce thought. He could see Yankus joking with some of the men standing nearby, and saw a few take positions in a row beside the plane as if they were planning to challenge it in a foot race.

Lieutenant Spence turned on the fuel booster pump and opened the throttle for number 3 one-third, then repeatedly pressed the primer switch for engine number 3, causing fuel to squirt into the combustion chambers of the number 3 engine's cylinders, then held the number 3 starter energizer to "ACCEL."

"Starting 3," Lieutenant Spence said, and he turned the switch from ACCEL to CRANK. Number 3's propeller began to rotate, slowly, and the men of CASU-16 quieted. "Here we go," they said, almost in unison.

Number 3 repeated a high-pitched mewing sound as each propeller blade turned, the prop turning too slowly it seemed for the engine to come to life at all when it suddenly rumbled and coughed and the entire airframe shuddered. Lieutenant Spence switched the mixture setting to AUTO-LEAN from IDLE CUT OFF so the fuel pumps would deliver fuel to the engine. The propeller spun faster and the airplane vibrated with the engine cylinders firing and a cloud of white smoke gathering behind the plane was blown back by the accelerating propeller's wash, and the men behind the plane inhaled the powerful rich thick smell of oil and exhaust of high octane aviation fuel mixed with the air blown back by number 3.

The propeller was no longer visible as three blades but was now a great powerful dangerous circle, and the airframe's vibrations smoothed as the engine whined, the cylinders now firing in perfect pitch as a single loud growling voice.

"Four," Lieutenant Spence said, and the number 4 engine mewed and whined and turned, then a spark caused a cylinder to fire, then the next, and the airframe shook again as the right outboard engine came to life.

Yankus walked across to the front of number 2, and Lieutenant Spence repeated the starting procedure with the inboard engine on the left side, then number 1, and all four mighty engines spun with a confident roar.

The CASU-16 men watched with approval and admiration the way mechanics will when they have had the chance to work on something special, because this B-24 was a rare bird for them, Navy mechanics more accustomed to working on the smaller single-engined aircraft carried by Navy ships. Four fourteen-cylinder engines running up in concert was special, the mighty sound and power and vibration an awesome thing, which was just as much felt as seen or heard.

Lieutenant Spence watched the oil temperature climb past 40 degrees Celsius while the engines turned at a leisurely 1,000 revolutions per minute. Lieutenant Pratte checked the vacuum gauge on his left and confirmed four and a half inches of pressure for operation of the instruments, then checked the brake gauges to make sure there was at least 850 pounds of pressure in each of the two systems.

Yankus climbed into the plane through the bomb bay and pulled the bomb bay door handle located on the right under the flight deck. The bomb bay doors closed behind him as he pulled himself up through the pilot's escape hatch just behind the cockpit and ahead of the top turret, where he sat on top of the plane with his legs dangling inside. He glanced at the CASU-16 men and made sure there was nothing and no one in front of the plane, leaned down and in and shouted, "You're clear!"

Lieutenant Pratte pressed the parking brake pedals to disengage the brakes and *Belle of Texas* began to roll. Pratte throttled up number 1 engine and turned to the right to taxi to the end of the runway and the big bomber responded smoothly, gently rising and falling on its big rubber tires as the shock absorbing landing gear struts traveled up and down with the plane's advance. Pratte pulled number 1's throttle back down and straightened the plane toward the end of Mullinnix Field.

Navy men waved to the bomber as it taxied away from them, and finally Yankus smiled and waved back at them. At the end of the runway, Lieutenant Pratte ran up number 4 and turned the plane to the left 180 degrees, faced it into the wind, and braked the plane to a stop.

Lieutenant Spence exercised the propellers through their full range to make certain they worked correctly, the indicator lights flashing on when they reached the limits of their travel. Lieutenant Pratte called for tab settings for take off: elevators 1 degree tail heavy, aileron tab neutral, one degree of right rudder. Lieutenant Spence casually and coolly repeated the settings as he manipulated the controls.

"Mix—rich" Lieutenant Spence set the mixture to Auto Rich for full power at take off. He switched the booster pumps on and ran the engines up to 2000 RPMs.

The pilots checked the engine magnetos and pushed the number 3 throttle to the stops.

"Supercharger . . . on." The turbo-superchargers increased the pressure of air rammed into the engines for greater power.

"Ten degrees of flaps." The pilots looked left and right confirming the flaps were extended by hydraulic pressure from number 3 engine's pump.

One at a time the other three engines were run up to full power. Yankus dropped into the plane, closed the escape hatch and turned on the engine generators. "Cowl flaps to one third." Lieutenant Spence closed the cowl flaps to one third open so the engines would stay cool but the air flow around them wouldn't create drag or cause the tail to buffet.

"Ready for take-off, boys."

Pratte held the brakes and Spence held the throttles to the stops so they couldn't creep back with the plane's vibration. The big bomber was poised like a runner at the starting block, and with take-off permission from Mullinnix Field, Lieutenant Pratte released the brakes and the big plane began to roll, gaining speed quickly because it had no bomb load and carried half a crew.

The CASU-16 men shouted and ran alongside, keeping pace for a moment until *Belle of Texas* passed them and the men trotted to a stop and spread out on the runway behind the plane. They watched as the wonderful rich exhaust smell drifted away and the powerful engine sounds grew distant. They watched and waved hats and shirts as the bomber's landing gear snugged up under the plane, and finally the bomber climbed out of sight and the Navy men sighed and walked back to their duties, talking about the fine things these lucky Air Corps men must have planned, once they get back to Oahu.

Chapter 14

Last Flights

THE RADIO OPERATOR'S TABLE DROPPED, Sergeant Scearce's stomach leaped, and he braced his knees against the table to keep from falling into the heaving cockpit floor. Just outside his window, Scearce could see the silver propeller hub of *Belle of Texas'* number 3 engine turning so fast it seemed to be standing still. On sunny days the hub spinners were shiny bright enough to blind you, but today they were grubby gray like a well-worn nickel. Rain pelted and spread across the cockpit glass and streaking rivulets raced across the radio operator's window. Just past number 3 the outboard engine was a ghostly dark shadow and the wingtip beyond wasn't visible at all.

Lt. Charlie Pratte and co-pilot Lt. Reginald Spence pushed the plane's nose down to reduce altitude because they had been unable to get above the weather and decided to try downstairs. The long, thin wings of the Liberator fluttered up and down, an unsettling vision that knotted the stomachs and choked the throats of green airmen the first time they saw a B-24 flex like this, but Yankus, Findle, Scearce, Pratte, Spence, and navigator Ball weren't green airmen. They weren't rattled because the wings were flexing; they were rattled because the bomber was on its first flight after major repairs by men who didn't usually work on

B-24s and they were in the middle of the worst flying weather any of them had ever experienced.

At altitude the big plane was tossed about, dropped, and snatched up again like a toy in a child's hands. Descending through one thousand feet the wingtips flashed into view, gray-white misty patches rushing across them and past the windows of the plane as if some unseen jester was quickly opening and closing thick gray curtains. The right wing rose suddenly, the plane banked left, and it felt like the aircraft was going to roll completely over, but Scearce could see the artificial horizon in the middle of the instrument panel already coming slowly back to level and the sensation they were still rolling left was just an illusion. The gyroscopic horizon was the only visible reference for the plane's attitude, and Scearce watched it until the ball showed level and his stomach stopped trying to convince him that the plane was on its side and still going over. He thought the fellows in CASU-16's mess hall would be disappointed to know that the food they had prepared so carefully for the flight wouldn't be eaten.

At 500 feet the flashes of gray mist across the wings were less frequent and the splashes of rain on the windows eased enough to reveal a choppy swirling dark sea. Lieutenant Pratte pushed the bomber even lower and leveled out at fifty feet because it was the smoothest place he could find to ride out the storm. At fifty feet the plane rocked back and forth as the wind buffeted it and the six men aboard shifted their weight first one way and then the other. "We're just going to have to stick it out," Pratte said, and no one else spoke for a long time. Instead each man tried to find some place on the ocean's surface for his eyes to focus, because there was no discernible horizon, the horizon's line hidden by smudged gray sameness from overhead right down to the water just yards from the plane in any direction. "Visibility zero," Scearce could picture in the pilot's log.

Finally Charlie Pratte turned to Scearce and said, "Go ahead and get
an update from Hickam."

Scearce tried, but there was no reply. Or if there was a reply, it was
buried in static so noisy and loud that he quickly pushed the headset
up on his head. He followed up the request: "Weather bad, can't receive
you. Will try later," and he dutifully recorded the transmission on his
Form 35 Radio Log in the log book which had been creeping from one
side of the radio operator's table to the other.

Belle of Texas made noises Scearce had never heard from an airplane,
low rumbles and waves of metallic vibrations that seemed to move
diagonally through the plane from one quadrant to another. The sounds
of the plane and the storm mixed to produce a concert that was strange
and ominous and interesting because there was little else to occupy the
radio man or the engineers, and every new groan and creak by the old
bomber tossed by the wicked storm renewed their hope that the Navy
boys on Tarawa had gotten things right.

Just a couple of hours out of Oahu, Belle of Texas burst suddenly into
beautiful, blinding sunlight, floating, with no more feeling of motion
and no clouds flashing between the windows and the mirror-shiny
propeller spinners. The plane was suspended above the calmed ocean
as if Hawaii's gentle blue sky was welcoming it home after a long and
troubled absence. Pratte and Spence reached for their sunglasses and
Jack Yankus knelt on his jump seat, looked out the cockpit windows
and said, "That's nice."

The flight line at Hickam in February 1944 had changed in the weeks
Belle of Texas spent at Tarawa. If the Belle had feelings, she would have
wondered powerfully at the bright silver newcomers to the airfield, shiny
new B-24-J Liberators standing near Hickam's hangars. *Belle of Texas*

would have felt proud and experienced but at the same time older and blemished. The new J models contrasted sharply with the planes they would replace, older planes like *Belle of Texas*.

The sparkling aluminum J models gleamed newness. They were bolder, not hiding inside a coat of dull green paint, and faster because they had shed the weight of the paint. They were better because they incorporated design changes learned from Army Air Forces experience with the older D models. The olive-drab D models seemed to shrink from the self-assured new bombers muscling their way onto flight lines on Hawaiian bases. J models had an air of complete confidence, poised and modern and ready while *Belle of Texas* looked like a proud but tired prize fighter deciding whether to come out for the next round.

Depot men met *Belle of Texas* where it taxied to a stop, walking around the veteran aircraft while one of them made notations on a clipboard. Those notes marked the end of the bomber's fight; it was over for the *Belle*, the Hickam Air Depot had thrown in the towel. CASU-16's weeks of labor, the flight to Tarawa with the repair parts, sleepless threatening nights when the Japanese dropped bombs and might invade, and the harrowing flight from Tarawa, were all for nothing because the plane could have been salvaged right where it sat after the parachute landing on Mullinnix Field back in December.

Major General Willis Hale's letter of commendation to Lt. Charlie Pratte's crew had praised them for saving "a valuable bomber from certain destruction," but as it turned out they hadn't saved the bomber at all. *Belle of Texas* would not avenge Rear Admiral Mullinnix' death aboard the carrier *Liscome Bay* or Commander Tilghman's horrible accident on the Mullinnix Field flight line. In fact, *Belle of Texas* would never fly again. Scearce and Yankus climbed down from *Belle of Texas*, *"Patches"* to the CASU-16 men, and agreed that it would be better if the Navy boys never learned that the bomber they cheered and so proudly

watched take to the sky earlier that day was on its last flight. Pilot Charlie Pratte gratefully patted *Belle of Texas* on its side and walked away.

During the first week of February 1944, while Scearce and Yankus
and the other four airmen were on Detached Service to Tarawa, two
regiments of the Army Seventh Infantry Division invaded and took
Japanese-held Kwajalein.[1] The invasion began on February 1 after an
intense bombardment, and this time there was no foul-up in communications with the 7th Air Force as there had been at Tarawa. Liberators staging through Mullinnix Field delivered massive 2000-pound
bombs just before the troops went ashore, and an early report said the
advance was so quick that American forces were hampered more by
fire and debris from their own operations than by Japanese resistance.[2]
The Japanese defense stiffened, but the Americans advanced me-
thodically and the island was secured by February 4. Combat patrols
confirmed there was no further resistance, work details unceremoniously buried Japanese dead, and soldiers surveying enemy positions
found Japanese documents. The captured documents were delivered
to intelligence officers for translation and analysis, and something
within their pages warranted summoning the commanding officer of
the 11th Bombardment Group's 42nd Bomb Squadron, Captain Joe
Deasy, to Kwajalein.

On February 24, Captain Deasy, Lt. Robert Bean, Lt. Randolph Ball,
and Sgt. Herman Scearce flew to Kwajalein.[3] The men met with Army
intelligence officers there to discuss a report concerning two American
flight officers captured by the Japanese and interrogated there on Kwajalein before being shipped to Japan. The report indicated that the men
had survived the crash of a plane that had been flying at low altitude
when an engine quit and the aircraft engineer made the tragic mistake

of cutting off the gas to the adjoining engine.[4] The translated papers were a prisoner of war interrogation report.

Clues in the interrogation report about civilian schooling and details about Army Air Forces training bases identified the two American flight officers as bombardier Lt. Louis Zamperini, the 1936 Olympian, and his pilot Lt. Russell Phillips. Apparently a third man had also survived the crash but died on the thirty-third day as the three men drifted across the ocean in a raft.[5] The men now gathered on Kwajalein could not determine who the third man was, except that he was an enlisted crewman. The other two survivors drifted forty-seven days and were nearly dead when the Japanese discovered them and brought them to Kwajalein.

Lieutenant Phillips' plane, *The Green Hornet*, was the aircraft that had become overdue to Palmyra in May of the previous year while on a search mission with Lieutenant Deasy's crew, and these were the men Deasy and Scearce and the rest of their crew had so desperately tried to find until they were forced to give up because of maintenance problems with their own plane.

As they reviewed the translated evidence they understood that these two men, Zamperini and Phillips, were now suffering in a Japanese prison camp, if they were still alive. The facts hit them hard, because they had failed to see the men when they must have been there to be seen, drifting in their raft, and Scearce and Deasy felt profoundly sad, but there was nothing, not a damned thing they could do about it now.

Scearce and Deasy had no idea how close they had come to spotting the survivors of *The Green Hornet's* crash. On the third day after the crash, the third day of forty-seven, a B-24 flew directly over the three downed airmen. When the B-24 approached, Zamperini recognized it as one from his own squadron. He fired flares from a Very pistol and watched hopefully as the B-24 turned.[6] Zamperini saw the B-24 turn and was convinced they'd been seen, but he was mistaken.[7]

On that day, besides Phillips and Zamperini, the raft held Sgt. Francis McNamara, "Mac" he was called, a gunner on Phillips' crew. Mac was the enlisted man who couldn't be identified from the captured Japanese records. Mac died after a full month more of exposure and hunger and thirst, and was buried at sea by Zamperini and Phillips on the thirty-third day.

On Kwajalein, Scearce and Deasy reminded themselves that they had done their best, that ocean surface chop can obscure a raft just when a searching airman's eyes might otherwise glimpse it, and that no matter how hard they tried, sometimes circumstances simply conspired against them. Circumstance and error built upon circumstance and error until a critical mass was suddenly reached and men died.

In Zamperini and Phillips' case, a B-24 bound for Australia had already gone down in the water, so a low-level search was necessary. The low altitude Phillips flew eliminated the margin of safety higher altitude provides when a plane gets in trouble. An engine died, and the engineer's apparent mistake cut power to a second engine, a frightening but recoverable error at high altitude.

Years of hindsight change perspectives, and it is possible now to suppose that the failure to see the raft from *The Green Hornet's* crash worked out for good and might have been providential because of the lives Phillips and Zamperini lived. Had they been spotted in the raft, rescued and returned to service, they may not have survived the war. There simply is no way to know, but even in hindsight it is hard to imagine a scenario in which rescue wouldn't have brought a better outcome for Sergeant McNamara. Scearce felt as if they had let their friends down, and a sick, sorrowful feeling about it lingered for many years.[8]

The training regimen implemented by Captain Joe Deasy and the 42nd Bomb Squadron in January 1944—six weeks of training tailored to Pacific operations—supplemented the phase training completed by air crews stateside. As B-24 crews came over from the States they were attached to the 42nd , given a Training Crew number, and completed the additional training before going on to fight with the 26th, 98th, or 431st Squadron. Each crew completed three weeks of flight training including gunnery, formation flying, strange field landings, bombing, navigation, and search missions, followed by three weeks of ground school including water landing procedures, radar, communications, photo interpretation, ordnance, aircraft and sea craft recognition and identification, and the geography of the Central Pacific.[9] Even during the three weeks of ground school, crews were expected to fly every day.[10] This Hawaii-based supplemental training would equip green crews with the brass tacks of B-24 operations in the Pacific and expose them to unique challenges they would face, challenges like navigating alone over large expanses of water.

Many crews found the training flights terribly boring, and at least one whiled away the hours by watching flying fish to see how high they could jump.[11] But the training was short, just six weeks, because the other three squadrons of the Group needed replacements at the front. For some, six weeks wasn't enough.

Training Crew 18 was 2nd Lt. Edwin Szczypinski's crew. They completed their training with the 42nd during February and March 1944 before being assigned to the 26th Squadron at Eniwetok on March 29. At that time the 26th was regularly bombing Truk, home to the Japanese

Combined Fleet. Truk was a staging base for Japanese aircraft flying from Japan to other parts of the Pacific, and it was defended by forty anti-aircraft guns.[12] Another concern for B-24 crewmen was the big Japanese battleship *Musahi*, stationed at Truk. Bomber crews wanted nothing to do with enemy ships because gunners on ships, Japanese and American, were well trained and accurate. Bomber pilots would usually give a wide berth even to American ships, just to avoid the chance of being mistaken for Japanese by an overzealous anti-aircraft gunner. One way to reduce the effectiveness of the anti-aircraft guns concentrated on Truk was to hit the powerful Japanese base at night.

At the end of their second week with the 26th Squadron, Szczypinski's crew was returning from a night bombing mission against Truk flying the B-24 J *Heavy Date*. They were on their way home to Eniwetok where a ground-based radio operator named Hagen relieved his buddy and began a shift that was uneventful for the first six hours. But at nineteen minutes past 8:00 on April 16, *Heavy Date* broke the monotony for the Eniwetok station.[13]

"SOS SOS SOS DITCHING FLYING COURSE 73"

Eniwetok responded, "WHAT IS YOUR POSITION, OVER"

"POS 09 DEG 25 MIN NORTH 163 DEG 25 MIN (R)" The letter "R" was a request for a response.

Eniwetok's operator Hagen replied, "HELP ON WAY, OVER."

"HELP ON WAY?"

"YES HELP ON WAY." Hagen then asked, "ARE YOU SOUTH OF US?"

"WE ARE WEST."

"STAND BY WITH ME," Hagen responded, and he began contacting another ground station in an effort to triangulate a fix on the aircraft.

Heavy Date's radio operator, Sgt. Carl B. Swift, quickly tapped another message with his Morse key to let the ground station know they had turned on their emergency identification system (EMG IFF) and to update the plane's position: POSITION AT 2030 GCT EMG IFF ON 09 DEG 25 NORTH 163 DEG 25 MIN EAST R R R"

Eniwetok's Hagen asked, "ARE YOU 170 MILES?"

Swift typed desperately, "YOU ARE ON WAY RIGHT?" Then "POSITION NOW 09 51 NORTH APP 162 30 EAST R R"

Swift added the time of the position fixed by navigator 2nd Lt. Bernard Wienckowski: "2100 GCT R R"

Eniwetok replied, "DUMBO ON WAY."

Aboard *Heavy Date,* Swift typed a message he hoped would get a response from a Navy flying boat: "DUMBO CHIEF R . . . DUMBO IS THAT YOU CHIEF?"

Eniwetok sent, "DUMBO IS ON WAY IS ALL OK R R" And two minutes later, the ground station asked Swift how much more time the plane had in the air.

"NOT OVER 1 HR AT MOST R"

Hagen asked, "WHAT IS TROUBLE?"

Swift replied, "GAS LOW R"

Hagen requested Swift send him another position, and Swift responded, "FLYING TRUE COURSE OF 73 DEG R"

Swift had sent a heading, not a position, so Hagen asked again for a position. It had now been forty-five minutes since Szczypinski ordered Swift to send an SOS and the fuel gauges aboard *Heavy Date* would by now show nothing left. There would be no new position updates from the navigator. Sgt. Carl Swift, from *Heavy Date's* radio operator's table, replied to the position request.

"UNABLE TO SEND TRUE POS OVER R"

Hagen requested, "CLIMB TO 8000 IF POSSIBLE R"

Swift replied that they were "AT 10,000 NOW R"

Hagen asked, "ARE U USING YOUR HOMING?"

Swift replied that yes, they were using their homing and another ground station, code named WVNE2 got the plane's bearing and reported, "BEARING 299 TRUE FROM WVNE2 OVER"

Eniwetok's Hagen asked Sergeant Swift to send the letters "MO" repeatedly, so the two ground stations could fix the plane's position. WVNE2 advised Hagen the plane was "NOW 300 TRUE OVER" The time was 2136, one hour and 17 minutes after Swift's SOS. At 2139, Hagen recorded in his radio log that the plane "SENT SCRAMBLED, NERVOUS, UNABLE TO MAKE SENSE OUT OF TRANSMISSIONS"

And at 2144, Hagen recorded, "AT THIS TIME TRANSMITTER EMITTED STEADY TONE FOR APPROXIMATELY 4 MINUTES . . . ENDED AT EXACTLY AT 2148 WITH GARBLED SQUEAL, NO MORE HEARD FROM"

Swift had screwed down his wireless transmitter key, just as radio operators were trained to do when they were about to crash. It took four minutes from the time Swift screwed down his key to brace for ditching until the rush of the sea into the bomber shorted the radio equipment and the transmission ended.

Pilot Edwin Szczypinski got out of the sinking plane and climbed into a raft with his bombardier, the assistant engineer, and one of the crew's gunners. Sgt. John Refy, the assistant radio operator, also managed to get out of the sinking plane, but he clung desperately to a wing. His pilot called for Refy to let go of the wing and come to him, but Refy could not make himself do it, and he sank with the wreckage of the plane. Radio Operator Sgt. Carl Swift and four other men were also pulled down, trapped inside the bomber.

Four B-24s of the 26th Squadron and a Navy Dumbo flying boat searched *Heavy Date's* last reported position for five hours and found nothing. On the morning of April 19, the third day after their crash, a Dumbo plane spotted the airmen's raft and rescued the four survivors. They were transferred from the plane to the Navy destroyer USS *Gansevoort* and later returned to their squadron. By the twenty-eighth, Szczypinski and two of his crew were at the 204th General Hospital on Oahu, recovering from injuries they suffered when *Heavy Date* hit the water.[14]

The crash was directly a result of fuel starvation, but the fuel was exhausted because the plane was lost. The positions reported by Swift to the Eniwetok ground station were wrong. Six weeks' supplemental training with the 42nd had not been enough for the crew of *Heavy Date*. Sometimes green crews simply had too little skill and too little experience to survive.

Chapter 15

Ask the Man Who Owns One

THE ROLE OF THE 42ND SQUADRON as a replacement crew training unit gave the old timers in the squadron the feeling that they were more in business than in combat. New crews came through and went to the front, but the 42nd stayed put, at least for now. The old timers, men who had arrived a full year before, been in combat and returned to Hawaii, understood that the 42nd was also gradually being rebuilt around a core of experience, and as that core they knew that sooner or later they would be called upon to lead the squadron into battle again.

In March 1944, Capt. Joe Deasy got sick. He was feverish, didn't have much appetite and felt tired all the time. His symptoms were like a mild case of dengue fever, similar to flu symptoms, except that they wouldn't go away. Dengue fever was spread by mosquitoes in some of the forward areas where the 11th Group operated, and the crew had assumed Deasy would recover from it in a week or two. But on April 10 Deasy was admitted to Oahu's Tripler General Hospital and diagnosed not with dengue fever but with tuberculosis, and as the next most senior pilot, Capt. Jesse Stay assumed command of the squadron.[1] Deasy's crew was shocked by the news and they were concerned about their pilot's welfare, but they were also very worried what this unfortunate turn of events would mean for them if their pilot could not return to flying status. The men liked and respected Captain Stay but they knew it was up to him, if he officially succeeded Deasy as squadron commander, whether he would take a crew. Some squadron commanders preferred to run their squadrons without an assigned crew of their own.

Herman Scearce and Jack Yankus collected money from the rest of the crew and bought a leather toiletry kit for their pilot. They had "Capt. John J. Deasy" embossed into it in gold letters, and Scearce and Yankus went together to visit their friend, pilot, and squadron commander in the Tripler General Hospital.

The two men stopped at a desk and got directions from a heavyset, serious woman in a white nurse's uniform. They were on the right floor, she said, and she pointed them down a hall. Scearce and Yankus walked the hall, reading room numbers and names beside doors as they passed, careful not to look inside the rooms with open doors because someone's injury or illness seemed like such a personal thing.

"If he's sleeping, we won't stay," Yankus said.

"We don't need to stay long anyway, Jack," Scearce replied. "I expect he needs to rest."

The men walked side by side, silent because Deasy's room number was coming up and the door was partway open. Yankus stopped, Scearce leaning in beside him, and Yankus pressed one hand flat against the door and knocked gently with the other.

"Knock, knock, Captain!" Yankus tried to sound upbeat. "You awake?"

"Come on in here, fellas!" Deasy said.

Scearce and Yankus entered their pilot's hospital room where Deasy rested in bed, looking strangely small and out of place.

"They treating you good in here, Joe?" Scearce asked, while Yankus clutched the toiletry kit.

Deasy pushed himself to sit up and stuffed a pillow behind him. "Yes, but they won't let me go far. That nurse at the desk—the big one—was she there?"

"Yessir, there was a big one at the desk," Yankus said.

"She threatened to put a cow bell on me if I didn't stay put."

"I believe she could do it," Scearce said.

"Well, I do too, and I don't want to test her."

"I bet she could keep you warm at night, Captain, if you play your cards right," Yankus said, grinning his big grin. Deasy laughed; Scearce smiled and shook his head.

"We brought you a little something, Joe, the boys all went in together."

Yankus had forgotten he was holding the toiletry kit. Scearce looked at Yankus and Yankus paused for a heartbeat then held the brown leather toiletry kit out to his captain. Deasy took the kit and admired the lettering on the side while his radio man and flight engineer stood silently, self consciously watching him. "That's nice," Deasy said, and he unzipped the top of the toiletry kit and peered inside, the same cast to his blue eyes that Scearce had seen countless times confidently checking instruments or throttle settings on a Liberator.

"It's a toiletry kit," Yankus said. Scearce and Deasy laughed, Yankus grinned sheepishly. "Well . . . but you can put whatever you want in it," Yankus offered next.

Deasy smiled gratefully. "It was really nice of you to do this."

Scearce extended his hand. "Get better, Joe," he said. Yankus shook Deasy's hand and the bomber pilot's blue eyes got very wet. "I'll be all right, boys."

"We better go before the big one runs us off," Scearce said.

"Okay, fellas, thanks again for coming to see me."

Scearce and Yankus stopped beside the open door and turned to their captain and saluted him. Capt. Joe Deasy shifted the leather toiletry kit to the crook of his left arm, looked up at his crewmen and saluted them back.

Deasy's radio man and flight engineer left Tripler General Hospital wondering quietly whether they would see him again and what a fine man and great pilot he was, feeling sorry for him and for themselves because Deasy's eyes seemed to say he would not return.

Deasy was the man who had so serendipitously stepped forward just as the crew was finishing phase training, back when they were green and naïve. He was experienced and skilled and the men liked him from the very beginning. Even then, wet behind the ears as they were, they knew that flying with a 1st lieutenant pilot had to be better than flying with one of the dozens of 2nd lieutenants. From that point forward they enjoyed the perks of being a lead crew in the squadron. Deasy had always treated them well, respected their skills, and listened to their concerns. He was cool and unruffled in combat and the crew had complete confidence in him. He had earned their absolute trust.

When Joe Deasy was transferred from Tripler General Hospital on Oahu to Fitzsimons Army Hospital in Colorado in May 1944, the squadron had been actively engaged in training and rebuilding for four months, and the operation was running smoothly. Assigning Deasy's crew to another pilot wasn't a problem that the squadron needed to solve right away. Scearce and Yankus and the rest of Deasy's crew were suddenly leaderless and their pilot's assignment to the States meant they had lost their best friend and protector. They were also keenly aware of the difference a good pilot made for his crew's survival, and serving with a command pilot who could choose from among the best co-pilots and navigators and men for every other position was better still. The many implications of Deasy's illness and losing him as their pilot upset his crew, now his former crew, and not knowing who they might end up with was especially troubling. It seemed unlikely their reassignment to any other pilot could possibly work out as well.

Had they lost their pilot in the middle of combat missions at a forward base, the crew would have been scattered around as replacements for other men lost or injured or sick, or a pilot with no crew would have been plugged in to fly with them. For the moment, though, they weren't flying missions, and they pushed their anxieties about the future to the back of their minds. Scearce and Yankus agreed on the simple and straightforward truth that no amount of worry would help and there was nothing they could do about Deasy or their future crew assignment anyway, and their sense that the squadron's respite in Hawaii was only temporary motivated the men to make the most of the time. For the present they would enjoy the distractions around Oahu, and just as experienced men knew how to handle themselves in combat, they had also learned how to handle themselves around the island.

Mokuleia was on the opposite side of Oahu from Honolulu, and Mokuleia had little to offer an Air Corps man with a weekend pass. The situation was no better when the squadron moved by truck on March 19, 1944, from Mokuleia to Kahuku.[2] Kahuku was no closer to Honolulu, clubs, girls, or anything else a man with a pass wanted to find. Kahuku was across the island from Honolulu, like Mokuleia, just in a different direction. There was no organized transportation system such as buses or rail, and taxis were expensive. When Scearce and any of his buddies got a pass, the main topics of discussion were what they were going to do, which was the fun part, and how they were going to get there, which was the hard part. Solving the how to get there problem was a constant struggle.

There was the daily mail truck, but the truck was often crowded, it was tedious and slow because it had stops to make, and it didn't go into the club or hotel district in Honolulu. It got close, but the airmen had to hoof it the last several blocks, take a taxi, or catch a ride with someone if they were lucky. With precious short time for whatever they had in mind, a poorly thought-out transportation plan was costly. The return trip had the same challenges with the added risk of getting written up and incurring "squadron duty" assignments for being late, assignments like pulling guard duty or scrubbing pots and pans in the mess hall. If a man waited until the night he had to get back, it was too late to catch a ride on the mail truck. It was possible to waste a full day of a three-day pass just completing the round trip.

Since men were compelled to get back to their squadrons on time, they would pile on to whatever conveyance was available, often a GI truck. After enjoying themselves right up to the last minute, men coming off a weekend pass could be anywhere from sober to tipsy to sloppy. Since the trucks were usually crowded, soldiers would sometimes stand on the back and hold on for the ride, an especially dangerous idea for men who were more sloppy than sober because the trucks were jarring and hard and the roads were rough. A 42nd Squadron cook, Corp. Harold Shadbolt, died from head injuries after an unfortunate fall from the back of a crowded truck in March.[3] A jolt through the truck's stiff suspension would test the grip of any man, even sober.

When they got a pass, Yankus and Scearce planned most of their extracurricular activities together. On one occasion, Scearce complained that he was hungry, and their first order of business ought to be getting something to eat. Once in Honolulu, Yankus made matters worse for Scearce by insisting on finishing some piddling errand before they went to eat. Scearce got increasingly impatient, pestering Yankus to hurry up, reminding him that if they waited much longer they might have to wait for a table. Finally done with his errand, Yankus suggested a nearby restaurant that offered a huge steak dinner. Yankus called it a "plank" steak and he estimated it was more than four pounds, cooked, and if you could eat all of it in one sitting, with a huge helping of potatoes and gravy on the side, and keep it down, it was on the house. Yankus challenged Scearce to order the plank steak since he was so damned hungry.

Everything was fine until halfway through when Scearce's confidence began to wane. Most of the potatoes were gone, but there were easily two pounds of meat left on the plate, and Yankus tried to pour more sauce on the steak but Scearce parried the attempt with his elbow. "Ain't funny, Jack."

Yankus, who Scearce liked to say could make a seven-course meal out of a sandwich and six bottles of beer, was dispatching cold beers and thoroughly enjoying himself at Scearce's expense. He forked the pineapple garnish off Scearce's plate and stuffed it in his mouth. "Here, I'll help ya out, buddy!" Scearce muttered something about not wanting his help.

"What's a matter, Herman? You said you were hungry!" And he laughed his room-filling laugh while Scearce smiled weakly and tried to keep chewing. Each bite took longer to swallow and beads of sweat popped out of Scearce's forehead from the thick spicy steak sauce.

"I can't do it."

"Sure you can! You got it half gone, Herman! Don't give up now!" And Yankus swilled some more beer and laughed at Herman.

"It ain't funny."

"Excuse me ma'am! Could you bring my buddy here some more steak sauce?"

"Dammit, it ain't funny, Jack."

"Herman! Do you really want to disappoint your fans?" Everyone in the place knew what was going on.

Scearce dropped his fork and glowered at the waitress with the steak sauce in her hand. "Ged id oud ub 'ere," Scearce mumbled, head held low with a mouthful of meat and he waved away the waitress with the full bottle of steak sauce. He couldn't look at the steak any longer and the smell of it was about to make him throw up. Yankus swallowed some beer and wiped his eyes from laughing.

Scearce finally tossed his napkin across his plate, a white flag of surrender to the portion he couldn't force himself to eat, and continued very slowly chewing the last bite he had put in his mouth, bile rising in his throat.

"Let's get some girls and go dancing!"

"You go ahead," Scearce groaned, "I'm going back to Kahuku." Yankus laughed again at his miserable friend, paid the bill, then made an elaborate show of helping Scearce up from his seat and good-naturedly agreed to hitchhike back to the squadron with him.

An infantry officer in a black 1932 Packard stopped to give the Air Corps men a ride. The Packard was a big car with four doors. "Whole damn crew could ride in this," Yankus said, and he climbed comfortably into the back and reclined as if he might go to sleep. Scearce asked about the car and how the officer had come to own it, because cars were hard to come by. There was no used car market on Oahu, and when cars did change hands it was by word of mouth. No new models were being built since the car companies were making tanks and planes and trucks for the war effort, so the chance to buy a car was rare, especially a good one.

The infantry officer explained that he had bought the car from a doctor in Honolulu, but he'd have to sell it because he was shipping out soon.

"How much you want for it?" Scearce asked. "I'd let it go for $400," the officer replied, and Scearce quickly said, "Sold, I want it."

"Where you gon' get *four hunner* dollars, Herman?" Yankus slurred from the back seat, "Tha's two, three months pay!" "I'll get it, Yank." Scearce was glad his friend's mind was a little slowed by the beer, otherwise Yankus might have jumped in and the car deal discussion could have escalated into a bidding war or a complicated half-ownership arrangement. With Yankus in the back seat staring off into space for the most part, Scearce was able to nail it down on his own. Scearce was thrilled with this sudden turn of events because the night had looked like it was going to end with a bloated early collapse into his bunk, but now he was on the verge of passing from the desperate ranks of riff-raff soldiers constantly fretting about ride arrangements to the freedom and royalty of car ownership. The possibilities filled Scearce's mind immediately and the plank steak was suddenly far enough in the past that it was okay to laugh about it. Car ownership meant that anything on the island was within reach. Restaurants, shops, and shopkeepers' daughters were all within reach for a man with a car of his own.

Yankus was right: Scearce didn't have "four hunner dollars," and it was true that $400 was almost three months' pay for a man earning $144 a month. But Scearce had confidently jumped on the Packard offer because he knew that his friend Charlie Bunn, the squadron's radar officer, would float him a loan for the deal.

Capt. Charlie Bunn was from Stanhope, North Carolina, a small town in the next county over from Roanoke Rapids, where Scearce's father lived. Captain Bunn and Sergeant Scearce hit it off well when they met, because they knew each other's home towns. Bunn had a lot of respect for Scearce's skill with radio and the new radar sets, and he needed a technically strong enlisted man to help him work with the equipment, ask intelligent questions, and give feedback to its civilian developers. Scearce spent weeks working with Captain Bunn, experimenting with radar, learning its capabilities and how it could be used to their greatest advantage. Bunn took Scearce to meetings and briefings with the Army Air Forces brass and civilians who were installing the new radar systems and often Scearce would be the only enlisted man in the group.

Scearce borrowed the Packard money from Bunn in exchange for his word that he would pay the money back, and took possession of the car from the infantry officer who had picked up Scearce and Yankus hitchhiking the day before.

Scearce had learned to drive during the squadron's first stint on Oahu in '43, thanks to squadron navigator Lt. Charles Amory. Scearce practiced in Amory's beautiful red 1935 Ford Touring convertible, driving the Ford around the base until he got the hang of it. The flashy '35 Ford was a temptingly fast car to drive, equipped with a V-8 engine. Amory good-naturedly reminded Scearce that his Ford was similar to the cars outlaws Bonnie and Clyde liked to steal. "Don't run off with it, Herman!"

Scearce was grateful that Amory trusted him with the car, not because he might steal it but because he wasn't a very experienced driver. He had driven the stovewood truck back in Danville a few times, and took the wheel of a jeep once or twice, but that was about it. Just the same, Scearce was a quick learner, and Lieutenant Amory's pretty red Ford never got a scratch.

On July 1, 1944, Scearce passed a Territory of Hawaii, City and County of Honolulu driving test and received his first driver's license. In a box on the right side of the paper license Scearce placed his right thumb print and listed his birth date as May 22, 1922, three years before his actual birth date, because the license had to match the Army's record started back in December 1941 when sixteen-year-old Scearce lied to the recruiter at the Danville post office and said that he was nineteen.

Herman Scearce had joined the few and privileged enlisted men on Oahu who owned his own car, and now he had a license to drive it. No more mail trucks, no more hitchhiking, no expensive taxis, no time wasted as buffer for iffy plans to get back to the squadron on time. The multitude of problems associated with transportation was solved, except for the problem of how to fill the Packard's gas tank.

The Rationing Board decided who got gasoline ration cards, and Scearce didn't think they would be very sympathetic to his pleasure-seeking purposes because gas ration cards were issued based on need. "A" cards were given to car owners whose driving was considered nonessential, "B" cards were for driving that was necessary to the war effort, such as plant employees getting back and forth to work. "B" card holders could buy eight gallons a week. "C" cards went to doctors, mail carriers, railroad employees, and other essential workers, and "T" cards with no limit were for truckers.[4] Scearce figured he might be able to get an "A" card, which was good for four gallons of gas a week, not much for a 1932 Packard. But Scearce didn't bother with application to the Rationing Board because there was a large supply of gas near his quarters on base, sitting right there next to the flight line in Army Air Forces tanker trucks full of 100-octane aviation fuel.

Scearce didn't know what the consequences might be if he got caught with aviation gas in his car, but he knew it must be bad. It had to be worse than his penalty for driving after curfew, when a civilian police officer stopped him and ticketed him for using his headlights after dark. For that offense Scearce had to appear before an officer in a military court and pay an eight-dollar fine and promise he'd never drive after hours with his lights on again and yes sir, he understood it could have been his headlights that some Japanese submariner with a deck gun might have used for target practice that night. At the very least, Scearce was sure that the Packard would be impounded if he was caught driving with aviation gas in the tank, and what punishment he might suffer beyond that, he didn't know, but he balanced the risk against an assumption that he could outsmart the military police on Oahu.

The MPs were most active in Honolulu. They carried a siphon bulb with a clear hose, and they would remove a car's gas filler cap and slide the hose down the filler neck, squeeze the bulb, and watch the gasoline rise in the hose. If the gas was gold, it was automobile gas, and it was legal. If the gas was green, it was stolen government aviation fuel and the driver was in trouble.

The key to running the Packard on aviation gas, in Scearce's mind, was simply a matter of avoiding military police checkpoints and, for the most part, that meant steering clear of Honolulu.

Scearce and Yankus gassed up the Packard at night. Scearce drove the car with lights off from the crew quarters across the end of the runway and eased in behind a tanker where the trucks were parked in bunkers on one end of the flight line. There was little danger of a guard spotting them, because guards weren't posted at the trucks. If a soldier got a "squadron duty" guard assignment for missing curfew or breaking some other rule, odds were he would be pacing with his rifle in front of the airplanes backed into their dirt-banked revetments on the other side of the flight line and besides, he wouldn't give a damn if a couple of guys helped themselves to some government gas.

On June 23, 1944, the squadron posted new crew assignments, and Scearce was assigned to Crew #1, Squadron Commander Capt. Jesse Stay's crew.[5] Gunner Ed Hess was also assigned to Captain Stay's crew. Jack Yankus was assigned to Crew #2 piloted by 1st Lt. Jordan Churchill, another experienced and well-respected pilot, and the rest of Joe Deasy's men were assigned to other crews. 1st Lt. Sam Catanzarite, Deasy's original co-pilot, had been reassigned to the States back in February.[6] Catanzarite had the mildly embarrassing but potentially troublesome problem of getting airsick whenever he could not see the horizon, especially if the plane was getting bounced around by bad weather. In combat the aircraft might be deliberately pitched suddenly down or to one side to evade Japanese searchlights or to get below flak bursts, and during these evasive actions Catanzarite would groan and get pasty until things calmed down. The crew heard that the flight surgeon had diagnosed Catanzarite with an inner ear problem, but they believed the co-pilot had simply gotten fed up with flying and getting queasy and that his friendly relationship with the flight surgeon became his ticket home.

Scearce took it as a compliment that he had been selected for Jesse Stay's crew, assuming it had been the commander's choice. He and Yankus were very pleased with their new crew assignments, and both men let go of anxieties they had felt since Deasy's diagnosis with tuberculosis. They didn't have to worry any more about being assigned to a replacement crew with a green pilot, and that would be especially important when the squadron returned to the front and began flying combat missions again. For both men the new crew assignments meant that the comfortably familiar benefits of being on lead crews would also continue, and for now, one of those benefits was the quiet acquiescence of comrades who admired these men in their bold misdeed of stealing gas. His position on the squadron commander's crew allowed Scearce and his buddies to get away with it when others might not. You could count the car owners in the squadron on one hand, so everyone knew whose black '32 Packard that was, and if they did see the thirsty old car creeping toward the gas trucks, Scearce's squadron mates would wink and nod and keep quiet.

It was important that Scearce and his friends didn't flaunt these freedoms, because doing so might breed resentment in place of respect and a man who would otherwise wink and nod could just as easily make a quiet report to the squadron executive officer.

The executive officer, Maj. William J. Farris (name changed), was not a flying officer, and he didn't like aircrews, enlisted men in particular. At least that is how it seemed to Scearce and his buddies who thought it was odd that an officer who didn't like aircrews would be assigned to a bomb squadron in the first place. Surely there was some infantry assignment better suited for Farris, and the airmen in the squadron would have been happy for Farris to find it, but of course they had no say.

Since Farris wasn't a flying officer, he never went on bombing missions. Ground officers had their own jobs to do, and they might have been in the bomber crew's way during a strike mission. Farris flew with the squadron from time to time as a passenger, because it was the only way to get from one place to another. Whether he was afraid to fly, the men couldn't be sure, and they would never have been so bold as to ask Farris why he hadn't gone to any of the schools necessary to become a bombardier, navigator, or pilot. But back in June they had found mean humor in the fact that Farris was along as a passenger with Lt. George Smith when the overloaded B-24 *Thumper II* crashed on take-off from Kualoa. Everyone in the squadron was relieved that no one had been killed, but this didn't inhibit the men from joking privately that the Exec must have soiled his neatly pressed pants and probably had to change his too-tight drawers.

While the aircrews were operating from Funafuti, Scearce and Yankus would crawl the 25 yards or so from their tent to the nearest officers' tent, which happened to house Deasy and the rest of their crew's officers, digging a little trench in the sandy crushed coral by hand as they went. Lipe and Hess stood watch while Scearce and Yankus laid wire, connected it to the power going into the officers' tent, and then filled in the trench to cover the wire as they backtracked to their own tent. For the night and maybe for a few nights if they were lucky, they would have light in their tent to read by, write a letter, or play cards.

Their own flight officers knew what was going on, and didn't object, but when Farris made his rounds during the day and discovered the connection, he would unceremoniously yank the wire out of the ground and pull the connection loose and the men would have to start all over again after dark. Electricity in tents was a privilege reserved for officers, and Farris seemed to enjoy walking through the enlisted men's area looking for ways to assert his authority enforcing such rules.

Farris walked into the airmen's tent one afternoon on Funafuti and found Scearce alone on his cot. Scearce stood to attention, because enlisted men were taught to respect the rank no matter how they felt about the man. The major sniffed around for a moment, and without turning toward Sergeant Scearce, he asked, "Why are flyboys' tents always so messy?" And Scearce could have stayed silent, because it was probably a rhetorical question, but he answered. "Sir, we've got all this flight gear. We can't leave it on the plane, and we've got nowhere else to put it. What would you like for us to do with it?" And the Executive Officer left the tent without responding.

During an interval of three days on Funafuti when Deasy's crew wasn't scheduled to fly, Scearce and Hess got the idea that they could build a boat from readily available materials, and with the boat, they could fish in the lagoon. It was against regulations to use the natives' boats, but watching the natives it was easy to see there were plenty of fish to be caught in Funafuti's lagoon, and fresh fish would make them the envy of all the other men, every one of them tired of eating corned beef hash, corn willy as they called it. Hess thought they might even be able to reach Navy boats anchored in the lagoon and trade with them, but Scearce didn't think they would want to risk taking a homemade boat that far out, and besides, they didn't have anything to trade to a Navy man. Air Corps men had only what they could bring along on their planes, mostly mission-essential things with little room for extras. Sailors had ships, and as far as airmen were concerned, sailors had everything.

Scearce and Hess scrounged through squadron supplies and took tarpaulins, airplane dope used to waterproof the fabric-covered elevators and rudders of B-24s, wood from supply pallets, twine, nails, and tools. They made a boxy wooden frame from the used pallet wood, planning to cover it with tarpaulins cut to fit, and then waterproof the whole thing with the dope sealer.

On the morning after building the boat frame Scearce and Hess sat on the ground by their tent, busily cutting the tarpaulins into the pattern they needed. Scearce was thinking about how Bob Lipe had said that his mother supervised a shop in Columbiana, Ohio, making tarps like these when, in his peripheral vision, Scearce saw smartly-creased long khaki pants and shiny black shoes step up. The long pants could only mean "officer," and the mirror finish on the black shoes could only mean Major Farris. Scearce felt suddenly ill at ease about butchering stolen tarpaulins, but he didn't let on and kept at it. Hess also didn't flinch and neither man looked up. Finally the officer spoke.

"What are you working with there?" The officer's voice confirmed the men's recognition of the shiny shoes and creased khakis.

Hess didn't hesitate. "A canvas-like material."

In a moment, Major Farris moved on, just as he had moved on after the exchange with Scearce about why flyboys' tents were always so messy, and Scearce squinted up at Hess, and Hess just grinned. The two airmen happily resumed cutting their tarps, tarps which for all they knew might have come from Columbiana, Ohio, and the shop supervised by Bob Lipe's mother.

The two aspiring sailor airmen got the boat finished and with high hopes carried it out to the lagoon. They had tried to be low-key about the project but it was hard to hide. Word traveled fast, especially when something out of the ordinary was afoot, and inevitably the boat builders had quickly drawn enough attention to become a source of amusement for the rest of the squadron. Like Noah with his ark, Scearce and Hess endured doubters and hecklers and drew snide comments and advice laced with sarcasm. They didn't respond, but silently Scearce made mental notes about who might have to wait a very long time before tasting any fried fish. A side business of betting sprang up around the possible outcomes, from immediate sinking failure to outright success, with a range of bets about how long the boat would stay afloat in between.

More than likely Farris was aware of the buzz in the squadron about the boat under construction and the anticipation of the launch, and surely he had recognized the tarps Hess and Scearce were ruining in the process. But Farris didn't assert his authority to stop it, maybe because of the buzz and the fun the squadron seemed to be having with it and to avoid making himself a morale-killing stick in the mud over something so inconsequential. Farris was certainly aware of the men's status as operations officer's crewmen, so being on Deasy's crew could not have hurt. It is unlikely that just any two enlisted men would have gotten away with destroying the tarps and wasting the paint sealer. But it is also possible, after the messy flyboy tent discussion, that Farris relished the idea that Scearce and his friend were about to get in front of a tough audience and make complete fools of themselves.

Sure enough, Hess and Scearce drew a small crowd for the maiden voyage launch. They carried the boat past the gentle waves washing on the lagoon beach and set it in the water, where it floated more or less on an even keel. Scearce stood and held the sides of the boat while Hess tried to climb in, but the sad, boxy contraption rolled under his weight and swamped. The two men lifted their creation from the surface and emptied the salty water from it for another try, and Scearce put his foot in the very center of the boat's bottom and then quickly shifted his weight into the boat while holding both sides. The sudden movement caused the boat to slip wildly sideways, sending Scearce splashing into the water and drawing hoots and applause from the squadron's observers on the beach. "Kiss my ass!" Hess growled, with perfect Chicago clarity, and the two wet airmen abandoned ship and dragged their waterlogged invention straight to the island's garbage dump.

Farris was the man someone with a burr in his saddle might talk to if they wanted to make trouble for a soldier stealing aviation gas, but Scearce didn't think the risk was very high. Most everybody felt the same way about the executive officer, and there were unwritten rules about not ratting out your buddy, and no enlisted man wanted to be a rat.

Since Yankus was a flight engineer, and flight engineers were responsible for gassing up their aircraft, he knew the fuel trucks and their operation inside and out. He and Scearce would pull enough hose off the reel on the back of a fuel truck to reach the Packard, open the valve into the mouth of a funnel and let gravity do its work. There was no need to start the truck, because there was always enough gas left in the hose to drain into the car's tank.

Sometimes filling the tank took finesse, because there were times when the men didn't want to get it too full, maybe half a tank or a little less. The siphon bulbs used by the MPs reached about halfway into a tank, so if Scearce planned to take the car into Honolulu, where there were more MPs and the risk of detection was greatest, he would make sure that the level of gas in the tank was too low for the siphon hose to reach. Scearce and his buddies strategized as if stealing government gas was a necessity rather than something more akin to juvenile delinquency.

The Packard belonged to Sergeant Scearce but crewmates and friends could have it for the asking any time he didn't need it. "Let's *ask the man who owns one*," they would say as they made their time-off plans, borrowing Packard's trademark advertising line. The men enjoyed the freedom and ease of transportation the car provided, and they were proud of it as if it was their very own staff car. For Scearce and his buddies, the Packard was a vehicle for living in the present. Their time on Oahu training replacement crews and rebuilding their strength was a time for forgetting their losses and setting aside their own mortality, but just for right now, because deep down they knew it couldn't last.

Chapter 16

The Meaning of Boxes

IN LATE JULY 1944, the 42nd Bomb Squadron had been on alert for a return to combat for almost three months. The unusual length of their alert status caused it to be largely forgotten, so for most of the squadron's men, the arrival of shipping boxes in each squadron section caused quite a buzz.

A letter from Headquarters dated May 1 had placed the ground echelon of the squadron on alert and led to rumor and speculation about their next combat station.[1] With no follow-up orders, interest waned until late June when the alert status was modified to include the air echelon. The June orders also relieved the squadron of its training duties, significant because this was an important step toward returning the 42nd to true fighting trim. It wasn't that they had been idle, but for most of the 42nd's crews there hadn't been a combat mission in six months and there is something unquantifiably different about flying strike missions, something which focuses the mind and sharpens skills unlike any training or patrol mission ever could, possibly the awareness that another nation's fighting men were committed to shooting you down, killing you on the ground, denying you your objective any way they could. Being relieved of training duties meant that the 42nd could focus on preparing themselves for combat, and the knowledge

221

that combat would come sooner now than later heightened their sense of purpose.

The June orders moved the squadron back to Mokuleia Air Base, a better location for the 42nd because Mokuleia was occupied by just one other unit, a fighter outfit.[2] There the 42nd would not be crowded for maintenance and support facilities or flight operations by another bomber unit. The Engineering Section of the squadron had been responsible for maintaining as many as sixty heavy bombers, the 42nd's assigned aircraft plus those on detached service to the squadron for training.[3] At Mokuleia, the mechanics of the Engineering Section were down to the squadron's normal complement of fifteen aircraft, a much more manageable work load.

Three 42nd Squadron aircrews wouldn't make the move to Mokuleia. Capt. Alf Storm, Capt. Warren Sands, and Lt. Robert Kerr were the first three pilots in the squadron to complete thirty strike missions, the quota for furlough back to the States at that time.[4] A few men on each of these three crews had missed a mission or two along the way, so these crewmen stayed behind to finish their mission credits. Men like Scearce, with only six mission credits, regarded these veteran crewmen with respect, tinged with a hint of jealousy.

Storm, Sands, and Kerr were old timers in the squadron. Storm and Kerr had piloted one of the B-24s in the February 1943 six-plane flight to Hickam from Hamilton Field, California, when the crews were fresh out of training and they still expected to gas up and head down to the combat zone, that first flight to Hawaii led by Joe Deasy and a crack navigator borrowed from the Air Transport Command.[5] At the time, Kerr was Storm's copilot, transitioning to first pilot in the fall of '43.

Sands had been lucky to survive a crash landing in July '43 that destroyed a B-24 because a faulty air speed indicator caused him to come down too fast on a wet steel runway. Storm was one of only three pilots to reach Mille on the ill-fated December 1, 1943, mission with Stay and Dechert, when Dechert flew with Assistant Engineer Bob Lipe borrowed from Joe Deasy's crew and never made it back. Dechert's crew was short its own assistant engineer because the man had broken his collarbone after *Naughty Nanette's* desperate crash landing on Nanumea. Scearce had been along on that mission and swore he'd never fly with Dechert again.

All three of these thirty-mission pilots—Storm, Sands, and Kerr— had been on the December 20 mission with Lt. George Smith flying *Dogpatch Express* when Smith had been shot down ninety miles off the target, near the combat time and range limit of the Zero pilots pressing home the attack, and all three had been among those valiant crews who turned back to form up on the struggling plane in a heartrending effort to protect it.

The fact that three pilots and most of their crews had completed thirty missions was a milestone for the squadron. The 42nd had matured as a heavy bomber unit, improving and advancing as the war in the Pacific also improved for American forces advancing toward Japan. Three pilots finishing their missions proved it could be done. Three pilots had earned their way east to the States while the rest of the squadron looked west into the battle zone of the Pacific and wondered where they would go to meet the enemy again. As the 42nd considered the meaning of boxes arriving in July, their westerly destination was already shaped by decisions at the highest levels of government.

Whatever their destination, the squadron was experienced enough to know that the new shipping boxes were too big to be transferred to shore by lighter. Just getting them across Oahu would be a challenge; the boxes were so big and heavy that they would have to be lifted onto flat railcars by Cletrac, the tracked vehicles used for towing aircraft, with rigged cables and A-frames.[6] Other boxes would take ten men to muscle onto the railcars. It only made sense if the destination was some place with a deep water port, some place where ships' cranes could unload huge boxes and crates directly to shore. The men of the 42nd weren't told where they were going, but it seemed unlikely they were going to another pretty little atoll with a reef-ringed, shallow lagoon.

The Joint Chiefs of Staff had already chosen the next American objectives in the Pacific. Their directive of March 12, 1944, stated that "the most feasible approach to Formosa, Luzon and China is by way of the Marianas, the Carolines, Palau and Mindanao."[7] With respect to the Marianas, the Joint Chiefs directive required "Occupation of Saipan, Tinian and Guam, starting 15 June . . . with the object of controlling the eastern approaches to the Philippines and Formosa, and establishing fleet and air bases."[8]

Wresting the Marianas from Japanese control would satisfy the U.S. Navy's need for advanced naval bases while providing the Army Air Forces with bases close enough for their new B-29 Superfortress bombers to strike Japan.

B-29s had been in development since before America's entry into the war. They would surpass in performance the B-17 and B-24 workhorses of the Army Air Forces strategic bombing groups, carrying more than twice the bomb load of a B-24 Liberator with more than a thousand miles' greater range. Even the most grizzled flight line veteran might stand in awe of the new Superfortress, towering ten feet taller at the tail than a B-24, with a wingspan over 141 feet, more than thirty feet greater than a B-24, and at 99 feet long, also more than thirty feet the length of a Liberator.[9] B-29 Superfortresses were massive aircraft and a devastating new weapon. Superfortress development and production accelerated in 1943, and the first missions were flown in June 1944.

The Japanese knew enough about the B-29 to appreciate its fearsome power, because a Superfortress had been shot down in May 1943, during a test flight over the Solomons. The captured American pilot divulged enough to convince the Japanese that B-29s must never be allowed to reach Japanese air space.[10] The Joint Chiefs took the opposite view: just 1100 miles from Tokyo, the Marianas would provide excellent bases for B-29 operations against Japan.

Sentiment also favored the Marianas, especially within the U.S. Navy. An American possession since the Treaty of Paris ended the Spanish-American War in 1898, Guam was fiercely loyal to the United States.[11] Guam's native Chamorros were well respected in the U.S. Navy, where they had been serving for years as stewards and mess attendants.[12] Recovering American territory and liberating Guam's loyal people was a noble objective.

Japanese forces had bombed Guam during their opening offensive of the war; bombers from their base in Saipan hit the island, while nearly 4,000 miles to the east, their Pearl Harbor strike aircraft were returning to their aircraft carriers.[13] After bombing Guam for two days, a force of seven hundred Japanese landed and rushed to engage U.S. Marines and native Chamorros defenders. The Japanese invasion coincided with the most sacred Chamorros religious holiday, the Feast of the Immaculate Conception.[14]

Rumors of fighting reached Guam's capital city ahead of the invading Japanese as Bishop Miguel Olano led mass in the cathedral. As he finished the mass, the bishop told his people to leave the city, and they fled to the countryside in droves. The fighting lasted less than half an hour, with just ten Japanese and seventeen Americans killed. When he learned that 5,000 more Japanese troops were landing, the American governor of the island surrendered Guam rather than face annihilation.[15]

The Americans captured on Guam were the first to become prisoners of war of the Japanese.[16] The Japanese confined their prisoners in the Catholic basilica, an utter desecration of the church from the Chamorros' point of view.[17]

Inside the cathedral is a statue of Guam's patroness Saint Mary, and it is she the people were preparing to celebrate when the Japanese rushed ashore. According to the folklore of Guam, the statue was a gift from God presented to a fisherman who received it from the back of a crab, and legend says that salty tears appear on the cheeks of the statue when the island feels great sorrow.[18]

Among the prisoners in the cathedral were five American nurses of the United States Navy Nurse Corps who taught nursing skills to Chamorros women serving with them in the Naval Hospital.[19] One of the five nurses imprisoned by the Japanese was Leona Jackson, later transferred by ship to Japan and confined in Kobe. There she became one of just a handful of Americans to witness the Doolittle raid. She was repatriated in June 1942 in an exchange of nationals; the Japanese considered her a noncombatant.[20] At that time, she observed prophetically, "It is going to be a nasty fight, and it is going to be a dirty fight, because they don't fight according to our rules, they make their own as they go along and they aren't pretty . . . I think it is going to take an awful lot, I think we all know."[21]

Jackson and her Navy medical staff comrades had come to love the native women who worked with them on Guam and prayed that God would protect "our people whom we would be powerless to aid in the dark hours ahead."[22]

But now the awesome power of America's forces in the Pacific would be brought to bear on the Japanese occupiers of Guam and the rest of the Marianas. Five hundred thirty-five American ships and 127,571 American troops were assembled in the greatest assault force of the

Pacific war.[23] On June 15, the American assault on the Marianas was set to begin with carrier aircraft strikes on Japanese air bases on the islands, followed by an amphibious invasion of Saipan. Opposing this massive American force was the Japanese 31st Army, 32,000 men, supported by a small local navy under the command of Vice-Admiral Chuichi Nagumo, the once highly-esteemed commander of the Pearl Harbor strike force. Japan's 31st Army on Saipan had not completed construction of fixed defenses, and American submarines had torpedoed and sunk Japanese ships carrying supplies and equipment intended for Saipan's defenders. Carrier-based American planes sortied and engaged Japanese aircraft as early as June 11, and American battleships pounding Saipan on June 13 and 14 meant that invasion was imminent. Nagumo suffered the irony that three of these American battleships had been targeted by his forces during his attack on Pearl Harbor.[24]

If the commander of the 31st Army, Lt. General Yoshitsugu Saito, hadn't vigorously prepared his defenses, it may have been because he didn't expect an American assault of this size this soon, operating more than 1000 miles from its advance base at Eniwetok and 3500 miles from its headquarters in Hawaii.[25] The invasion of Europe at Normandy was now barely more than a week old and America's ability to commence a second massive invasion on the opposite side of the world was as staggering as it was unexpected. Just the same, Saipan's defenders numbered twice what the Americans anticipated.[26] On June 14, 1944, Japan's English-speaking propaganda broadcaster Tokyo Rose announced to the American forces, "We're ready for you."[27]

The next day, eight thousand U.S. Marines from more than seven hundred landing craft hit the four-mile-wide beach front on Saipan in less than twenty minutes.[28] The Japanese reception was accurate and intense, and the Americans were caught in a crossfire of shells from

Saipan's guns and coordinated batteries on nearby Tinian. American forces that quickly grew to 40,000 men needed three days to reach their first-day objective, repelling Japanese counterattacks and enduring skillful Japanese artillery and mortar fire during their advance.[29] As the American beachhead grew and his counterattacks failed to drive the invading forces back into the sea, Lieutenant General Saito conceded the beachfront and concentrated his defenses in Saipan's rugged interior.[30] There he would await relief from the Japanese Mobile Fleet, steaming toward Saipan to engage the Americans.

As the American invasion forces were storming Saipan, the first B-29 raid on Japan's home islands struck the Imperial Iron and Steel Works on the island of Kyushu.[31] The June 15 raid, staged through China from India, had little effect on the steel works because most of the bombs missed their target. Civilian casualties were high, and while the steel works remained in operation, the psychological effect on the Japanese was significant.[32] This was the first time since the April 1942 Doolittle raid that American bombers hit the home islands, but unlike the Doolittle raiders, these weren't medium bombers on a one-way trip with a symbolic mission. The June 15 B-29 raid foreshadowed what was surely to come if the Marianas were lost.

Also during June, Liberators from the 26th, 98th, and 431st Bombardment Squadrons based on Kwajalein hit the big Japanese base at Truk as often as possible in order to neutralize airfields there.[33] Bombing the airfields was intended to prevent enemy planes from staging from Truk to attack the American forces trying to wrest control of the Marianas from the Japanese. And beginning in June, Liberators carried bombs specially fused to explode just above ground.[34] Bombs exploding on the ground were good for punching holes in runways, but bomb blasts above parked aircraft would damage many more planes, if the planes were there.

The Americans had been optimistic that Saipan would be secured within a few days and that the assault on Guam could begin right away.[35] But the Japanese resistance on Saipan was much tougher than expected, and American submarines patrolling off the Philippines observed two large formations of Japanese ships moving toward the Marianas. Admiral Raymond Spruance cancelled the invasion of Guam and turned his attention to securing Saipan while preparing to meet the approaching Japanese fleet.[36]

Just after Vice Admiral Jisaburo Ozawa's Japanese fleet began its cruise toward the Marianas and the relief of Saipan, a torpedo bomber pilot crash-landed his plane on the flagship carrier *Taiho*. The out-of-control aircraft struck another bomber on the carrier's deck and the planes burst into flames. Before the fire could be extinguished, two dive bombers, two torpedo planes, and two Zero fighters burned.[37]

Six aircraft destroyed before the Americans had even been engaged in combat was a significant loss. Coming just as their ships were making way to engage the Americans, the Japanese considered the disaster an omen.[38]

A B-24 raid against Truk on June 19 included planes from the 26th, 98th, and 431st with crews on Detached Service from the 42nd joining aircraft from the 13th Air Force, a total of fifty-six bombers. From Kwajalein the three forward squadrons of the 11th Bomb Group flew 852 miles to Eniwetok, and after refueling, they flew 1,565 miles farther to reach Truk.

The Liberators hit Truk, but the nineteen planes based there escaped destruction. They had flown that morning to Guam in support of Ozawa's fleet steaming toward the Marianas, and they took off before the American planes arrived over their airfields.[39] Close to their target on Truk's island of Moen, one B-24 element of the 431st Squadron saw three single-engined Japanese planes flying low, about fifteen miles north, north west of the island.[40] These three planes may have been the last of Kakuta's nineteen to leave for Guam.

Writing later about their June 19 raid on Truk, the 26th Squadron's historian recorded, "Strangely enough we received no interception but the antiaircraft fire was unusually intense . . ."[41] Japanese anti-aircraft gunners must have been well motivated that day, since they had witnessed the morning's departure of planes that might otherwise have intercepted the American bombers. Nineteen planes would raise the number of Japanese land-based planes on Guam to fifty, but fifty was far short of the 500 Ozawa expected.[42]

The squadron historian for the 98th recorded, "On June 19 our aircraft departed for Eniwetok for another daylight strike on Truk. There was no interception this time and all planes returned safely, coming back to home base the morning of June 21."[43] The ease of the June 19 raid and its lack of enemy aircraft made the mission almost unremarkable. The mission got two quick lines in the historian's narrative, and where he might otherwise have been compelled to describe enemy fighter action, damage to his squadron's planes, or casualties in his squadron's ranks, he instead recorded an update on squadron dog Queenie, last mentioned when the squadron moved up from Funafuti to Tarawa:

One of the squadron pets, Queenie, by name, has started once more to launch a series of major engagements. The period starting now has been her first active participation since she gave birth to a litter of puppies early in March at our base on Tarawa. Since the father of these puppies had died immediately after contact with our Queenie, the field was wide open for new lovers to appear on the scene. Nine

dogs, male variety, with Tojo—another squadron pet—being ably
assisted by his many friends, have taken advantage of Queenie's
impartiality. A scoreboard has been proposed to keep tabs on her
escapades, this to be maintained in the operations office by S/Sgt.
George V. Tamburrelli, section chief.[44]

As the B-24s returned to their bases and Kakuta's Truk-based planes
approached Guam, American fleet radar detected the Japanese aircraft
and Hellcat fighters were launched from their aircraft carriers to intercept them. Hellcats attacked the Japanese as they approached Guam,
and more Japanese planes already based on Guam rose to join the fight.
Waves of aircraft fought for two days while the opposing fleets never
sighted one another.

When the final Japanese sortie of the battle ran low on fuel, failing
to find American ships to attack, most headed for Guam. Thirty of
forty-nine Japanese planes trying to reach Guam were shot down. Two
American pilots boldly swung their fighters into a landing circle of Aichi
"Val" dive bombers and shot down five.[45] American aircraft overhead
repeatedly bombed Guam's airfield, making it dangerously holed and
cratered as Japanese pilots with no place else to go tried to land.

A Japanese soldier's diary, later captured on Guam, revealed the
demoralizing effect of this spectacle:

The enemy, circling overhead, bombed our airfield the whole day
long. When evening came our carrier bombers returned, but the
airfield had just been destroyed by the enemy and they could not
land. Having neither fuel nor ammunition the 15 or 16 planes
were unable to land and had to crash . . . It was certainly a shame.
I was unable to watch dry-eyed. The tragedy of war was never so
real . . .[46]

During the two-day battle, the Japanese lost 426 fleet aircraft plus some 50 more from the land-based group on Guam, and an estimated 445 airmen.[47] The Americans lost 130 planes, most to water landings due to fuel exhaustion. Seventy-six American aviators were lost.[48]

Some American Hellcat pilot returning from engaging one of Ozawa's four waves of aircraft may have been the first to refer to the rout as a turkey shoot, and if so, his name is lost to history, but the reference is immortal. Officially the engagement was called the Battle of the Philippine Sea, but it will always be known by the name given to the single day that saw so many Japanese aircraft go down. The Marianas Turkey Shoot left Admiral Ozawa without air cover for his fleet and with no choice except to steam toward Okinawa and away from Saipan, leaving Saipan's defenders to face the invading American forces alone.[49]

The dramatic loss of Japanese pilots and aircraft and the impressive air superiority of the Americans resulted from differences in philosophy dating from the beginning of the war. The Japanese wanted a decisive victory in a short war, so they deployed pilots for the duration of the conflict. American pilots learned from experienced aviators rotated from the front, and fighting tactics improved as aircraft design also advanced. The Zero, so formidable in 1941, was no longer the superior design but it remained the mainstay Japanese fighter aircraft.

America's aviation combat strength increased as surely as Japan's declined. While Japanese pilot losses mounted, experience and skill was also lost, and demand for replacements increased. Japanese pilot quali-fications were relaxed and training hours reduced to meet the demand until front line pilots were hopelessly inexperienced and unskilled, so losses increased, demand rose again, and Japan's aviation strength spiraled downward like so many of their young pilots.

The Battle of the Philippine Sea was similar to the Battle of Midway two years before, from the point of view of bomber crewmen of the 42nd Bombardment Squadron. In each case, while the 42nd trained from a Hawaiian base, waiting for a future deployment, the United States Navy engaged the Japanese in a decisive battle. And in each case, the loss of hundreds of Japanese aircraft and pilots was welcome news for bomber crews and men like Sgt. Herman Scearce, about to head to the combat front.

In June, 1944 the 42nd waited for the Marianas to be secured. Lt. General Yoshitsugu Saito's stubborn defense of Saipan was doomed by the power and freedom of maneuver of naval forces supporting the advancing American troops, yet it was effective enough to delay America's plans for the Marianas.

Tinian, Saipan's nearby smaller neighbor, was bombed and shelled for forty-three days before United States Marines stormed ashore.[50] Tinian was invaded July 24 while fighting continued on Saipan, and it was secured by August 1.[51] Tinian's airfields and flat ground would be perfect for B-29 Superfortress operations against Japan.

Guam and its long-suffering Chamorros people waited. The principal island of the Marianas, the one that had been an American territory before the Japanese invasion in 1941, would be the last of the island group to be taken. American planners had intended to invade Guam within days of the Saipan invasion, but the arrival of the Japanese Mobile Fleet and the tenacity of Saipan's Japanese defense delayed the operation until July 21.[52] The capture of Saipan was finally announced complete by Admiral Spruance on August 10, and the last organized Japanese defense on Guam was wiped out on August 12.[53]

As the Marianas were finally secured, the 42nd Bombardment Squadron's heavily packed shipping boxes and equipment crates were loaded aboard ship on Oahu, thousands of miles away.

Chapter 17

Guam

ON AUGUST 21, 1944, 183 men, the ground echelon of the 42nd Bombardment Squadron, climbed aboard freshly painted green troop trucks and drove across Oahu from Mokuleia to the docks at Honolulu.[1] Men breathed the strong smell of the trucks' new enamel coats and the scent evoked a powerful sense of renewed purpose. The aroma of fresh government paint mixed with rich truck exhaust smelled like readiness for combat.

By 8:00 that morning they were aboard the transport ship *Cape Perpetua*, right on schedule, and most of the squadron's equipment was loaded aboard another ship, the *Joseph Priestley*.[2] The squadron's ground support was ready to ship out and set up another forward base while the aircrews and planes were left behind, waiting at Mokuleia for the new base to be ready. No one in the squadron knew where that next base would be, though bets were on Saipan, Tinian, or Guam.

Eight months had passed since the 42nd was deployed to a combat zone. Their mission on Oahu made important contributions to the war effort in a strategic sense, reorganizing and rebuilding while training replacement crews for the other three squadrons of the group, but it wasn't the same as being in action, doing what a bomber outfit is trained and equipped to do. Relieving the 42nd of their training duties back in June had increased their anticipation of a move, and when orders to ship out hadn't come quickly, the anticipation became pent-up energy, stored like a compressed steel spring.

The 42nd's men had already taken every step required of them to be ready to return to combat. During July they inventoried clothing and equipment so that worn or missing items could be replaced. They endured dental exams and updated immunizations. They were issued new gas masks just in case the Japanese decided to use mustard gas. The men practiced shooting with carbines, Thompson sub-machine guns and .45 caliber pistols. The squadron's trucks and other motor vehicles were washed, sanded, and repainted, then loaded with squadron equipment. And since the trucks were loaded for shipment, 7th Bomber Command Headquarters loaned their single-engine Cessna aircraft to the 42nd to serve as a courier vehicle between the base and Hickam Field.[3]

Scearce and the other radio operators spent three days working the squadron's ground station, improving their understanding of the ground operator's role in communications with aircraft and practicing their code speed and touch.[4] Navigators became familiar with a promising new radio navigation system called LORAN, Long Range Aid to Navigation, which would help them determine their aircraft's position relative to radio transmitters on the ground.[5]

The squadron's pilots watched training films called "Thunderstorms" and "Aerology," a film about weather forecasting based on atmospheric observations. The whole squadron sat through presentations on security and censorship and attended lectures about sanitation and insect-borne diseases, emphasizing the importance of controlling flies. Newer crews watched water landing films and the flight surgeon gave talks on emergency first aid. Aircrew gunners made certain their airplane's weapons were in perfect working order.[6]

Crews practiced high and low altitude bombing with radar, a new technique they expected to use increasingly in the coming months.[7] The squadron needed a training aid to help radar operators recognize islands as they appeared on the radar scope, so the photo section developed a camera attachment that could be placed over the scope for taking pictures of the radar image.

Photographing the scope and labeling the ghostly images of islands was an idea developed in meetings during the early months of 1944, meetings and discussions between Capt. Charlie Bunn, Sergeant Scearce, and civilian technicians. The camera attachment produced by the photo section was cumbersome and there was no way to see the radar image once the camera and its boxy attachment were placed over the scope.[8] Scearce learned to time placing the camera attachment over the scope just as the radar beam was sweeping across to light up the islands below. A blurry image in the center was sea return, a reflection of the radar beam from the ocean's surface directly below. Scearce took dozens of radar photos of islands, at different altitudes and from various angles of approach, and these photos were used to train crews in radar navigation and island recognition. The photos depicted targets within range of Guam.

For six men of the 42nd's ground echelon, the arrival of shipping boxes during the last week of July 1944 and the packing and loading activities in early August boosted the pent-up energy of their anticipated move to the breaking point. On August 8 they sprung themselves from the base, absent without leave.

The six AWOL soldiers would have returned to base and it is unlikely they would have been reported missing, let alone disciplined for their adventure, had the one driving kept their car under control. But the car crashed near Waialua on an unpaved, twisting road, killing a young private named Edward Bales who had been standing on the vehicle's running board when the speeding driver lost control. Another man was seriously hurt, and while the injured man recovered in the hospital, the other four were demoted.[9] The accident happened just a few miles from base; they had almost made it back. These were men who needed a mission, a return to combat, but it came too late for Private Bales.

Three new aircrews joined the squadron during the first week of August.[10] They came over to the 42nd from the Training Detachment that the squadron had left behind on Kahuku, and they would be the squadron's greenest crews when they finally took off for their new base, wherever it was going to be.

While the thirty men of the three new aircrews were moving their gear and setting up bunks in the 42nd's barracks areas, a few of the old timer crews were granted a week of rest and relaxation at Kilauea's rest camp on the big island of Hawaii. They hopped over to a civilian air strip near Kilauea in B-24s and crews leaving the rest camp ferried the planes back to Oahu.

Kilauea's rest camp was hosted by a pretty American girl named Trixie Ecklund. Trixie was fair skinned and blonde, unlike the shop girls so familiar around the air bases on Oahu. She was like girls back in the States, back in home towns, and she somehow seemed familiar to Herman Scearce and Joe Hyson, friends who happened to get a week at Kilauea together. Hyson and Scearce flirted with Trixie and Trixie smiled and wrote her address for the two men just as she had done for countless service men before them and would for countless more to come.

When Scearce and Hyson were at Kilauea, aircrew men were outnumbered by a noisy group of U.S. Marines. Airmen typically didn't enjoy the company of Marines, and the feeling was probably mutual, but

Scearce and his friend Hyson chatted with the Marines when meal time brought them together in the dining room of the nearby Volcano House.

Volcano House served sweet breads and cereals for breakfast, bacon and eggs cooked any way you wanted, sausages and hash browns, fruit, pancakes, French toast, coffee and juices and milk. At lunch they offered seafood, pork, chicken, vegetable and fruit platters, salads, soft rolls and butter, desserts, soft drinks and tea. Each meal's wonderful palette of aromas filled Volcano House and lifted the spirits of the men being served, but the evening meal was the one no man wanted to miss: prime rib, steak, filet mignon and crab legs served in a room with floor to ceiling windows overlooking ancient volcano craters and Hawaii's verdant landscape, set before a blue and red-orange Hawaiian sunset. As the orange hues darkened and a star-filled night sky appeared over Kilauea, fresh with the lush scent of the island's flora on a breath of ocean air, it occurred to Scearce how perfect the place would be if he had a girl, an American girl to share it with, a girl like Trixie, or a girl like the one who lived across the street from his dad's place in Roanoke Rapids.

The last time he had seen the girl in Roanoke Rapids, he was on her tiny front porch overlooking her tiny front yard and Madison Street with the rotten-egg stink of the J. P. Stevens mill fouling the air. How impressed she would be with the view from Volcano House! But instead of a pretty girl Scearce had the company of rowdy Marines getting liquored up, and every one of them, make no mistake about it, sir, had gone ashore with the first wave at Tarawa.

Scearce and his friend Joe Hyson were wading through Marines drinking at the Volcano House bar when a leatherneck sergeant elbowed one of his buddies and called out to the two Air Corps men. "Hey, flyboys! Settle a bet for us here, would ya?"

Scearce and Hyson stopped and turned to face the Marine.

"What's the wager?" Hyson asked.

The Marine sergeant struggled to keep a straight face. He asked, "How does a fly land on the ceiling upside down? I mean, does he do a half-loop with a stall at the top, or is it a half-slow roll?" And with that, the Marine and his buddies guffawed at the outnumbered Air Corps men. Scearce and Hyson smiled and nodded, and Hyson said, "Sorry guys, it's classified—Air Corps secret."

Scearce and Hyson surrendered Volcano House to the Marines and slipped away to a quiet game of gin rummy. Maybe tomorrow they would ride Kilauea's horses. They'd have the horses to themselves if they went early enough; Tarawa's heroes would be sleeping off their drunk.

The troop ships *Joseph Priestley* and *Cape Perpetua* left Oahu on August 21 after spending the morning taking on the 42nd's ground support men and equipment.[11] Most of the men had been aboard the *George W. Julian* for the trip from Funafuti to Oahu nine months earlier, a miserable ruination of Christmas 1943 and New Year's 1944 rolled into one heaving thirteen-day voyage. But at the very least, on that eastbound trip, even the sickest landlubber among them had the destination, Hawaii, to lift their spirits.

Spirits were also high on the westbound trip because the squadron was getting back in the game, like athletes temporarily sidelined. On the last day of August, the squadron reached Eniwetok.[12] The men knew this wasn't their final destination, but after ten days aboard ship it felt good to be *somewhere*. But word soon spread that they wouldn't be allowed to go ashore, so the happy prospect of getting off the boat, walking on terra firma and having a little change of scenery quickly vanished. The optimists among the men voiced the opinion that if they weren't going ashore, surely that meant they would be forming up in convoy and sailing again very soon.

Optimism waned, however, as days at anchor in Eniwetok Atoll extended past a week. Word spread that the squadron's new base would be Tinian, but no one knew when the ships would get under way again. Rumors then spread that the Japanese were bombing the hell out of Saipan and Tinian every night and the squadron might be stuck at Eniwetok for a month.[13]

The highlight of every day in the Eniwetok lagoon was the arrival of a motor launch with the mail bag. Life aboard the troop ships revolved around mail and meals with napping, reading and card games in between. One card player said that "by the time we reach our destination, a lot of bridge will have passed over the water."[14]

Just before dark after twelve days at anchor, the *Cape Perpetua* and the *Joseph Priestley* finally nudged away from Eniwetok with their Navy escort. Four days later, and twenty-six days after boarding their ships at Oahu, the convoy reached the submarine net at Saipan.[15] The optimists among the men were disappointed again because, just like at Eniwetok, no one was allowed to leave their ship.

The mood was subtly different, though. Card games weren't quite so rowdy, books that had been engaging days before were easily put down, and meal times were a little less noisy. Eyes glanced north and west because that's where enemy planes might appear. There was an edge to the men aboard the troop ships now, and those who had been with the squadron longest knew the feeling. They were in the combat zone again.

On the nineteenth, Maj. William Farris, the squadron's executive officer, came over to the *Cape Perpetua* aboard a launch from Tinian.[16] He had flown to Tinian from Oahu to receive orders for his squadron's disposition. Groans greeted his news: as of now, he informed the squadron, there was no final decision. They would have to wait.

On September 21, 1944, five days after reaching Saipan, the 42nd was ordered to Guam.[17] The convoy sailed south to Guam from Saipan the same day, and on the way, the United States Navy treated them to a show.

The *Joseph Priestley* and the *Cape Perpetua* might have listed slightly to one side that day, because every man scrambled to watch a formation of Navy TBF Avenger aircraft bombing Rota, just five miles away.[18] Men shouted and cheered and pointed as the blue Navy planes swooped down and pulled up as bombs were released from the bellies of the Avengers, and they voiced echoes of each *whoomp* which soon followed. "There's one! Look, look, look! Boom! Oh, *Hell* yes!" The spectacle was wonderful to see and hear, because there were no Japanese aircraft in the sky to challenge the Avengers, and surely the convoy wouldn't pass the island so closely if the Americans didn't have complete control. Spirits soared, Guam it would be, and the ground echelon of the 42nd Bombardment Squadron was ready to set up an air base and bring their gallant aircrews and their mighty Liberators, still waiting on Oahu, forward again.

At midday on the twenty-second, the squadron entered Guam's Agana harbor and the men disembarked, walking on ground again thirty-two days after stepping from shore to ship on Oahu.[19] The men of the Transportation Section stayed on the pier for seventy-two hours straight, waiting for their trucks to be unloaded. As trucks came off the ships, they were serviced and put into action immediately, hauling gear for the squadron. Drivers worked in twelve-hour shifts while the trucks ran non-stop for three days to unload personnel and equipment from the ships, making round trips from the pier to the squadron's assigned area near the Agana airfield an hour's drive away.[20]

A work detail scoured the squadron area for live ammunition left by the Marines and the Japanese who fought there. The men assigned to this duty found helmets, bayonets, toilet articles and Japanese pornography.[21] Site cleanup included burial of putrid, dead and animal-scavenged

Japanese soldiers who had been rotting in the tropical climate since July.[22]

During the ground echelon's month-long voyage the weather was fair and the seas gentle, an answer to the prayers of men who had suffered so much during the trip from Funafuti to Oahu. But fair weather ended and rain began soon after the squadron reached Guam. Packing and loading in rain at Funafuti back in December had been unpleasant, but hindsight changes perspectives, and to the men trying to set up a base in the muck on Guam, working in the rain on Funafuti now seemed like a walk in the park.

One of the earliest squadron needs met was construction of a vehicle service depot, so the critically important trucks could be greased, serviced, and kept running.[23] Tent poles and Three Feathers whiskey bottles measured inches of standing muddy water and fresh rainfall every day. Sleep-deprived drivers struggled and slid their unwieldy heavy trucks through rutted, muddy roads, getting stuck, banging into one another, cursing, and then helping pull one another out of the mire. Some days the rain and standing water were so bad that work details were cancelled and the men did little more than sleep.

After a week of unloading and delivering squadron gear, the trucks were put to the task of hauling crushed coral for improving the muddy roadway from the harbor to the air base.[24] Roads in the 11th Bomb Group area remained thick, wheel- and boot-sucking muck because the Air Corps was not equipped for road construction. Progress was made in fits and starts when equipment could be scrounged from the Navy Seabees, who had bulldozers, rollers, a compressor, cement mixer, electricians, wire, prefabricated Quonset huts, plumbers, plus hundreds of men to handle the grunt work for their own base construction, a project that was about a third the size of the air base.[25] But the Seabees were working on their own base construction on Guam, and naturally, coralling roads in Air Corps squadron areas was not on their priority list.

Each night the 42nd showed a movie borrowed from the Seabees, projecting it on an improvised screen made from a mattress cover. Show time varied each night, because the movie didn't begin until the last work detail was finished for the day. Packing crates served as theater seating, and each night, seats were reserved for any Japanese sniper who might like to stop by to see the show.[26]

A passable, coral-paved roadway from the squadron area to Agana town, with the harbor beyond, improved the mood of the drivers and when signs were posted, painted by the industrious Seabees, the place started to look like it was becoming a real military base. Road building would continue for weeks, but for now at least the rain had subsided and base building by the 42nd's ground sections shifted into a higher gear.

Carpentry waited while the lumber dried out and seven and a half million more board-feet of Army Air Force lumber sat in ships in the harbor, unable to unload until storm-damaged dock facilities were repaired.[27] But by the first week of October, the squadron mess halls were coming along. The mess hall for the 42nd was complete by the sixth with screening, tarp coverings, hard packed coral floors and wooden door hinges because metal ones weren't available. The 431st Squadron mess hall was last, held up because two hospital tents brought in for the purpose had been thoroughly sabotaged by hungry rats aboard ship. The 57th Service Group, the outfit that would operate the islands' utilities, medical and firefighting services, financial operations, and motor transport, loaned the squadron a C-47 "Gooney Bird" cargo plane for a flight to Saipan to get two replacement tents.[28]

The 26th, 98th, and 431st remained on Kwajalein where they had been busy bombing Truk for months. In September, like the 42nd, these three squadrons expected to move to Tinian, but after they had already packed, the move orders were cancelled.[29] Wild rumors spread: the transport ships had been wiped out by a typhoon; horrible living conditions on Tinian caused the brass to rethink using the island as a base; Japanese bombers were wreaking havoc on pier facilities in the Marianas.

When new orders for a move to Guam came through, morale soared.[30] The men believed that Guam was better than Tinian, because Guam was bigger, not just another barren little speck of sand. It was a Navy base, which meant that there would be opportunities to barter, beg, borrow, or steal food and supplies from the always well-equipped Navy. Guam's Chamorros population liked Americans, and of course some of the Chamorros were women.

Spirits were already high on Kwajalein because of the Guam orders when, on October 5, a 98th Squadron B-24 returned from a routine training flight to Majuro loaded with 300 ice-cold cases of Primo beer.[31] The plane's crew had apparently been sworn to secrecy about the origin of the beer, giving rise to speculation that there were probably some very angry leathernecks back at Marine Aircraft Group 13's base on Majuro. Some suggested that the 98th was only planning to *borrow* the beer, and the Marines were welcome to have it back as soon as the Air Corps men were finished with it. Whether borrowed or stolen, the 98th wasn't going to let the beer get stale.

By noon on the fifth, word was out. "Beer Bust" notices were posted on squadron bulletin boards and soon officers armed with can openers were doing the honors for the men lined up in front of them. Most of the men drained eight or ten beers, but there was no limit other than each man's capacity to keep returning to the back of the line. Everyone was feeling very good and then the commanding officer of the 11th Bomb Group showed up.[32]

Four strong and happily inebriated men smirked at their commander. "Hey, Colonel! Wanna go for a ride?" And before he could answer, the four burly men lifted Col. Russell Waldron and carried him to the end of the nearest pier.

"One!" the four men shouted, swinging the colonel over the end of the pier. "Two!" the rest of the squadron joined the countdown. "THREE!" and the colonel splashed into the ocean. The game was on and no officer was safe. Once the officers were in the lagoon, the rest of the squadron joined in. With the officers in the drink and no one to guard the beer, whole cases disappeared. Boxes of empty bottles accumulated in the Ordnance Section area for loading on a B-24 for some future strike mission, because beer bottles were fun to dump over Japanese-held islands.[33] The party went on all night and for several nights beyond.

Three hundred cases of beer consumed by a small group of soldiers on a tiny, barren island could have been a recipe for disaster, but there were no casualties. A few men landed in the Kwajalein jail for their attempted invasion of the off-limits building designated Hell's Angels, the Army nurse's quarters. After they sobered up, the men guilty of this alcohol-induced misjudgment suffered more punishment along with the rest of the squadron: heads pounding, dehydrated and sick, they were compelled to load gear and move heavy crates aboard their transport ships, dreadfully hung over.

Before leaving Kwajalein, the three 11th Group squadrons based there were treated to their first look at one of the mighty new Boeing B-29 Superfortress aircraft, a plane that had taken on mythical proportions to them. Seeing the shiny silver monster firsthand amazed the B-24 men, especially when it taxied and parked beside an aging, olive drab Liberator. The sheer size of the new plane, the huge engines and massive four-bladed propellers, the enormous tires, the sleek rounded nose and exotic looking gun placements, the mammoth scale of the Superfortress beside the little old B-24 was incredible.

No sooner had the B-29 parked than its crew bounded out of the plane and a couple of corporals roped off their aircraft and placed a sign in front of it: "No Visitors Allowed."[34] And with that, whatever hospitality the 11th's men were ready to offer the B-29 crew evaporated. The B-24 men glanced at each other, amused by the apparent arrogance of the B-29 crew. The Liberator men walked around the new plane, trying not to act *too* impressed. They kept outside the ropes like patrons considering a freshly installed museum piece while the B-29 crew walked away from the flight line.

The weathered old B-24 parked beside the dazzling new B-29 was *Consolidated Mess*, named for the gigantic mess hall back at Hickam, serving the units based there. *Consolidated Mess* displayed a fat Pacific Islands woman painted on its nose, her black hair pulled back severely, huge sagging brown breasts exposed. She wore a white polka-dotted hula skirt and a broad, gleaming white smile, happily oblivious to how ridiculous she looked.[35] Fate could not have thumbed its nose at the new B-29 any better. *Consolidated Mess* stood in stark contrast to the Superfortress as if the village idiot had wandered up to the queen. The B-24 men made a sign of their own and posted it in front of *Consolidated Mess*: "This is a B-24J *Combat* Airplane. Visitors Welcome!"

The three Kwajalein-based squadrons boarded the transport ship *Cape Mendocino* on October 10 and sailed for Guam six days later in convoy with two submarine chasers and a destroyer escort, reaching Agana's port on the twenty-first.[36] The ground echelons had little time to prepare for the arrival of their flight crews; in fact, the 431st air echelon was ordered to fly to Guam on October 19 while their ground support was still at sea. The crews assumed that the orders were drawn quickly so that 11th Group Liberators from Guam could bomb Yap to prevent Japanese planes based there from harassing General MacArthur's forces as they followed through on his famous promise to return to the Philippines.[37] The ground echelon of the 42nd pulled double duty servicing the 431st's aircraft and helping the 431st's airmen set up temporary quarters.

The 98th's Squadron Dog, Queenie, veteran of Tarawa, made the move to Guam with her most recent offering, two squirming brown puppies born on Kwajalein in late August. Queenie's prolific contribution to the canine population on Kwajalein ended with her relocation to Guam, but surely there are dogs on Kwajalein and Tarawa today who could proudly trace their lineage to her.

Another 98th Squadron four-legged friend may not have survived the move: Porky the pig's history is obscure, but odds are she was an Imperial Japanese Army pig before she became a United States Army pig, and was probably already on Kwajalein when the Americans came ashore. During their occupation of Kwajalein, the Japanese kept livestock there and maintained a pig pen on the atoll's Ebeye Island.[38]

Plans to make Porky the centerpiece at a 98th Squadron luau were discussed as early as May, but Porky wasn't fat enough then. She enjoyed a special feast of her own that month when a carelessly tossed cigarette set fire to a rations tent next to the 98th's mess hall. The tent was ruined, bags filled with beans were scorched beyond salvage, and sacks of sugar were turned into a syrupy mess when the fire was put out. Porky slopped up the sugar sludge and the spilled beans. Watching Porky gorge herself in the aftermath of the fire, one soldier said, "I guess pork and beans go together anyway."[39]

Porky was rumored to have been "confiscated" by Kwajalein's island commander in August, but a reconnaissance patrol proved that Porky was sleeping in her usual spot under the 98th Squadron Mess Hall.[40]

Concern about Porky persisted, however, because she had a risky habit of meandering aimlessly through the squadron area.

Porky fattened herself on mess hall leavings while speculation about finding her name scrawled under the "Missing in Action" heading on the squadron scoreboard increased with her weight.[41] Whether Porky went from under the mess hall to the mess hall menu is unknown, because there is no mention of Porky in the squadron's record after September. There is a mildly suspicious reference to a B-24 arriving on Guam from Oahu in November with "a bomb bay full of ham and fresh fruit," but no indication the plane landed at Kwajalein first, or exactly where the ham was placed on the plane.[42] It's unlikely the 98th herded a fat pig into a landing craft and then onto a troop ship bound for Guam. The men were well aware of the unsettled conditions on Guam and their lack of a mess facility there. Even if they managed to keep Porky away from the merchant seamen and their galley on the *Cape Mendocino* en route, there was a chance they would have to share her with the 42nd since the 42nd had the only completed mess hall in the 11th Group area. It's also unlikely the 98th would have left Porky behind on Kwajalein. If she went down to a feast, it may very well have happened during the wild beer-soaked evening of October 5.

After unloading at the port, the men of the 26th, 98th, and 431st drove through Agana town, the same jarring truck ride the 42nd's ground sections had taken weeks before. Agana's buildings and homes lay in rubble, gutted by the American air assault and naval bombardment that preceded the invasion. The new arrivals saw Agana's people living in bombed-out remnants of their homes and they saw that in spite of the devastation the people looked clean, healthy, and proud.[43] The Americans riding their 11th Bomb Group trucks admired the Chamorros people who had toughed it out so long, and now the Group's bombers would carry on the fight against the Japanese.

There was no timetable for the arrival of supplies by ship, so logistical planning was next to impossible. Work was completed as much according to the tools and supplies available as according to need. It was an hour's drive from the port to the 11th Group area; making the trip daily was the only way to get accurate intelligence on the arrival of ships.

Sanitation was a serious problem because the weather turned open-pit latrines into vile, disease-breeding nastiness. Lectures the men sat through back at Mokuleia about sanitation, insect-borne diseases and the importance of controlling flies didn't take into account Guam's combination of climate, weather, and fly larvae, which were uniquely capable of resisting every effort to exterminate them. Guam's maggots were impervious to insecticides, chemical wastes, and repeated burning with gasoline and kerosene.[44]

Building proper latrines was no easy task because every second or third pit would reach a depth of a few feet and then strike a coral head. Most of the latrines in the 26th and 98th squadron areas had to be dug with the help of an air hammer to break through the coral, and privy construction was slow because lumber was earmarked for other projects. The 42nd's ground echelon lobbied for the dunnage from supply ships, but policy required using it to build and repair things for the Chamorros.[45]

The Army Engineers had their own logistical problems with shipping and supplies while setting up camp for themselves. They were supposed to help build the roads in the 11th Group's camps, but first they'd take care of their own. A bulldozer, one bulldozer, finally arrived on October 15 from the 1885th Engineering Battalion to build all the roads for two Groups, the 11th Bomb Group and the 57th Service Group.[46] Dozer men worked in shifts so it could run twenty-four hours a day. Coral for roadways came from borrow pits dug by the Seabees, and whenever they hit good coral, road work stopped and the coral was trucked to runways and taxi ways under construction.

Every night during the 11th Group's early days on Guam, there was gunfire. It was common knowledge that Japanese soldiers lurked about the island, and guards sometimes got jittery. The neighboring Seabees complained about bullets zipping through their area, so guards were posted in pairs and the shooting dropped off substantially.[47]

The ground sections of the four squadrons of the 11th Bomb Group, the 26th, the 98th, the 42nd and the 431st were hard at work and for the first time in the war, all four squadrons of the group would be together at the same forward base. There was a feeling among the ground crews of the 11th that they were really hitting their stride now. Bringing the combined strength of all four squadrons to bear on the enemy, the spectacle of the grateful Chamorros people in ruined Agana town, and the sight of B-24 Superfortresses with their massive bomb loads and the range to hit Japan said more to inspire the men than any officer's motivational talk ever could.

The old timers in the ground echelon sensed that the move to Guam would be their last before getting home. There was electric talk about new rules coming out, rules about furloughs and reassignments, and the rumors were confirmed when Lt. Frank Angel landed his B-24 *Umbriago!* on Guam on October 12, ferrying some of the ground echelon officers from Mokuleia. He brought copies of orders sending men with forty-five months' service in the Pacific Ocean Area to the 13th Replacement Pool on Oahu, and from there, these happy soldiers would be reassigned to the States.[48]

The new rules also changed the game for the aircrews still on Oahu, waiting for their base on Guam to be ready. When they went overseas in 1943, Lt. Joe Deasy and his new crew were anxious to get into combat, finish thirty missions, get medals, and go home. Somewhere along the line the number of missions was raised to thirty-five, but Sergeant Scearce and his buddies hardly noticed because they weren't flying combat missions anyway. Now the number was increased to forty, but it just didn't matter to Scearce. With only six strike mission credits in the twenty months since that flight from California to Hawaii, the last one almost a year before, Scearce figured that forty may as well be one hundred. He had no way to know that the pace would quicken very soon.

Chapter 18

Back in Business

THIRTY MILES EAST OF OAHU, a twin-engined B-25 Mitchell bomber towing a gunnery target entered airspace designated A-9 at 4,000 feet. Fifteen minutes later, three 42nd Bomb Squadron B-24s arrived in a V formation with Lt. Keeton Rhoades flying lead. Number two was 2nd Lt. Robert Davis and the third Liberator was piloted by Lt. Thomas Reale.

Reale was Capt. Jesse Stay's pick for co-pilot back in June when the new squadron commander decided to keep an aircrew of his own. Sgt. Herman Scearce was pleased to be on that crew as radio man because he had worried about getting stuck with a green pilot. Scearce was confident in the crew because Lieutenant Reale and the rest of the men were also hand-picked by Captain Stay. Since then, Lieutenant Reale had transitioned from co-pilot to first pilot, so Reale was in the left seat of the number three aircraft when the formation's gunners opened fire on the target towed by the B-25.

For the next half hour the three B-24 crews practiced formation gunnery on the towed target, but then Reale's plane began to turn out of formation to the right, away from the other two bombers. Davis saw Reale break formation but he had to keep his eye on the lead aircraft in order to hold his position. Rhoades, flying lead, saw Reale's plane bank away, trailing smoke.

In the barracks at Mokuleia, Scearce and Yankus looked for fresh victims to challenge to a game of pinochle. Since the squadron's ground crews were building a base on Guam, opponents had to be recruited from among aircrews, and it was hard to find players who weren't wise to Scearce and Yankus' subtle but effective cross-table communication tricks.

Joe Hyson was half asleep on his bunk when Jack Yankus leaned over, grinning, trying to see just how close he could get to Hyson's face before Hyson realized he was there. At half an inch, Yankus couldn't contain himself anymore and he snickered.

"Jesus, Jack! You scared the hell out of me!"

"You ought to be paying better attention," Yankus said. "We're s'posed to be on alert."

"Can't a guy get a little sack time around here?"

"Pinochle?" Scearce asked, holding up the deck of cards.

"I guess. Damn sure can't get to sleep now, bunch o' clowns," Hyson said. "Let me see if Farrell's around."

Hyson nearly collided with Bill Farrell as Farrell rushed inside.

"Damn, Bill! If Yank's not in my face you are! What's the hurry?"

"Gotta get my billfold. Eddie's takin' bets on whether the gate guard—the scrawny one?—can swig a pint o' liquor."

"Forget that and play pinochle with us."

"One of 'em drank a coupl'a shots out of it and filled it back up with tobacco juice, he and his boys don't know it. Come on guys, I want to see if he can do it. Says he can but he can't puke, either."

"That's dumber'n hell," Yankus said.

"Well, let's all go watch and then we'll play pinochle," Scearce said.

Farrell grabbed his billfold and rushed out the door, the other three followed.

A noisy mob crowded the latrine when Scearce, Hyson, and Yankus arrived. Bill Farrell was already up front where Ed Hess recorded bets on a little black note pad.

"He's gotta drink it all, he can't let it run down . . . an' he can't throw up."

The scrawny infantry guard looked like a flyweight fighter about to take the ring, pressing one fist and then the other into his hands and shifting his weight from side to side, staring straight ahead. Men betting with him gave him advice. "Deep breaths . . . turn it up quick and swallow steady . . . don't think about it . . ."

"Hold my shirt," the gate guard said. ". . . and my watch."

"He's gonna puke!"

"He ain't gonna puke, now shut the hell up," said a supporter.

"Both of ya shut the hell up and let him drink," Yankus replied.

"You boys want in?" Hess asked.

"No, just lookin'," Scearce said.

Hess nodded to the man holding the bottle and he held it up for all to see before unscrewing the cap. He handed the bottle to the gate guard. The gate guard took a long, deep breath, held it for a moment, then exhaled quickly and threw his head back, eyes squeezed shut, the bottle pressed to his lips.

Thirty miles off the coast, 42nd Squadron Flight Surgeon Capt. Woodie Hazel was a passenger on Lieutenant Reale's plane. He watched the right waist gunner firing on the target when suddenly an oxygen bottle mounted in the fuselage above him exploded. He smelled the pungent odor of burning wires and saw smoke rapidly filling the bomb bay ahead of him. Corp. Robert Saas, the flight engineer, hurried through the murky bomb bay as if he was looking for something. Just before Captain Hazel pulled his interphone headset off, he heard somebody say, "Take it easy, Saas."

Lieutenant Reale, his face covered with blood, appeared for just a moment in the opening between the smoke-filled bomb bay and the rear. He shouted, "Get the hell out of here!"

Hazel helped radio operator Sgt. Harold Martin bail out of the right waist window and saw Pvt. Carmen Rodriguez pull himself from the belly turret and head toward the rear of the airplane. Rodriguez didn't have a parachute. Hazel stepped on the gun mount to follow Martin out the right window and flames reaching from the bomb bay scorched his left hand as he jumped.

Staff Sergeant Stanley Chodkowski was at the left waist gun when the oxygen bottle blew. Looking forward, he saw flames under the flight deck where the auxiliary power unit, the putt-putt, was mounted. Smoke poured toward the rear when Lieutenant Reale came through and yelled for them to get the hell out. Chodkowski wanted to grab Reale and force him through the left window but decided against it when he saw that his pilot wasn't wearing a parachute. Chodkowski bailed out.

Corp. Thomas Hughes, the tow plane's target winch operator, saw four parachutes in the air as Reale's airplane banked and descended toward the water. The B-25 radio operator, Sgt. Harold Lawton, saw at least six, maybe eight. Lawton told his pilot, "Eight men got out."

Reale's bomber stayed in one piece as it nosed over, dropping fast through one thousand feet. At that point anyone left aboard risked having too little altitude for a parachute to open and heat from the fire on the flight deck caused the controls to stop responding at all. If Lawton was right and eight men got out, two were still in the burning plane.

Lieutenant Reale's B-24 exploded on impact with the water. The other three planes circled the area, dropped rafts, and contacted Mokuleia to request rescue service. Sergeant Lawson thought he saw four rafts in the water with at least one man in each raft, but he never saw all four rafts at the same time.

⇉⇇

The flyweight gate guard swallowed hard once, gagged, and coughed whiskey onto his undershirt and pants, prompting guffaws from most of the men in the latrine.

"That shit's got piss in it! Somebody pissed in it!"

"Nobody pissed in it," Hess said.

"Well it's got somethin' in it! It ain't right!"

One of the flyweight's corner men said, "Let me have that," and he took the bottle, sniffed it, held it up to the light and then put it to his lips for a taste. He was about to accuse the organizers of the betting pool of sabotage when another man stepped in to the latrine.

"Somebody's in the drink."

"What are you talking about?"

"The tow plane's comin' back to get more rafts. Somebody flyin' gunnery went into the drink."

"Bets are off, boys, show's over," Hess said, and he flipped his notebook shut. The crowd left the latrine with the gate guard still swishing water, cursing, and spitting into a sink. A few of the men headed toward the flight line. Scearce and his three barracks mates walked back to their building, quietly trying to remember who they knew who was flying that day. Back at the barracks, the men settled into chairs and Yankus absentmindedly shuffled the cards, but no one wanted to play.

Sea Rescue Control organized a search for Lt. Thomas Reale's crew. On the day of the crash and for two days following, aircraft from Seventh Fighter Command and Seventh Bomber Command covered the area. The Navy searched with fighter planes and surface vessels, including crash rescue boats, a sub chaser, a PT boat, and a destroyer. Captain Hazel, Sergeant Martin, and Sergeant Chodkowski were rescued on the first day. Day two of the search was fruitless and rescue efforts were called off after the third day.[1] Sergeant Lawton was mistaken: only three got out of the plane.

Among the dead was Pvt. Carmen Rodriguez, the belly turret gunner last seen by Captain Hazel moving toward the rear of the burning plane. Sgt. George Ebinger, assistant flight engineer, was also killed. Just the month before, Rodriguez was on Lt. Keeton Rhoades' crew and Ebinger was with Lt. Robert Davis' crew.[2] Their reassignment took them from the two aircrews witnessing the crash and placed them instead among the seven men who died in the ill-fated third plane.

Herman Scearce was mid-stroke pulling a carbon steel razor blade across his neck when a voice said, "Are you Herman Scearce?"

Scearce stopped shaving and glanced in the mirror at the man behind him. The man wore a Red Cross uniform with creased khaki pants, a neatly pressed shirt, and tie. "Yes, I'm Herman Scearce." The radio man bent toward the sink and pressed a hot, wet towel into his face. He turned toward his visitor and reached for his uniform shirt. "I'm done in here," he said. The two men walked out of the latrine and Scearce asked, "What's the Red Cross want with me?"

"Your mother and your sister said they hardly ever hear from you, Herman."

"That's why you came to see me, 'cause I don't write home?"

"I guess they're worried about you. We told 'em we'd check on you."

Scearce and the Red Cross man walked toward the barracks. Scearce eyed the olive green '40 Ford sedan parked next to the wooden building.

"You know, I got nothing against you personally. But you guys are crawling all over the place here on Oahu. You drive around in your staff cars with your girlfriends . . . but down in the combat zone, if somebody needs help writing a letter or getting an emergency furlough, there ain't a Red Cross man anywhere to be found."

The man didn't reply. Scearce stepped toward the barracks door and said, "I'll write home when I've got something to write home about."[3]

There was no way to know what caused the fire that brought Lieutenant Reale's plane down. It couldn't have helped that most of the squadron's ground crew and maintenance men were already at Guam. Engine changes, required every 200 hours, were a top priority and nine mechanics were on Detached Service to Wheeler Field where engine changes were performed, leaving just one man per airplane at Mokuleia for regular maintenance. Every ground section was shorthanded on Mokuleia, even the ordnance section. Ordnance had to borrow labor from Wheeler just to fill sand bombs for practice missions.[4]

The squadron flew more than three hundred training missions in September alone.[5] The pace didn't slow just because most of the ground support was gone or because a plane went down.

When Lt. Frank Angel returned to Mokuleia from a ferry mission to Guam his crew shared stories about the situation there. The 42nd's men still at Mokuleia heard about the rain, the muck, bad roads, and Japanese soldiers skulking around Guam, but it didn't matter. They wanted to move forward, anxious for a break in the routine, and Guam was almost ready to receive them. Since his deployment to Guam was imminent, Scearce parted with his '32 Packard, selling it to a soldier in another squadron for the same four hundred dollars that he had paid to the Army officer who owned it before.

On Guam, aircraft parking areas were a point of contention as the airfield neared completion. The 11th Bomb Group didn't have enough hardstands, paved parking areas for aircraft, set aside for all its planes; just twenty were designated for all four squadrons. The remaining planes would have to be parked and serviced on taxi ways unless plans were modified to make continuous hardstands rather than individual spaces with unpaved areas in between.[6]

While the advanced echelon worked on the aircraft parking problem, the main road from the port to the 11th Bomb Group area was almost finished. The last loads of coral for the main road were hauled while the first four bombers of the 42nd were en route to Guam, scheduled to arrive October 22. Scearce was with that first flight of four B-24s, riding along with Yankus and Lt. Jordan Churchill's crew for the three-day flight aboard a B-24 named *WRFTF.*[7]

When those first four planes took off from Mokuleia, each one was overloaded with equipment and supplies bound for Guam. Scearce breathed a sigh of relief just getting airborne on take-off; Lt. George Smith's crash trying to take off overloaded on a photo-recon mission from Kualoa was still a vivid memory. Churchill banked and buzzed the Mokuleia airfield at about 500 feet, a dangerous stunt as far as Scearce was concerned, but he figured the pilots were glad to be leaving.

Four and a half hours out of Oahu the bombers reached Johnston Island. After spending the night of the nineteenth at Johnston they flew nine and a quarter hours to Kwajalein, and on the third day took eight hours, forty minutes to finally reach Guam. Since they crossed the International Date Line on the second day, they arrived on the twenty-second. Lt. Phil Kroh landed first and taxied aircraft #662 to a stop, stuck his head out the sliding cockpit window, headset askew, and smiled for the ground crew's cameras. Churchill landed next in *WRFTF*.

Lt. Robert Davis' B-24 needed minor repairs before take-off from Kwajalein on October 21. The plane was fully loaded with fuel and ready for the third leg of the trip, but the last-minute repair work created a short circuit in the fuel transfer system. The short circuit caused fuel that had leaked into the bomb bay to ignite and there was little the crew could do except get away from the plane quickly and watch it burn. Fire consumed the plane completely, taking with it navigation maps, all the records of the Ordnance Department, Plexiglas turrets for radar antennae, three crates of fresh eggs, 600 pounds of potatoes, and three cases of beer.[8] Davis and his crew had seen Lieutenant Reale's plane go down in flames and they were profoundly relieved that their fire, if there had to be one, happened on the ground.

The dome-shaped radar antenna turrets were covers for the antenna on the newer SCR- 717 radar equipment, designed to be lowered into the slipstream from the aircraft's nose by a hydraulic hand pump when the radar was needed. The squadron's Radar Section was in bad enough shape on Guam, even without the loss of the Plexiglas turrets. Radar gear hadn't been stored properly in the supply area, allowing the relentless rain to soak several cases of equipment. It took a week of cleaning and drying to get just one radar set working.[9]

2nd Lt. Jack Henry was the B-25 tow plane pilot on September 12, the day Lieutenant Reale crashed thirty miles off Mokuleia. He was the pilot whose radio operator was sure that eight men had escaped from the falling B-24 and he was the pilot who had returned to Mokuleia to take on more rafts and rush them back to the scene. A month after Reale's crash, Henry became a B-24 first pilot with a crew of his own, and ten days later he was flying the Johnston-to-Kwajalein leg of the trip to Guam when his Liberator's fuel supply ran dangerously low.[10] Quick calculations between pilot, navigator, and engineer concluded that they weren't going to make it to Kwajalein at the rate they were using fuel. Visions of Lieutenant Reale's violent crash must have played in Lieutenant Henry's mind as he ordered the crew to lighten the load.

Spare parts went out the waist window. A beautiful new radio built into a cherry cabinet intended for the Officer's Club on Guam was dropped through the bomb bay. A second radio meant for the enlisted men's club was next. The second radio was purchased with money contributed by dozens of men; tossing the officer's club radio somehow didn't hurt quite as much. Technical Sergeant William Ellis' tools were thrown out, a one of a kind collection of radar maintenance tools he had carefully accumulated over the course of a year and a half and might never be able to replace.[11] Once again, the radar section suffered.

Lieutenant Henry's fuel situation remained critical, but the indicated level didn't drop lower. The crew sweated out the last hours of the trip until they sighted Kwajalein and finally touched down on the coral airstrip. Once the plane was parked, the flight engineer stepped onto the wing and checked the fuel supply: three hundred gallons remained. The fuel level indicators were wrong and the plane had never been in danger.

When the 11th's aircrews arrived on Guam, a barter system economy developed quickly and trade was brisk because the airmen had something the Marines wanted, and Marines guarded Navy supplies of things the airmen wanted. The system wouldn't have worked and the airmen would have had no bartering leverage at all if it had been easy for the Marines to get liquor on Guam. Aircrew officers got a fifth of Three Feathers every week, the benefit of being in the Locker Club back on Oahu, and officers often gave their bottles to the men. Well-connected enlisted men prospered in the economy and flights to and from Hawaii kept the liquor supply from running out.

Scearce and Hess borrowed a 2 1/2-ton truck and drove out to a Marine Corps supply depot, Hess downshifting as the truck bounced up to the Marine guard. The guard was supposed to check approved requisitions before allowing anyone access to the depot.

"How ya doin'?" Hess bellowed.

"Fine, sir. Do you have . . ."

"We'd like a few sheets of that plywood over there," Hess interrupted. Scearce displayed several bottles of Air Corps liquor, sort of fanned them out on his lap from the passenger side of the truck.

The Marine looked over his shoulder, then reached into the truck and grabbed the bottles.

"Do it quick," said the Marine.

"Nice doin' business with ya," Hess replied.

The Marine guard walked away. Hess backed up to the stacked plywood with the truck angled just right so that even if the guard looked, the truck would block his view while the airmen worked. Without a word Scearce and Hess threw back a tarp covering the plywood and Hess kicked the edge of the top sheet to knock it a few inches askew of the stack beneath. The men lifted the top sheet, slid it into the back of the truck, and dropped the end of the sheet to the truck bed. Kick, lift, slide, and drop, kick, lift, slide, and drop. Each sheet made a *shoof* sound as it slid forward into the truck and a *whoomp* as it dropped onto the stack that quickly grew larger than the stack on the ground.

Scearce leaned back and glanced past the truck toward the guard.

"He looks worried."

"Just keep goin'," Hess replied.

Both men's backs were sweaty wet, hands getting raw, but Scearce thought that loading a stovewood truck back in Danville had never been so much fun. When the entire stack of plywood was in the truck, Hess said, "Let's go!" and both airmen hopped into the cab and slammed the doors. The Marine guard walked briskly toward them, leaning, craning his neck to look past the truck when Hess gunned it away from the damp spot where the plywood stack had been. The airmen saw the Marine start to raise his hand and they could tell he was yelling something but they couldn't make it out over the roar of the truck engine.

"He looks pissed!"

"What's he sayin'?" Hess asked.

"I think he's saying he's gonna need a new job in the Air Corps!"

"We shoulda taken the tarp, too," Hess said.

"We got tarps, Eddie."

"Yeah, but he ain't usin' that one!"

Scearce and Hess laughed all the way back to their crew area. They floored their tent with plywood sheets, stacked the rest, and the enlisted men of the 42nd Squadron Commander's crew became the first in the area with a floored tent. They were quickly the envy of other crews. Men came by just to see the floor.

"Where'd you get that?"

"Supply requisition."

"What d'ya want for it?"

A couple bottles of liquor would buy enough plywood to floor one crew's tent. Scearce and Hess were in business, and the double digit inflation involved in the deal made them rich. But as fine as the wood floors were, aircrew tent interior furnishings were not complete. They had cots and blankets, but they didn't have mattresses.

Bomber crewmen discovered something that the ground echelon learned weeks before: Navy Seabees were a good bunch to know. Supplies the Seabees held seemed fantastic, sometimes exotic to airmen. Rumor had it that a particular Seabee supply hut was stacked floor to ceiling with Navy mattresses, but business with them could be challenging, like dealing with Mafiosi. Scearce was never sure if it was a matter of who's got the authority, who's got the keys, or just a question of the Seabees having to mull it over a while first.

When Scearce and Hyson took a truck to trade with the Seabees at the rumored mattress hut, they had to talk to two or three guys before finding someone willing to deal. "Geez, I don't know . . ." The burly Navy man rubbed his chin. "You gotta talk to the chief . . . you gotta talk to Tony."

"That's fine, where's Tony?" Scearce asked.

"I don't know . . . hey Bobby, you know where Tony is? No? Look guys, you find Tony. Tony can get you what you want."

"It ain't locked, boss," the Seabee named Bobby said.

"Oh? Well, hey, what the hell, flyboys, today's yer lucky day!"

Hyson and Scearce became instantly popular when they showed up in the squadron area with a truck load of a dozen mattresses. Bidding started before the truck stopped, but these mattresses weren't for sale. Scearce and Hyson stopped first at the tent occupied by Hyson and the rest of the enlisted men on Charlie Pratte's crew and unloaded six. The rest went into the enlisted tent quarters of the men on Jesse Stay's crew.

One of the new mattresses went to a replacement gunner on Charlie Pratte's crew, because waist gunner Sgt. Bill Findle had been grounded and sent home. His crewmates had seen Findle become easily tired and indecisive; they weren't sure they could rely on him to react quickly in combat and they became increasingly reluctant to fly with him. For the crew's sake and his, the flight surgeon agreed Sergeant Findle was no longer fit for duty.[12]

Findle was one of the men who attached a parachute to a gun mount in the waist of *Belle of Texas* in December '43, one of the men who miraculously escaped that mission without as much as a scratch while their plane was riddled by hundreds of bullet and flak holes. On the same mission he witnessed the death of *Dogpatch Express*, saw the bloody, blown-out top turret and after the crash saw Zeros mercilessly strafing survivors struggling in the water. He went with Scearce and Yankus back to Tarawa to fly *Belle of Texas*, renamed *Patches*, back to Hickam after CASU-16 finished repairs, and while at Tarawa he endured nightly bombings and threats of invasion while waiting for the plane to be ready.

Sergeant Findle's missions sent him through flak, unpredictable, sometimes heavy, sometimes light, sometimes accurate, sometimes too high or too wide, and the not knowing on approach to the target twisted men's stomachs with anxiety. Airmen were taught that "black puffs in the sky are spent shells . . . they're harmless."[13] But the black puffs warned of more shells hurtling skyward, unseen and deadly. Gunners would rather face a determined and aggressive Zero pilot than flak because they could fight back against the Zero; they could shoot him down. There was nothing to do about flak except hope it would miss and wish it was over.

Any of these experiences, or the sum of them all, might have caused Sgt. Bill Findle's fade away from combat readiness.

Besides pursuing creature comforts like wood floors and mattresses, there was a constant quest among aircrews to get something to eat, something better than C-rations, better than what the mess hall had, or just better than what the guys in the next tent had. It was a fact of life wherever they were in the combat zone, from Funafuti to Guam, and access to a jeep made the quest much more productive.

The jeep was a benefit of being on the squadron commander's crew. When Captain Stay didn't need it, Scearce borrowed it, and Scearce and Hyson spent down time exploring the island just to see what they might find. They agreed that if they came across a Japanese soldier, they would turn around and haul ass back to base.

Instead of an enemy soldier, on one particular evening they found a U.S. Marine smoking a cigarette in front of a Navy refrigeration unit. After some quick negotiations the Marine surrendered a large and tightly wrapped package of beef in exchange for two fifths of whiskey.

Scearce and Hyson were so thrilled to have real meat that they barged into the squadron cook's tent and woke him up.

"Missouri!"

"Whadd'ya want?"

"Missouri, we got some real beef! Come cook it for us! You can have some of it, too!"

Missouri was a good natured guy and a very good cook. Scearce and Hyson may have known his real name at some point, but everyone called him Missouri because that's where he was from. A wonderful aroma filled the air as Missouri cooked the meat, and there was enough for the enlisted men of Jesse Stay's crew, Charlie Pratte's crew, Missouri, and Missouri's cook's assistant. The men were tempted to charge admission to the jealous men who gathered to watch the production, so much to watch, so much to stand close and breathe in the mouth-watering smell of the meat as it cooked. The crewmen and the cooks ate and slept very well that night.

The base came together quickly after the aircrews reached Guam. Airmen pitched in extra labor to get the place in shape, and soon the surroundings looked very civilized, much better than the situation on tiny Funafuti. Sturdy wood frame huts were built to replace the tents, huts with raised floors and screened sides with canvas covers that rolled up. Each crew tried to outdo the others to make their huts homes. They built wood scrap fences enclosing little private yards set with packing crate lawn furniture. They lined sidewalk pathways with rocks and coral and landscaped with native plants. The Transportation Section named roads after streets back in the States, some famous and others from their home towns. They posted signs pointing the direction and mileage to Honolulu, New York City, and Tokyo.

Occasionally a plane would make the trip to Hawaii to pick up parts or ferry someone from the forward area. When a 42nd Squadron plane was making the trip, Scearce and his buddies pooled their money and placed an order, typically Campbell's soup, six cases: half chicken noodle and half tomato. They met the plane when it landed after its 4000-mile grocery run, loaded their canned soup in the back of the squadron commander's jeep, and hauled it to their crew area. They heated the soup over a simple stove made from a salvaged bean can from the mess hall. After filling the gallon-sized can about three quarters up with sand, all that remained was to pour in a liberal amount of kerosene, lean back, and light it. The men poured their soup into their GI mess kits, heated it over their bean-can stoves and soon it was hot and ready to eat.

Mail call was a big deal for a lot of guys. Mail wasn't delivered every day and complaints got louder every day that passed without it. There were men who were crushed if they didn't get a letter, at least one, every time.

The Red Cross visit hadn't changed the fact that Scearce rarely wrote to anyone, so he had no reason to expect mail. He got letters once every couple of months, and when he did, someone just dropped the letter on his cot. Scearce's letters were from his sister Hazel, usually, and once in a while there was a letter from his mother. A letter from his father was especially rare.

There was nothing encouraging in Scearce's letters from home. His mother or his sister complained about their jobs, complained that they couldn't get meat, couldn't get sugar. They always closed by saying they hoped he was all right, when in most ways he thought he was better off. He read these occasional letters while resting on his cot and for a moment he would feel the same indifference that had made it easy for him to leave home in the first place.

"The Moldy Fig" made its appearance in November. "The Moldy Fig" was a single-sheet newspaper, posted daily or almost every day, dealing with gossip and rumors. A loyal following developed quickly, and when the editor was knocked out of commission with dengue fever, he had a steady stream of well-wishers.[14] Island Command posted regulations about wearing proper uniforms; undershirts and trousers weren't good enough anymore. With the newspaper and the uniform regulations, some of the men thought the place was getting too civilized.

The finest buildings in the 11th Group area were among the last to be built: large Quonset huts with concrete floors. A Quonset hut was set up for the Radar Section, which had suffered so much in the rain during the preceding weeks. The Orderly Room got a Quonset hut. Intelligence shared another one with Headquarters, and soon the men would get one for an Enlisted Men's Day Room.

Another concrete-floored Quonset hut became the mission briefing room, with three rows of fifteen wooden benches separated by two aisles in between. There was a stage in front and ten electric light fixtures hung in two rows of five down the length of the hut.

The 11th Group's crest hung high over the stage. At top was a wooden banner in a wide, golden arc which read, "11th Bombardment Group (H)." Beneath the crest's banner were four smaller signs, one for each of the four squadrons, together now for the first time. The smaller signs were in numerical order: "26th Bombardment Squadron"; "42nd Bombardment Squadron"; "98th Bombardment Squadron"; and "431st Bombardment Squadron."

The crest's shield was blue crossed by a wide gold diagonal band, and on the gold band were three grey geese flying in echelon, wings on the down beat. Beneath the crest five wooden bomb profiles hung, each one commemorating the 11th Group's campaigns from the earliest weeks of the war, the topmost one dating back to the days the Group flew B-17 Flying Fortresses and Herman Scearce was a raw new recruit worried that the Army might find out he was just sixteen and send him home to his mother. The hanging bomb profiles were stenciled "Guadal-canal," "Northern Solomons," "Central Pacific Campaign," "Mandated Island Campaign," and the most recent one read "Japan Campaign Air Offensive."[15]

The Quonset hut mission briefing room served as a chapel, a concert hall, and a classroom, but there was no doubt about the building's main purpose. Whenever Scearce was there, an easel stood at center stage supporting a strategic bombing map of Iwo Jima.

Chapter 19

Halfway to Forty

BING CROSBY WAS ONE OF THE most popular performers among men in the service.[1] His radio broadcasts raised morale and inspired Americans at home and overseas. He often broadcast his *Kraft Music Hall* radio show from military bases across the United States, and during his shows, Bing talked to America about rationing plans, helped people understand them, and won their support. He toured with war bond drives and traveled to the front to sing for American troops. Bing performed songs written especially for branches of service and sometimes certain units, and while two fine new radios intended for the 42nd Squadron's Officers Club and Enlisted Men's Day Room lay at the bottom of the Pacific Ocean, Bing broadcast a song saluting the Seventh Air Force.

The song was rough, and Bing said so just before singing it.[2] The song described unbounded death and destruction rained upon the Japanese by the Seventh Air Force. The lyrics were written the day before recording for the broadcast, so it was quick and unpolished, but the men of the Seventh who were lucky enough to hear it were thrilled.

"Seventh Air Force Tribute" was not intended for commercial sale, but it was cut into a disc from the broadcast recording. Without the record, many aircrew and ground support men of the Seventh would never have heard the song. It was a hit when it reached Guam, and each unit altered the song's lyrics, replacing references to the Seventh Air Force with their own squadron number.

—≡≡⦓—

Six days after reaching Guam, Scearce flew with Captain Stay and eleven other Liberator crews to hit the Japanese airfield at Colonia on the island of Yap. A ship from the 98th dropped its bombs in the water because of a bad bombsight adjustment, but the remaining eleven B-24s had no trouble hitting the target. Ten planes struck the runway with frag clusters and General Purpose bombs while Captain Stay's plane dropped six 500-pound bombs on the anti-aircraft battery just north of the airfield. Most bombing results were obscured by clouds, but the string of bombs across the anti-aircraft gun emplacement was confirmed. The Japanese response was weak with inaccurate anti-aircraft fire, just thirty-six black flak bursts and there were no enemy aircraft at all.[3]

On touch down at Guam, Captain Stay's plane blew a hydraulic hose on the right landing gear. From his window at the radio operator's table Scearce saw the brownish fluid run down the strut onto the right main wheel and watched as the wheel splattered a dark streak on the underside of the wing. With the hydraulics out, the brakes were gone, a serious problem if they had been on a short runway. But at Guam's Agana airfield the plane just rolled long until it slowed and Captain Stay carefully taxied it to a hardstand to park.

This October 28, 1944, strike mission, six hours, twenty-five minutes from take-off to touch down, was the shortest bombing mission Scearce would fly, and it was his only mission to Yap. It had been a long eleven months since Scearce's last strike mission, but now he had seven.

Orders awarding the unit Good Conduct Medals, which were dated August 5, 1944, finally caught up with the squadron after they reached Guam. Headquarters also posted orders dated September 10, 1944, awarding Second Bronze Oak Leaf Cluster to Air Medals to some men and Third Bronze Oak Leaf Clusters to others. Oak Leaf Clusters were awarded to men who already had the medal but earned the decoration a second or third time, men like Sergeant Scearce, originally awarded the Air Medal on May 7, 1943. The order cited "meritorious achievement while participating in aerial flights over enemy controlled territory during the period 17 April 1943 to 24 April 1943." The Air Medal order listed everyone on Joe Deasy's original crew along with others who had been in action on those dates, the very first strike missions flown by the 11th Group's Liberators, flying from Funafuti to Nauru.

These medals didn't mean a lot to the men who had been around a while. Just being there, following orders, and simply surviving seemed to be the key to receiving them. Harold Brooks, Scearce's buddy killed on the April 1943 mission to Nauru, never got his Air Medal.

There were a few decorations that meant something to all the men, however, no matter how long they had been around. The Distinguished Flying Cross was one. Distinguished Flying Crosses weren't handed out for good conduct or for just showing up, and they weren't awarded for routine missions. In October 1944 the 42nd Squadron got a tough new assignment that would require a lot of missions, none of them routine, and dozens of Distinguished Flying Cross medals would be struck for the airmen flying these missions.

The men resented the dangerous new assignment. The missions, code-named MIKE, involved low-altitude flying when every man knew that altitude was safety; altitude bought time if something went wrong. Bombardiers, trained to aim at objects they wanted to hit, had to learn a new procedure because MIKE missions used indistinct bomb-release points, timed so many seconds after passing a certain place at a given altitude and airspeed in order to place the ordnance on a featureless target. Crews flying MIKE missions from Guam had to hop first to

Saipan where the special ordnance was loaded, an extra take-off and landing each time.[4]

MIKE missions sent the bombers directly over Japanese-held harbors and shipping, risky business at any altitude but especially flying low. The airmen's respect for ship's gunners was so great that they even flew out of their way to avoid American ships, just on the chance the bombers might be mistaken for enemy. The material construction of the ordnance, heavy at one and two thousand pounds but also fragile, required each device to be dropped not only from low altitude but also at airspeeds under 200 knots, compounding the problem of overflying ships by forcing the bombers to reduce speed. But the bitterest complaint about MIKE missions was the universal sentiment that this was the Navy's problem and the Navy ought to handle it.[5] MIKE missions were anti-shipping, mine-laying missions.

Chichi Jima, Haha Jima, and Ani Jima's natural harbors were critical to the Japanese garrison defending Iwo Jima because Iwo Jima had no harbor of its own. Iwo's lack of fresh water and its poor volcanic ash soil made the garrison's reliance on supply shipments almost absolute. The Japanese shipped supplies primarily to Chichi Jima where they were transferred to smaller vessels for the 150-mile trip over to Iwo. Mines placed in the harbor would sink supply ships and weaken the Iwo Jima garrison by depriving them of water, food, medicine, construction materials, guns, ammunition, and replacement troops.

Strike mission planners studied each enemy-held island, mapped its features, plotted bomb runs and designed release trajectories so that an aircraft flying a given heading and speed, after passing an identifiable feature, could put bombs on target. B-24 Liberators, designed for high altitude strategic bombing, instead cruised over the ocean on a heading meant to deceive Japanese spotters in the lower Volcano Islands. Once past the Volcanos, MIKE mission planes dropped altitude and turned for the run in to the target. Reaching the target island, the Liberators rose just enough to clear the island's land mass and the lead bombardier counted the seconds after passing a certain point on the shore line before releasing mines at specific intervals. As soon as the harbor came into view, waist and turret gunners aimed their machine guns low to sweep the harbor and shipping with bullets to suppress anti-aircraft fire while Japanese gunners on ships below and in gun emplacements on land shot at the American planes. As soon as the mines were away the Liberator pilots throttled up and dropped altitude again, pulling away at top speed just above the chop of the ocean to get away from the island as quickly as possible.

The 42nd got the MIKE project because their exhaustive training back on Oahu made them well suited for the job. New bombing techniques the squadron pioneered during their months in Hawaii, including radar bombing procedures that Sgt. Herman Scearce helped develop, prepared the squadron well for the new assignment. Sharpened skill and uncommon flexibility and creativity in getting ordnance on target moved the 42nd from the Group's rear on Hawaii to the leading edge of bomber operations.

The first MIKE mission was November 6, 1944, a seven-plane raid to Ani Jima carrying massive 2,000-pound mines, each one charged with 1,274 pounds of TNT. During pre-flight briefing, crewmen studied detailed photos and maps of the target area and bombardiers memorized mine release orders. On November 5, the seven aircraft, led by Capt. Jesse Stay, flew to Saipan where ground crews removed the conventional bomb racks from the bays and installed special racks for the mines. They also removed belly turrets to reduce weight for the flight the next day, and while the ground crews worked, Captain Stay's radio operator and flight engineer had a few hours to kill.

Scearce and Yankus, assigned to Stay's crew for the mission, approached a parked B-29 Superfortress where another man was tinkering with radio equipment. They chatted with the man, a corporal, and talked their way into a walk-through of the plane. It was impressive; the two friends figured Uncle Sam could have made two B-24s out of each B-29. Their tour guide for the walk-through revealed that he was the radio operator on the B-29, which the two B-24 Technical Sergeants thought was odd.

Yankus was blunt: "How come you're just a corporal?"

"If you were lucky enough to be on a B-29 crew, rank wouldn't matter to you," the tour guide replied.

"Really? Oh, okay. We didn't realize that," Yankus said, and the two B-24 men shared a furtive glance and a wink and left their new friend with his pride intact.

The rivalry between B-24 and B-29 crewmen was good natured, generally, but B-24 men felt pushed aside by B-29 operations. After all, the B-24 crews were the ones who'd been fighting their way up the Pacific since '43; they were the ones who had helped get the B-29s close enough to hit Japan and B-24 men thought the B-29 guys ought to be grateful. Instead, B-24 men got the impression that B-29 crews looked down their noses at B-24s and didn't like Liberators operating near their planes, "like we might get one of them dirty," Scearce thought.

The seven crews spent the night at Saipan, their aircraft ready for the next day's mission. Squadron Commander Jesse Stay felt the burden of responsibility for the air strike, well aware that the outcome had implications far beyond just one mission. Failure to place the mines on target or losses from low-altitude operations could hurt his men's morale and commitment, and might jeopardize the entire project.

Captain Stay took off first and the other six planes followed him, forming up on their leader for the five and a half hour flight, radios silent. Bombardiers mentally reviewed their instructions; gunners watched the sky for Japanese planes. The flight out was uneventful, routine except for the altitude and the strange ordnance shackled in the Liberator's bomb bays.

The seven planes approached the target in formation, diving toward their release point over the anchorage. Ani Jima's Japanese defenders were caught by surprise; anti-aircraft gun batteries opened up too late and the Liberators were already past the release point, speeding away. The mission was uneventful, the mines were in the harbor, and Captain Stay breathed a sigh of relief as the planes climbed to cruising altitude for the ride home.

Three days later, the second MIKE mission tested another mine-laying method in a nighttime raid using "pathfinders." Two B-24s went in to the target above and one minute ahead of the rest of the flight. These two lead planes, the pathfinders, used radar to identify the target and then dropped a string of fifteen brilliant white flares. The flares lit up the target for the bombardiers in the flight following below and behind, two formations of three aircraft flying line-abreast. Blinded by the dazzling white light, Chichi Jima's Japanese defenders fired at random between the two lines of flares. One B-24 took a flak hit to the main wheel tucked under the left wing, ripping the rubber tire to shreds.

The radar-assisted Pathfinder mission placed twelve, 2,000-pound mines in Chichi Jima's harbor and all eight aircraft returned safely, in spite of the lucky hit on one plane's landing gear. And as distasteful as the MIKE project was to the men assigned to fly them, the first missions were promising. The men flying these missions included experienced old timers like Charlie Pratte, Frank Angel, Jordan Churchill, Phil Kroh,

and Jesse Stay, but it was tactics, not just experience, which produced
good results. The tactics worked.

Sometimes a Distinguished Flying Cross was awarded because a man
earned it over time. He deserved it and finally got it when the right
mission came along to serve as a catalyst. The mission was written
up in the citation, but the board reviewing the selections knew the
complete, behind-the-scenes story. Sergeant Scearce was awarded the
Distinguished Flying Cross for the November 6, 1944, MIKE mission,
the squadron's first mine-laying mission, but his efforts developing
radar tactics set the stage:

AWARD OF DISTINGUISHED FLYING CROSS: —By direction
of the President, under the provisions of the Act of Congress approved 2 July 1926 (Bull. No. 8, WD, 1926) and pursuant to authority
contained in paragraph 14, AR 600-45, 22 September 1943 and Ltr
Hq AAFPOA, 18 October 1944, the Distinguished Flying Cross is
awarded by the Commanding General, Seventh Air Force, to the
following named officers and enlisted men, Air Corps, United States
Army, for extraordinary heroism in aerial flight against the enemy on
dates indicated. During these missions, each as a crew member of a
heavy bombardment type aircraft, participated in a highly successful medium altitude mine laying mission against the Bonin Islands.
The material construction of the mines necessitated extremely low
altitude flying and despite the danger of both heavy and medium
anti-aircraft weapons around the enemy held harbor, the mining
was carried out so successfully that the supplying of the enemy for
development of bases on this island was definitely retarded. Notwith-
standing the intense and accurate anti-aircraft fire and the possibility

of interception by enemy aircraft of fighter type, the mission was
successfully completed. The cool courage in the face of great danger,
the high degree of professional skill and devotion to duty displayed
by each exemplifies the highest traditions of the Army Air Forces:
6 November 1944

T SGT LESTER H SCEARCE JR 13033593

BY COMMAND OF MAJOR GENERAL DOUGLASS:

WILLIAM J. FLOOD,

Brigadier General, General Staff Corps,

Chief of Staff.

Through November 1944, the mine field intended to close the shipping channel between Chichi and Iwo Jima was incomplete. Cliffs at the
edges of Chichi Jima's harbor protected part of the channel and made it
difficult to finish the mine field. On November 29, 1944, a 42nd Bomb
Squadron MIKE mission would take a different route and with luck,
finish the mine field and get back to Guam. The day before the mission,
five planes made the hop from Guam to Saipan and each plane was
loaded with four 1,000-pound mines that afternoon.[6]

At Saipan, ground support men removed the B-24's belly gun turrets
but the planes still exceeded the maximum gross take-off weight for a
B-24J. During engine run-up for take-off, Lt. Frank Angel's *Umbriago!*
developed supercharger problems and had to abort. The remaining
four Liberators rose sluggishly into the sky. Burning fuel on the way
to the target reduced weight, so the ships would handle better when
they got close.

The four-plane flight started on a course toward Marcus Island as
a feint. After passing the Volcanos, the bombers dropped altitude to
fifty feet and test-fired the guns. Turning toward Chichi Jima, they
held fifty feet altitude for three hair-raising hours, the ocean's choppy

surface rushing toward then beneath and beyond the bombers like endless river rapids.

The bombers passed Haha Jima on the opposite side of Chichi to approach the harbor from the mountains. The mission routed the aircraft over the cliffs at the opposite end of Chichi Jima, across a saddle between mountain peaks, then through a narrow canyon leading directly to the harbor and the mine field. It was flying more suited for a nimble little fighter plane than a flight of heavy four-engined bombers.

The harbor was heavily defended with anti-aircraft guns and the combined firepower of Japanese ships anchored there at the time. Flying between the mountains was risky and difficult but it helped the bombers avoid detection until the moment they nosed over to rush down the slope toward the harbor.

They came in just off the water and then pulled up to clear the cliffs and ridges beyond. The area between the saddle peaks was covered by a low cloud and the pass was barely visible. Lt. Phil Kroh at the controls of #156, *Beanblossum*, flew the lead aircraft into the pass so tight that his wingtips overlapped those of wingmen Lt. Bob Strong and Lt. Herb Robinson. Lt. Reginald Spence followed close behind in the number four position of a tight diamond formation. Treacherous updrafts and turbulence bounced them up and dropped them down again. Waist gunners looked up from their positions at the canyon walls on either side. Flying one bomber along this route would have been wild enough; sending four together in formation was outrageous. The spectacle of it must have been incredible to the Japanese soldiers who spotted the American bombers roaring toward them down the mountain.

Kroh cleared the ridge line and pushed over hard, keeping his plane low, hugging the slope. In very tight formation in the canyon, his wingmen lost sight of their leader. Lieutenant Strong on the left and Lieutenant Robinson on the right suddenly had no reference for space and distance between their ships. They plunged down toward the harbor, blazing away with front and waist guns with anti-aircraft tracers streaming up toward them.

Strong banked right and felt a bump. His right wingtip folded up like the open top of a soup can and he thought it was a flak hit. At exactly the same time, something smacked the nose of Robinson's plane, knocking bombardier Lt. Ernest Miles down to the nose wheel compartment. Miles struggled up just in time to toggle the mine release switch on cue from Kroh's plane, now in view again. Robinson also assumed his plane had been hit by flak, but both pilots were mistaken.

At 350-feet altitude, Lieutenant Strong's right wingtip had slapped the nose of Lieutenant Robinson's ship, missing the whirling propellers of Robinson's number 1 and number 2 engines by a scant few feet while Robinson's left wing barely, miraculously, missed the right rudder of Strong's plane. Had either plane been a few feet forward or aft, or had their angles of attack differed ever so slightly, the collision would have sent both aircraft tumbling into a horrific mountainside crash. Robinson's aircraft was unscathed but seconds after the collision Strong's B-24 began to descend toward the water and the controls wouldn't respond.[7]

Aboard Strong's B-24, waist gunner Corp. Vince Sutter called to his pilot on the intercom, "We've got a bomb in our laps back here."

Strong wasn't amused. "This is no time for cracks, get the hell off the intercom."

Sutter and Corp. Al Newell, the other waist gunner, were so busy strafing ground positions that it took precious seconds for them to realize what had happened.

One of the thousand-pound mines from Robinson's ship was lodged in the side of Strong's plane. Lieutenant Miles had released the mine just as Strong's aircraft passed laterally in a bank beneath Robinson's ship and the mine crashed into the fuselage, punching an ugly hole three by six-feet wide just behind the right waist gun. A six-foot parachute attached to the mine, designed to slow its descent to the water, billowed out full behind the aircraft, dragging the plane down while the mine in the fuselage pinched the elevator and rudder control cables to a stop and a frightening crack raced across the top of the fuselage.

Newell and Sutter anxiously grappled with the mine, wrestling and pushing, sweating and swearing, but the stubborn device wouldn't budge. They grabbed an axe mounted in the fuselage and chopped the parachute shroud lines and the parachute fell away, relieving vicious drag on the plane, but they continued losing altitude with the mine jammed into the control cables. Newell and Sutter knew that the mine was designed to arm itself after contact with water, but they feared they could set off the 465 pounds of TNT if they handled the mine roughly. No training, tech orders or precedent prepared the men for getting a mine out of the side of a B-24.

In the lead plane, Kroh was just above the water's surface, throttles pushed to the stops. His waist gunners could see the sea foam blown back by their propellers. As soon as they were out of range of Japanese gunners, Kroh, Robinson, and Spence climbed to altitude for the ride home. Aboard Lieutenant Strong's struggling B-24, waist gunners Newell and Sutter worked fast to wrench the barrels from their .50 caliber machine guns.

The crack in the side of Strong's plane where the mine had crashed through turned and began to run down the fuselage toward the rear. The tail section was in constant motion; it shook and swayed on its own while Newell and Sutter worked their gun barrels as improvised crowbars. They pried and lifted the mine up and out of the side of the plane, and as it fell away the exhausted gunners moved forward to the bomb bay, watching transfixed as the tail of their plane trembled.

They could see daylight through the crack as it alternately widened and closed and grew longer toward the rear. If the tail wrenched free, the Liberator would pitch forward with such force and violence that no one would get out. There was nothing more Newell and Sutter could do except watch and pray the ship held together for the 800-mile ride home. Gently, carefully, Strong finally gained precious altitude and set a course for Saipan.

Word spread fast at Saipan's Isely Field after the crash crews were alerted that a badly damaged plane was coming in. A crowd of ground crew and airmen gathered to watch and hope while Lieutenant Strong piloted as smoothly and gracefully as he could with slow, deliberate inputs, sweet talking the plane into final approach. The crew wondered: would the tail break off on landing? Would it drag along the runway and twist the plane into a crash?

Strong eased the plane down to Isely Field. It settled lightly and rolled smoothly and held together, and Strong taxied the plane to the same hardstand he left when the mission began. Squadron Commander Capt. Jesse Stay met the crew and congratulated Lieutenant Strong and his men. Standing under the tail of the plane, Stay could move the tail up and down with one hand. The aircraft would not fly again, but it served in another vital way, as the Engineering Section's report for November 1944 explained:

Supplies have been critical, getting down to rock bottom and having to ground airplanes for lack of critical items such as main landing wheels. Airplane #377 will put a lot of airplanes in commission. It will fix up #280 with engine parts, #871 with engine and airplane parts, #682 with a new nose section, #521 with necessary parts to repair wing damage. It will help numerous airplanes in other squadrons. Airplane #377 will be named "Miss Tech Supply."[8]

Through the end of 1944, the 11th flew 102 MIKE missions, laying 227 mines in Japanese harbors. Shipping between Chichi Jima and Iwo Jima dropped off substantially. Lieutenant Strong's plane, #377, was one of just five damaged on MIKE missions. As much as the aircrews dreaded MIKE missions, losses were not heavy. The 42nd wouldn't lose a crew to a MIKE mission until late January 1945.

Sergeant Scearce flew nine consecutive MIKE missions, each one staged through Saipan to Ani Jima, Chichi Jima, or Haha Jima. He participated in the first and the second, which was the first mission relying on radar to find the target. Just one of Scearce's nine MIKE missions was anything but routine, and the problem he and his crewmates faced on the return leg of that mission, a December flight to Haha Jima, had nothing to do with low altitude, ships' gunners, or the widespread belief that MIKE missions were the Navy's responsibility. The problem came from a familiar adversary, one the 11th Bomb Group faced from the very beginning: distance.

Haha Jima was too far away for a B-24 flying from the Marianas unless the plane carried extra fuel, so auxiliary fuel tanks were mounted in the bomb bays. Bomb bay tanks weren't unique to MIKE missions; Scearce had flown many long-distance missions with bomb bays loaded with fuel. Just the same, he would rather have walked past racks of bombs on either side of the catwalk than gas tanks. He never quite got used to the idea of hundreds of gallons of aviation fuel hanging in the bomb bay, and no crewman liked having to sacrifice bomb load for fuel.

On a return flight from Haha Jima, out of danger of searchlights, fighters, or anti-aircraft gunners, at the time fighter pilots liked to imagine bomber crews breaking out the coffee and doughnuts, Flight Engineer John T. Durden knelt on the bomb bay catwalk and moved the bomb bay fuel tank selector valve from "BOTH OFF" to "BOTH ON." He paused for a moment, turned the valve off, and tried again. He tapped the pump, but it made no sound. He turned the valve selector to "LH ON," then "RH ON," but the pump still did not start. The fuel in the bomb bay tanks wasn't going anywhere, not through the pump, not to the wing tanks, and not to the four fourteen-cylinder engines burning 170 precious gallons every hour.

Durden, pilot Capt. Jesse Stay, and navigator Capt. Bernard McPartland discussed position, distance, fuel consumption, and the fuel remaining in the wing tanks while Scearce leaned in from his radio operator's position.

"It's not going to be enough," Stay said.

"I'll transfer it with the hand pump," Durden replied, and he stepped through the cockpit toward the bomb bay again, removed a hand crank from its stowed position on the bomb bay bulkhead, inserted it into a socket on the pump, and tried to turn it.

"You gotta be kiddin' me," Durden muttered.

He repositioned himself, knees on the metal catwalk, and grasped the pump handle with both hands. Rocking with the weight of his upper body, Durden managed to turn the pump just a few revolutions before he realized this wasn't a one-man job. He returned to the cockpit to brief his pilot:

"Takes everything I've got to turn it, Captain. We'll have to tag-team it."

"Okay, John, you boys get it flowing."

Durden returned to the bomb bay; Scearce followed and stood on the catwalk while the engineer leaned through the opening into the rear fuselage section and gestured for Sgt. Earl Dooley and Sgt. Robert Hollis dozing fitfully there to follow him. "Bring your blankie, sleepyhead," Durden said to Dooley.

Each crewman knelt on Dooley's flak jacket in turn, cranking the balky pump handle just a few revolutions, pushing gasoline up from the bottom of the auxiliary tanks, up through narrow fuel lines through the center of the plane, through the fuel transfer unit mounted over the center wing section, and finally into the main tanks. One man could turn the crank just a minute or two before stepping aside for the next man, and then the next, and after each exhausting effort the men stepped through the bomb bay racks to get in line again, and they continued to crank for three grueling hours. They turned the pump crank and pushed fuel through the lines until the Liberator entered the traffic pattern over Saipan. On the ground, Captain Stay thanked his crew. "If they gave Purple Hearts for sore muscles, I'd put you all in for one."

In nineteen months from April 1943 and the first mission from Funafuti to Nauru, to the October 1944 raid from Guam against Yap, Scearce's mission count had crawled to seven. After nine MIKE missions in less than six weeks, his count was suddenly sixteen.

On November 24, while the 42nd was busy with the MIKE project, 111 B-29 Superfortresses staged the first mass air raid from the Marianas to Tokyo.[9] Three days later Japanese twin-engine bombers paid a return visit, striking Saipan while B-29s were being bombed-up for a mission. One B-29 was destroyed and eleven more damaged. A second Japanese raid hit later the same day, destroying three more B-29s. Another three were wiped out in a raid on December 7, and two dozen more were damaged.[10]

Japanese bomber crews staged through Iwo Jima for their raids against Saipan. Stopping them, protecting the B-29s and American operations in the Marianas, meant that the airfields on Iwo Jima had to be kept out of commission. Every mission flown against Iwo Jima designated the airfields as primary targets, and the missions had to be frequent because Japanese soldiers rushed to fill the bomb craters just as quickly as the American planes moved away from the target.[11]

December 8 was Pearl Harbor Day on the Japanese side of the International Date Line. Iwo Jima's Japanese commander, Gen. Tadamichi Kuribayashi, expected an American attack marking the anniversary, and the Seventh Air Force did not disappoint. In a letter to his wife that afternoon, Kuribayashi described the attack coming "in thirteen waves . . . followed by a naval bombardment lasting one and a half hours."[12] Twin-engined P-38 Lightning fighter planes hit ground targets that morning in the first low-level fighter sweep of Iwo Jima. One of the P-38s shot down a Zero fighter climbing up to intercept; another Zero was caught while taxiing. A twin-engined Japanese plane unlucky enough to approach Iwo Jima while the P-38s were attacking tried to turn and speed away, but faster Lightning pilots caught it and shot it down.[13]

Next came sixty-two B-29s unloading 620 tons of bombs. One hundred and two B-24s followed in the afternoon, and finally, U. S. Navy Cruiser Division 5 shelled the island with six destroyers and the heavy cruisers *Chester, Pensacola,* and *Salt Lake City.*[14] But as soon as the American ships and planes moved away, work details of Japanese soldiers once again rushed to each airfield bomb crater. They filled the holes with dirt, rocks, and gravel, returning the runways to operational status within hours.

Sergeant Scearce's seventeenth strike mission, December 21, 1944, was his first against Iwo Jima. In the Quonset hut that served as the squadron briefing room, the map standing just to the right of center stage showed the pork-chop-shaped outline that was Iwo Jima, and the two heavy black lines crossing its middle were Iwo's runways. Those heavy black lines illustrated the target for every B-24 mission to Iwo Jima, from single-plane night "snooper" radar missions to raids involving more than thirty aircraft.[15] Iwo Jima was halfway to Japan from Saipan, and there was no way for B-29 formations flying the route they called the Hirohito Highway to avoid detection by Japanese radar based there. Iwo transmitted air raid warnings to the mainland where a reception would be prepared for the incoming American bombers, and on the return flight, Japanese fighters operating from Iwo's hastily repaired runways intercepted the B-29s, sometimes finishing off damaged American planes struggling home. The 3,000-mile round trip was tiresome for B-29 crews, but the problems created by the Japanese possession of Iwo made many missions harrowing. Suppression of Iwo and its airfields was a short-term answer; possession of Iwo Jima was the solution.[16]

Nighttime snooper and daylight raids against Iwo Jima intensified in September as the 11th began operations from Guam, and beginning with the December 8 raid, 11th Bomb Group B-24s hit Iwo's airfields at least once every day, including December 25. There was no Silent Night over Iwo Jima, but the squadron celebrated Christmas on Guam.

Corp. Ralph Schnepf, the mail orderly, did double duty all month, driving twice daily to the Army Garrison Force to pick up Christmas packages sent from the States. On Christmas Eve, most of the officers and enlisted men gathered in the Squadron Day Room. Enlisted men brought their beer rations; officers brought the hard stuff. Squadron Commanding Officer Col. Russell Waldron contributed ten cases of beer. The men sang Christmas carols but the selections became tawdrier as the alcohol had its increasing effect well into the night, and the next morning, tomato juice was popular at breakfast. Later in the day the squadron enjoyed a turkey dinner with apple pie for dessert.[17] Morale was good among the aircrews; things were humming along nicely and everyone was getting missions.

On Iwo Jima, Japanese General Kuribayashi wrote home: "we're getting air raids every day . . . usually one or two planes in the night, and about twenty in the daytime. Our airstrips and our defense positions are damaged every time."[18] On another occasion, Kuribayashi wrote, "The awfulness, damage, and chaos of air raids are inexpressible and beyond the imagination of people living peaceful lives in Tokyo."[19]

Sergeant Scearce was over Iwo Jima three more times as the year ended. His December 27, 29, and 31 missions delivered 5,000 pounds of fragmentation clusters from 12,000 feet. In addition to protecting B-29s and American operations in the Marianas, repeatedly bombing the Japanese airfields on Iwo Jima denied the enemy the opportunity to resupply from the air while mines in Chichi Jima's harbor limited shipping.

Kuribayashi's artillery officer, Col. Chosaku Kaido, reported in mid-December that "Ammunition is short, and there is no hope of replenishment." Anticipating an American invasion, Kaido said, "It is vital that direct hits be scored by all fire."[20] The supply situation was so desperate that Japanese ships destined for Iwo Jima were filled with green bamboo on top of whatever supplies were aboard: if the ship was sunk, sailors could cling to the bamboo, and if the ship got through, Iwo Jima's defenders could sharpen the bamboo into spears.[21]

Ammunition supplies were not a problem on Guam. At midnight on December 31, the 11th Bomb Group greeted the New Year with the unauthorized discharge of a wide variety of weapons, from small arms and rifles to anti-aircraft guns and artillery.[22] Scearce's buddies on the island said they wouldn't have known it had the Japanese come ashore with guns blazing, but Scearce wasn't there during the midnight revelry. New Year's Day 1945 arrived for Sergeant Scearce somewhere over the black Pacific Ocean while he worked at the radio operator's table in a B-24 returning from a nine and a quarter-hour mission to Iwo Jima. It was his twentieth mission, he was halfway to forty.

≡≣

On a sunny January afternoon exploring Guam in the squadron commander's jeep, Scearce and his buddy Joe Hyson discovered that the
Seabees had an ice machine. Plywood and mattresses were wonderful
finds, but ice really was exotic. The men had no need for ice, no way to
keep it, and nothing to put it in, but none of that mattered; it was ice,
and the ice felt good and tasted good because it was cold and clean and
no one else in the squadron, maybe the whole bomb group, had any.

Scearce and Hyson got some Navy ice and rushed with it back to the
crew area where they joined a rowdy group listening to music in the
squadron's Day Room. "We got ice!" Scearce said, and Hyson held up a
chunk for all the men to see. "Where'd you get that?" a man asked, and
Hyson stopped mid-slurp, bent forward, his mouth full and dripping
cold water: "F'm *Navy* guy." The two friends showed off their ice, sucked
on it, chewed it until their heads ached, swallowed the cold ice melt
water and watched the rest of it disappear from their hands.

Gathered around the phonograph after a few rounds of beer, someone put Bing Crosby's "Seventh Air Force Tribute" on the turntable,
set the needle gently onto the spinning disc, then turned, smiling, arms
raised toward his buddies as if to lead a choir, and they sang. What they
lacked in harmony they made up in volume, and at each mention of
the Seventh Air Force, their singing gave way to shouting, "the Forty-
Second Squadron!"

This singular event, the afternoon he and Joe Hyson got some ice,
became one of the most memorable experiences for Herman Scearce
during the war. For just a little while the two friends had something
simple and still so special, something they enjoyed for just a moment
before it was gone.

Chapter 20

January 1945

THE GAMBLER'S PARADOX is a product of our tendency to see patterns in events. The gambler might make his wager based on a pattern he sees in the turn of a roulette wheel, just as a child might guess that the next coin flip will land heads because the last two were tails. But the patterns aren't really there; the odds don't change on each successive turn of the wheel or flip of the coin. Winning streaks in games of chance are illusions, and the loss that ends a streak is heartbreaking because the momentum of winning felt so real, it seemed bound to continue.

On January 22, Lt. Charlie Pratte and his crew took the nameless B-24-J #42-109871 on a mine-laying mission to Chichi Jima, staging through Saipan. Pratte and his men were old timers, around as long as anyone in the squadron, averaging thirty missions per man. When Pratte's crew went overseas, and before the rules were changed, thirty missions earned a ticket home.

Scearce's buddy Joe Hyson, radar operator on Pratte's crew, was with them when they crashed the Navy's dedication party at Mullinnix Field a year before, landing *Belle of Texas* with brakes out, no hydraulics and hundreds of flak and bullet holes, using parachutes to slow the plane. Pratte's crew had its brush with death that day and survived, and since

291

then they had a winning streak going. Nothing bad was supposed to happen to a crew like Charlie Pratte's.

Also on January 22, Japanese anti-aircraft gunners on Chichi Jima scored hits on an American four-engined bomber flying over the harbor and saw the plane begin to smoke and lose altitude. The plane crashed into the cliffs above Maruen Wan, a bay on the south side of Chichi Jima, and part of the plane fell to the beach below the cliffs.[1]

Scearce returned from a bombing mission to Iwo Jima and learned that Pratte's plane was overdue. There had been no contact from Pratte by radio. Capt. Jordan Churchill sent two B-24s to search for them, and one reported sighting some smoke and a life raft nine hours after Pratte left Saipan. Col. Russell Waldron stepped up the search effort and ordered twenty-one B-24s to cover the area between Guam and Iwo Jima at 2,000 feet. Army and Navy aircraft from Saipan also looked for any sign of Pratte's crew.[2]

On the twenty-fourth, Scearce's crew and seven others from the 42nd were joined by two from the 26th for a night snooper mission. All ten planes got over Iwo Jima and most of their bombs hit the targeted runways. There were no searchlights and no anti-aircraft fire. The mission was unremarkable, forgettable, except that before "bombs away" men aboard the planes droning through the blackness over Iwo Jima that night saw things that put them on edge.

All ten crews reported a fire on Iwo Jima's southeast shore, a fire that started before any of their bombs fell. It was as if someone below heard the American planes approaching and wanted to signal them. Someone else on the flight saw a white flare, then a yellow one, but the flares arced and burned out and then there was nothing more to see. Could Pratte's crew have ditched and reached Iwo Jima? The squadron was convinced there were survivors from Charlie Pratte's crew and they desperately wanted something more to be done for them.

On Chichi Jima, Japanese Capt. Fumio Kudo sent a search party to investigate the wreck of the bomber shot down on January 22. His soldiers followed the beach to the site, but they could not reach the plane where it rested on the cliffs. They assumed the American flyers were dead; it seemed unlikely anyone could have survived such a violent crash.[3]

Two days later, the 42nd hit Iwo from 20,000 feet in daylight. From that altitude there was little opportunity to make observations and little hope that a downed airman could signal an aircraft. There was nothing more the lost airmen's friends could do except go about their business and hope for the best. They imagined a clandestine mission; maybe by night a submarine or a fast patrol boat would pluck Pratte's men from the island. Weighing the odds or seriously considering the prospects of rescue was depressing, so they hoped their friends would be okay and tried not to dwell on the chances.

On January 26, Sergeant Scearce was over Iwo Jima on a snooper mission with Capt. Jesse Stay when suddenly the aircraft was bathed in blinding light. Japanese searchlights tracked the plane for several anxious seconds while the bombardier finished his bomb run, Scearce spread his feet wide for stability because he knew what was coming and at the moment the last bomb fell from its rack, Jack Yankus standing on the bomb bay catwalk and the bombardier from his position in the nose called "Bombs away!" Captain Stay said, "Brace!" and pushed the plane down hard and to the left in a steep, turning dive. The searchlight beam suddenly flashed past beneath the right wing and was gone, and Captain Stay leveled the wings for the ride home and asked if everyone was okay.

Searchlight beams blinded bombardiers and gunners, but they also helped Japanese anti-aircraft batteries solve altitude and direction and get accurate bursts in a bomber's path. Searchlights during the bomb run were as unnerving as flak or fighters, and evasive action was impossible until the bomb run was over. Violent evasive action to get out of searchlight beams was unsettling and sometimes caused falls and bruises, but a pilot did anything he had to do to get out of the light.

Sergeant Scearce had flown many missions with Stay, serving as his squadron commander's radio man since Joe Deasy's reassignment to the States months before. During that time Stay led most of his squadron's missions and had actively assisted planning them all.[4] The January 26 mission was Captain Stay's fortieth, and Scearce felt honored to shake his commander's hand after they taxied back to their hardstand and shut down the engines at the end of the flight.

Missions came fast once the 42nd moved to Guam and the pace accelerated through the end of 1944 and the beginning of '45. Scearce got sixteen strike mission credits in January, by far his most active combat month of the war.[5] The missions were long, typically nine hours apiece, and these didn't count flights to Okinawa, which were even longer.

The 11th frequently bombed Okinawa, but crewmen didn't get strike mission credit for these raids because Okinawa was a "milk run," too easy to merit strike credit, according to Group Command. There was no Japanese opposition on bombing raids to Okinawa, but all the hazards of long flights over water were as real as with any better-defended target. Crews groused about Okinawa assignments because no one wanted to go on a bombing mission without getting credit, but no one wanted to get shot down either. The cynics among the men said that a chance of getting shot down was required for strike mission credit.

Sometimes there was no mystery to the loss of an aircraft. The gut-wrenching drama of witnessing a plane crash at least avoided lingering, not-knowing aches and sad, fading hopes. When Bobby Lipe disappeared with George Dechert's crew in December 1943 there was only speculation, no real answers. *Dogpatch Express* was shot down the same month with other B-24s flying on its wings and every man in the squadron accepted the finality of it in his own way.

Charlie Pratte's failure to return was similar to Dechert's because the crew's fate in each case was a mystery. The important difference between the two losses was that Dechert's crew was green and had a bad streak going. Pratte's crew was solid and skilled, and in a game where experience favored good outcomes, a gambler would have bet on Pratte's crew to make it.

News about the crash of another B-24 just two days after Pratte's failure to return hastened talk about Pratte's loss from the lips of air and ground crews and it settled into the back of the minds of men who had been close to the crew, men like Herman Scearce. Discussion of Pratte's unexplained disappearance and the troubling sights over Iwo Jima was replaced by reports of 2nd Lt. James Fagan's crash, and this time there was no mystery.

Lieutenant Fagan, piloting a B-24 named *Bird of Paradise*, had just finished his bomb run over Iwo Jima when a flak burst sent mean metal shards ripping through his aileron and rudder control cables. The plane suddenly slid out of control and dropped out of formation, rocking violently. Flight leader Capt. Robert Edwards followed Fagan down and took position on Fagan's right wing, but Edwards had a hard time staying with Fagan because the stricken plane swerved wildly back and forth across a wide track of sky. Fagan had his hands full keeping his B-24 airborne, but twenty miles off Iwo Jima at 14,000 feet and still falling, Edwards finally established voice contact with Fagan. Fagan told Edwards he expected to go down and asked Edwards to call Dumbo.[6]

There are three axes of rotation around the center of gravity of an aircraft: pitch, yaw, and roll. By extending an arm horizontally, hand flat with thumb and little finger extended like the wings of a plane, waving the hand up and down at the wrist mimics pitch. Holding the hand flat, turning the wrist from left to right is yaw. Twisting the arm so that the thumb and little finger rock up and down is roll.

Elevators are movable surfaces on the trailing edge of the horizontal tail that control pitch, the nose up or down attitude of the plane. Rudders, moving surfaces on the B-24's twin vertical tail sections, control yaw. Ailerons, moving parts on the outer wing trailing edges, control roll.

Lieutenant Fagan had no rudder or aileron controls. Holding a hand level, then rotating it through yaw and roll at the same time, angling forward and downward like a leaf driven before the wind, imitates Fagan's bomber and explains why Captain Edwards had to keep his distance.

Bracing himself in the crazily swinging and rocking fuselage of his Liberator, flight engineer Corp. Calvin C. Bryant worked feverishly to splice and clamp the severed rudder cables. There was no way to repair damaged lines in the wings and no way to know how badly damaged the flaps were; they wouldn't need the extra lift from extended flaps until the plane slowed for ditching.

Fagan adjusted throttles to put his plane on course toward home, increasing power left or right to slowly turn the aircraft. Corporal Bryant succeeded in clamping a cable splice, restoring partial rudder control, but the aileron cables were severed in the wings where they could not be reached. The plane limped ahead, one wing low, threatening to fall into a spiral at any moment.

Fagan asked Edwards to fly above and in front of him to provide a reference to level, his own plane's vicious behavior too much for its swinging instruments to make sense. Fagan coaxed *Bird of Paradise* on a heading toward Saipan and began to think he might make it there. Two

Navy Catalina flying boats were ten miles ahead and closing, vectored on an intercepting course toward the two B-24s when Fagan reported a new problem: gasoline was leaking from the tanks for number 3 and number 4 engines.

Fagan considered ordering his crew to bail out over Saipan and crash landing with his co-pilot and engineer. At 120 miles out, the two Dumbo planes made visual contact and followed Fagan as he continued to lose altitude. At 6,000 feet, Fagan got clearance to land at Saipan's Isely Field, Runway #1. The crew, parachutes strapped on, remained aboard for the landing attempt while Isely's alerted fire and ambulance crews stood by, their trucks idling beside the runway, ready to rush ahead to a plane crash.

Fagan attempted to lower the landing gear but the right main wheel didn't extend; the hydraulics were out. Remaining fuel was enough for a second landing attempt, so Fagan banked in a wide circle for another approach while his crew kicked the nose wheel out and tried to lower the right main gear manually. At 1,500 feet Fagan turned on the down-wind leg of his second landing attempt and ordered 12 degrees of flaps lowered. Co-pilot Lt. Johnnie Grant pumped the flaps but only the left wing flap came down. Sudden lift on the left wing caused it to rise and the plane spiraled out of control to the right. Fagan and Grant stood on left rudder, shoved the throttles full on engines 3 and 4 and cut power to 1 and 2 completely, but it didn't work.

The Liberator's right wing hit the water first, just a quarter mile off the northeast coast of Tinian, and the plane broke up as it spun into the water. Edwards made a low pass and reported the downed plane's position. He dropped a life raft from 300 feet and circled the site until rescue boats arrived.

Four of Fagan's crew were hospitalized and four more, including both pilots and the heroic flight engineer, returned to duty right away.

Corp. Ernest Bradley and Corp. Frank Maressa, gunners, were killed. A third man killed in the crash was Capt. John Bowers, along on the mission as a passenger.

The saga of Fagan's flight home from Iwo Jima inspired a variety of story lines. Men discussed whether the crew should have bailed out, whether Fagan should have brought his crippled B-24 down on the runway without landing gear, whether he should have risked going around. All agreed that it was a hell of a bad luck deal for Captain Bowers and all agreed Corporal Bryant deserved a medal. For now and at least until the next big story came along, Fagan's flight was the hot topic and talk of Charlie Pratte's disappearance faded.

Had the Japanese search party been able to reach the bomber that crashed on the cliffs of Chichi Jima on January 22, they would have found clothing with an American airman's name sewn inside: William Farrell, a gunner on Charlie Pratte's crew. They would also have found the tattered remains of four letters written to Farrell.[7] The letters may have been from a girlfriend, maybe they were from his mother in New York; the authors of the letters are unknown but they must have been very special to Sergeant William Farrell.

In January 1945 Herman Scearce had been in the Army three years. His strike mission record showed the progress of the war in those months, flying from Funafuti, Midway, Guam, and Saipan against targets increasingly closer to Japan: Nauru, Wake, Tarawa, Jaluit, Yap, Ani Jima, Chichi Jima, Haha Jima, Iwo Jima.

Drawing a finger across a map of the Central Pacific, Scearce started at a point south of the equator and traced a line from Funafuti north to Tarawa, then northwest to the Marianas, then up to Iwo Jima. With a metal ruler, Scearce compared distances. By the scale of his map the distance from Oahu to Funafuti measured six inches, Funafuti to Tarawa was just two. From there westerly across the Pacific to the Marianas was five inches, then two again up to Iwo Jima. Japan was just an inch and a half away.

As the end of January approached, it became harder for Sergeant Scearce to keep his mission count out of mind. It was considered bad luck, or at least bad form, to talk about mission counts. It was an unspoken rule, a corollary to the illusory pattern seen in the Gambler's Paradox: talking about a winning streak might cause it to end.

Scearce was assigned a night snooper mission for January 31. The counter in the back of his mind was ready to roll to thirty-six and he caught himself thinking, "Four more."

Chapter 21

Endings for Some

IT WAS NEVER MORE CLEAR how alone an aircrew was than when they were in trouble. Men flying a stricken plane had only their aircraft and all the skill and resourcefulness they could muster, but sometimes the plane was too broken for any heroic effort to save it. At the moment the aircraft could no longer fly, and its crew could no longer function as pilot, navigator, engineer, radio man, gunner or bombardier, the crew became individual men with their own thoughts, reactions, and emotions.

Bailing out was the last resort, but even bailing out was sometimes hopeless. Injured men might be unable to get out, or violent forces acting on the tumbling, spiraling, falling wreckage of a plane might make it impossible for a man to take any action at all, and his survivors would shudder to imagine his feelings and fears as the plane went down. If the stricken plane was in formation with other aircraft, the contrast was gut-wrenching. Men aboard a struggling aircraft were in a completely different world, alone.

Japanese losses of aircraft and experienced pilots were good fortune for American bomber crews. Hundreds lost at Midway and during the Marianas Turkey Shoot, with attrition through 1944 and into 1945, made enemy skies more survivable for Americans. But with their home islands under attack and their battles becoming more desperate, Japanese defenders committed themselves to a fight to the death. On Iwo Jima, Gen. Tadamichi Kuribayashi created a list of six vows and distributed them to his men, and they repeated them every morning:[1]

1. We shall defend this place with all our strength to the end.
2. We shall fling ourselves against enemy tanks clutching explosives to destroy them.
3. We shall slaughter the enemy, dashing in among them to kill them.
4. Every one of our shots shall be on target and kill the enemy.
5. We shall not die until we have killed ten of the enemy.
6. We shall continue to harass the enemy with guerilla tactics even if only one of us remains alive.

Surely it occurred to Iwo Jima's anti-aircraft gunners and Zero pilots operating from Iwo Jima's airfields that B-24 Liberators usually carried ten men. Zero pilots able to get airborne from Iwo Jima to intercept American bombers knew there was a good chance their airfields would be too badly cratered by those bombers for them to land again, and they understood the implications of their recent losses quite well. They did not expect to survive the war, and in the sky over Iwo Jima, some of them employed a devastating new tactic.

On a daylight raid in mid-January, nine B-24s near Iwo Jima broke from the safety of their formation because ice had begun forming on the wings. Lt. Herman Bierwirth at the controls of *Catherine* dropped down to 13,000 feet, followed by another B-24, *Tarfu*, on his wing.[2] As the two planes left Iwo Jima, Zero fighters attacked.

The first Japanese fighter made a pass from 4:00 but broke off at about 300 yards. He made two more halfhearted passes then turned toward Iwo Jima. A second fighter made three passes from 3:00, then another from 2:00. The plane broke toward 5:00 at about 300 yards away and then circled as if to get in position for another pass. White smoke streamed from the Zero's cowling.

At 500 yards ahead of the two B-24s, the Zero dropped its left wing and turned toward the bombers. It streaked in from 2:00, guns firing. Gunners on both B-24s fired into the Zero and Bierwirth nosed down hard, banking left, and his wing man followed. Waist and top turret gunners risked warping their gun barrels, they were pouring so many rounds into the attacking Zero. They had never seen one so close, so aggressive. Tracers zipped past and into the Zero as Liberator gunners turned to track the plane, by now so near that the gunners could see the radial engine cylinder heads within their circular cowling, the stripes on the Zero's propeller blades spinning a red circle and the Japanese pilot's face behind his cockpit glass. The Zero's guns blinked fast at the Liberators but the fighter pilot's weapon of choice was the mass and velocity of his entire plane. The Zero pilot intended to ram the lead B-24 with an angle of attack meant to drive through both American bombers.

Sgt. Richard Carton expected the Japanese plane to race through his 8 to 7 o'clock within seconds. He couldn't see the Zero from his tail gun position, but he held his twin .50 caliber guns to the right and level for a shot as the fighter passed. Suddenly 7.7 millimeter bullets from the Zero raked the side of Bierwirth's B-24 and pierced the tail from behind and to the left of Sergeant Carton, and Carton immediately felt a sharp pain in his right eye.

The Zero's near-perpendicular angle of attack required precise timing and control, and the B-24's last-second evasive action dropped the American planes below the fast closing fighter's line of attack just enough. The Japanese pilot pushed his control stick right and forward and kicked right rudder to compensate and his Zero's right wing hit *Tarfu* in the number 4 engine, then struck the number 3 engine cowling, and as the Zero flipped over, it ripped out the bomber's whip antenna. The Japanese plane appeared to be under control as it passed inverted sixty feet to the rear of Bierwirth's B-24. Sergeant Carton struggled to see well enough to fire a burst into the Zero as it sped by, and a moment later the enemy fighter went into a spin, nosed down, and fell into the ocean more than two miles below.

Carton felt sure something was in his right eye, a piece of fragmented bullet or splintered Plexiglas. As soon as they were away from Iwo Jima and out of danger Carton moved forward and got a crewmate to check him out, but his buddy could see only a watery, red, and irritated eye. After returning to Guam the flight surgeon diagnosed Carton with a scratched right cornea and told him he was damned lucky. Lieutenant Bierwirth recommended Carton for a Purple Heart.[3]

Twenty B-24 crewmen had survived a determined suicide attack by a Japanese fighter pilot, and it had been as close as it could possibly be without bringing down a bomber. *Tarfu* limped home with number 4 engine feathered, *Catherine* needed some bullet holes patched, and Carton's scratched cornea was the only injury. The Japanese pilot had been greedy; an angle of attack in line with the heading of just one of the bombers had a better chance of success. Another Zero pilot might not make the same mistake.

On January 31, 1945, ten B-24s assigned to hit the dispersal area between Airfields 1 and 2 on Iwo Jima left Guam at forty-five-minute intervals in the early morning, just as the Pacific sky shaded from purple to blue. Two planes from the 26th Squadron joined eight from the 42nd, Sgt. Herman Scearce flying with Capt. Jordan Churchill since Captain Stay had finished his missions on the twenty-sixth. It felt good, Scearce thought, flying on a crew with his friend Yankus again, "Just like the good ol' days!" Yankus said as they boarded the plane, calling to mind the "good ol' days" of just two years before, flying with Joe Deasy aboard the long lost *Dogpatch Express*.

Hours away from the target, one of the Liberators lost number 4 engine. On three engines with number 4 feathered, the plane dropped its load of seven 500-pound bombs into the ocean and the crew threw out machine guns, ammunition, and flak suits, anything loose to lighten the ship, and turned back to land at Saipan since Saipan was an hour closer than Guam.

The nine remaining bombers got over Iwo Jima individually, approaching on separate compass headings: 133, 360, 135, 180, 345, 90, 100, 000, and 350 degrees; the lines of attack looked like the letter "X" drawn repeatedly over a map of Iwo Jima. Varying approaches and altitudes made it difficult for the Japanese to train their guns on the American planes. The nine bombers dropped sixty-two 500-pound General Purpose bombs and forty 125-pound fragmentation clusters from 10,000 to 12,700 feet altitude.[4]

Seconds after their bomb release, standing at his waist gun position, Yankus saw a bright white shell burst with white vapor lines shooting out beneath like the tentacles of a jellyfish. He nudged Scearce in the side and when Scearce turned, Yankus gestured toward the strange apparition at the 10:00 position outside the left waist window. On the flight deck Capt. Jordan Churchill saw the burst, too, and said through the interphone, "Phosphorous bomb at 10:00."

Most of the crew had not seen this Japanese anti-aircraft weapon before, phosphorous bombs dropped by aircraft flying above American planes. The bombs were set to detonate above their target aircraft, and the white streaks shooting from beneath the bursts were left by searing-hot pieces of phosphorous able to burn a hole through a bomber like a bullet scorching through a paper target. Scearce and Yankus took pictures of the burst now drifting through 9:00, grateful the bomb hadn't been closer.

The crew of *Miss Nadine*, another aircraft from the 42nd, saw tracers streaking skyward from a Japanese ship while en route to the target, but the gunfire was inaccurate. The nine aircraft on the mission unloaded over Iwo Jima and landed individually at Guam eight and a half hours after their staggered departures, and returning to his crew quarters, Scearce thought, *"thirty- six."* With the exception of the engine failure forcing one aircraft to abort, the mission was like Scearce's next, his thirty-seventh, a nine-hour night snooper mission on February 6: uneventful, unremarkable, like most of the missions flown against Iwo Jima.

On February 8, 1945, Lieutenant Bierwirth, survivor of the near-miss suicide attack in January, led "C" flight, the third element of planes on the mission, in a ten-plane raid against Iwo. Bierwirth's nameless bomber was a new B-24 L, similar to the "J" models except that the tail turret was replaced by twin hand-held machine guns. Losing the tail turret saved weight and gave the tail gunner a larger cone of fire.

After "bombs away" the planes banked to the east, circling around to a course of 164 degrees to take them back to base. Sunlight glinted off the bright aluminum skin of the planes in "A" and "B" flights as they turned through 120 degrees.

Two minutes from the target, Lt. Harry McCallam, leading "B" flight, saw a bright flash to his left. Lt. Howard Bettis, flying on Bierwirth's right wing, saw a streak cross very close above him and to his left. Lt. William Wright, on Bierwirth's left, saw the same streak, a Japanese fighter, coming down from 1:00 high. The Zero rolled until it was belly-up and smashed into Bierwirth's plane at the top turret, precisely where the main wing spar intersected the fuselage.[5]

The impact broke the Liberator's back and it crumpled immediately. The right wing broke off, engines and propellers still turning, and as the broken wing fluttered away the rest of the plane exploded. Gunners in the waist of Bettis' ship felt the flash of the explosion hot on their faces. The tail section of Bierwirth's aircraft fell as one piece, tumbling 15,000 feet toward the ocean with gunner Sgt. Richard Carton trapped inside. Carton's scratched cornea had healed quickly, just as the flight surgeon predicted three weeks before when he told Carton he was damned lucky.

Lieutenant Bettis' crew saw two parachutes open. The parachutes may have been soaked with aviation fuel or they may have been too near the heat of the explosion, whatever the reason, as soon as they opened the parachutes burst into flames. Bettis called the strike commander, leader of "A" flight, and informed him of the crash. Bettis also tried to contact rescue service, but it was no use. Eleven American airmen died, each of them on his thirty-ninth mission, just days from finishing forty and going home to their futures.[6] Broken pieces of B-24 and Zero splashed into the water about ten miles east of Iwo Jima while the other nine planes tightened formation to fill the void and headed back to Guam.

That night Scearce flew with Captain Churchill to strike Iwo's airfields with 100-pound General Purpose bombs.[7] Six planes from the 42nd and four from the 431st took off at intervals and hit the target individually, bombing by radar with Kama Iwa Rock off the north-west coast as a course checkpoint. Four searchlights on the north end of the island came on just as the bombs fell away, then two searchlights on the south end caught Churchill's plane. Churchill nosed down steeply and swerved sharply left and right while the crew braced, but in spite of the bomber's evasive action the lights held the plane for a nerve-wracking half minute. Yankus exhaled hard when the lights finally flashed away from the plane, and Scearce patted his friend on the back, both men relieved to get out of the light, safely into the blackness and away from the island.

Scearce tried to get some sleep on the four-hour ride home. He thought about the pinochle game he and Yankus had been playing earlier in the day and smiled at the thought of the signals he and Yankus used and how innocently and naively their latest victims agreed to place wagers on the game. Drifting in the subconscious place between wakefulness and sleep, the cards reminded him of his mission count: thirty-seven, thirty-eight when this plane touched down, can't count it until it's done. He had been dealt a good hand from the start, two points for a King and Queen marriage on the deal, two points, two more missions. Two sets of Jacks on the deal was worth forty, man, that really would be a good hand.

They hadn't finished the game before time to get to the plane. They closed the hand and Scearce said, "Okay, Yank, your deal tomorrow."

On February 10, Lt. Edwin Brashear flew lead on a strike against Haha Jima in a new B-24 L named *Royal Flush*. *Royal Flush* featured an unhappy Japanese soldier peering from the bowl of a toilet overshadowed by an ominous royal flush poker hand.[8] Maj. Robert Holland flew with Lieutenant Brashear on the mission. Holland had finished forty missions but stayed on, taking a promotion to major, and became commanding officer of the 26th Bomb Squadron on January 27.[9]

This was the first mission organized under the direction of Major Holland.[10] Haha Jima was considered a milk run, especially compared to the better defended air space over Iwo Jima. Haha Jima's greater distance required auxiliary fuel tanks to be mounted inside the Liberator's bomb bay, and Operations made sure the auxiliary tanks were in place and the planes fueled properly for the mission.

At 16,000 feet the ten-plane B-24 formation held a course of 270 degrees at the beginning of the bomb run, bomb bay doors open. *Royal Flush* Bombardier 2nd Lt. Albert Reynolds concentrated on the target through his Norden bomb sight. As he focused on his target, a Japanese anti-aircraft gun battery tracked *Royal Flush*. An anti-aircraft gun crew could compute the lead for their guns after tracking an aircraft for twenty seconds, maybe less, maybe as fast as ten seconds for skilled gunners, as long as the enemy aircraft maintained a predictable course.[11] *Royal Flush* flew a predictable course a few seconds too long, and the Japanese gun crew on the island below fired.

Airmen knew that an anti-aircraft shell needed about one second for every thousand feet of altitude to reach their plane. At 16,000 feet, *Royal Flush* continued on a predictable course for another sixteen seconds after the Japanese gun crew fired.

Aboard *Royal Flush*, Lieutenant Reynolds toggled his bomb release lever when an explosion behind him caused him to turn on his seat and look toward the bomb bays.

Lt. Howard Bettis, witness to Lieutenant Bierwirth's ramming loss two days before, flew behind *Royal Flush* in "D" flight when he saw flames coming out of the lead plane's bomb bay. Lt. David Watson saw the lead aircraft nose down, and for a fleeting, hopeful moment the fire seemed to be out. *Royal Flush* then banked right, its nose rising, bringing the flames into view again, and then "C" flight flew through the smoky white streamers left by the phosphorous shell that had exploded inside the lead plane's bomb bay.[12]

At the tail gun position, Sgt. Richard Chandler turned to move forward as soon as he realized *Royal Flush* was in serious trouble. Chandler saw flames forward, filling the bomb bay. The two waist gunners were slumped over their guns when Chandler bailed out.

Dense black smoke poured from Lieutenant Brashear's plane. Fifty seconds after the bomb bay auxiliary fuel tanks took a direct hit, the plane crumpled, nose high, as if desperately struggling to keep flying. But *Royal Flush* broke apart, trailing a fiery orange pillar 150 feet above the Liberator now falling in pieces toward the ocean more than three miles below.

The Japanese gun crew surely saw the flaming American bomber fall, and they must have shouted to their comrades, pointing to the place in the sky where the flaming bomber plummeted. The gun crew must have been pleased, satisfied that they had kept their vow to kill ten of the enemy before dying. In fact, they had killed ten of their enemy before the inevitable American invasion had even begun.

Lieutenant Bettis saw four men get clear and reported two parachutes open. Lt. Dewey Williams reported three. Lieutenant Watson also saw three parachutes open, but thought he saw four more men get out of the plane. Eight remaining B-24s closed formation and headed away from the target, all except Lieutenant Bettis who released his bombs and dropped altitude as soon as he saw Brashear's plane burning. At 200 feet above the ocean, Bettis saw a parachute floating in the water with one man struggling nearby. Lieutenant Bettis' crew dropped two life rafts and his radio operator called for help. The radio operator gave the time, location, a brief description of the action, and asked for Dumbo service:

11V535: 100200Z GR 9 BT 3 V HIT BY FLAK ONE GOT OUT CONTACT DUMBO OVER.

The ground station asked for a bearing from Fanny's Foxhole, code name for a fixed point on Haha Jima: 00V535: INT BEARING FROM FANNYS FOXHOLE OVER.

The response: BEARING 166 FANNYS FOXHOLE. Then the ground station asked for clarity, who went down? INT QUF 13V535 OR 3V535 OVER.

Lieutenant Bettis confirmed that it was Lieutenant Brashear's plane that had gone down: 13V535 DOWN OVER.

The ground station replied, ROGER AT 0312Z WE ARE NOW MONITORING SEARCH FREQUENCY OF 7920 KCS.

Dumbo, the Navy Catalina flying boat, reached the location: CONTINUING IN COMPANY WITH PB4Y2 WILL SEARCH AREA AS LONG AS POSSIBLE. The Catalina searched with a Privateer escort, a PB4Y2 single-tailed Navy version of a Liberator. Two and a half hours after Brashear's plane went down, the Navy Dumbo aircraft reported: PICKED UP ONE SURVIVOR OFF HAHA JIMA HAVE AMBULANCE WAITING MAN BADLY BURNED ETA 1930 OVER.

Sergeant Chandler had first and second degree burns to his face.[13] He spent two and a half anxious hours in the water, fearing a Japanese plane would spot him before Dumbo could save him. Hospitalized and recovering from his burns, Chandler completed an Individual Casualty Questionnaire, AF form number 6-3861, for his crew. The form was meant to be completed for each man lost, but Chandler filled out only one. It began with his pilot's name: BRASHEAR, Edwin E, followed by rank, serial number and crew position.

The first question was, "Did he bail out?"

"No," Chandler wrote.

"If not, why not?"

"The plane blew up too soon."

"Where was he last seen?"

"In plane."

The form provided five lines for "Any hearsay information." Chandler wrote: "The plane was hit in the bomb-bay by phosphorous ack ack and blew up almost immediately." The next question asked for an explanation of Lieutenant Brashear's fate.

"Believe he was killed when plane blew up." And at the bottom of the page, Chandler added, "Note—all the rest of the crew is the same information."

Brashear's crew had flown thirty-three missions; Major Holland was on his forty-first. Had Chandler been in the tail of a "J" model Liberator, closed inside a turret, he might not have survived.

Lt. Howard Bettis received a First Bronze Oak Leaf Cluster to Distinguished Flying Cross, his second award of the DFC, for his efforts after Brashear's plane was hit:

For meritorious achievement during a daylight bombardment strike against the Japanese held base of Haha Jima . . . The leading plane of the formation was hit by enemy anti-aircraft fire and burst into flames . . . Lt. Bettis, with utter disregard for his own safety, immediately left the formation and dove his plane through enemy fire to give assistance to any survivors of the ill-fated plane. He remained in the vicinity under continuous fire from shore batteries, searched for survivors, dropped life rafts and sent position reports to the Air Sea Rescue Service, leaving only when he had done everything possible to aid the rescue. These actions were responsible for saving the life of one crew member . . .[14]

In the same set of General Orders is the posthumous award of a Silver Star for Maj. Robert Holland. Headquarters reached back to June 1943, citing a mission against Nauru as a basis for the award, a disastrous mission that was cancelled when two bombers crashed on

take-off from Funafuti and only Holland and Jesse Stay, both lieutenants
then, reached Nauru.

Lt. Harry Gibbons, a Liberator co-pilot, was in the cockpit of the
B-24 *Dangerous Critter* in B flight behind the strike leader when Lieutenant Brashear's plane went down. Later that day he recorded in his
diary:

> Another rough one. I feel a little uneasy. No appetite . . . we were
> supposed to have an easy mission today but the lead ship picked up
> some ack ack in the bomb bay tank . . . it was just a flying torch, a few
> fellows got out but some of them didn't have chutes on . . . had some
> good friends on it, too. I sometimes wonder if we'll ever get home.[15]

In the 26th Squadron's records for January 1945, Lt. Edwin Brashear's
photograph appears on page five. In the photo Brashear is smiling,
walking tall across the stage of the 11th Group's "Bomber Bowl" outdoor
theater to receive an Oak Leaf Cluster to the Air Medal from Maj. Gen.
Robert Douglass, commander of the Seventh Air Force. On the last page
of the January record, Lieutenant Brashear is mentioned again in a section titled "Special Orders," where a fellow officer is assigned responsibility for inventory and disposition of Brashear's personal belongings.[16]

February 10, the day *Royal Flush* went down, was a very busy day in Iwo
Jima's air space. 28th Photo Reconnaissance Squadron F-5s, modified
P-38 Lightnings with cameras in place of nose guns, began their second
week of low-level photo mapping of Iwo Jima, photographing Japanese
defenses before the coming Marine invasion. The F-5s, "Photo Joes" as

P-38 pilots called them, were escorted by four Lightnings of the 318th Fighter Group.[17] High above the photo runs, eight Liberators of the 431st Bomb Squadron approached Iwo to strike airfield taxiways with 500-pound General Purpose bombs. Ten B-24s were scheduled for the raid, but one suffered a fuel pump failure and didn't take off from Guam, another aborted and returned to base with number 3 engine vibrating badly and cutting out.

One of the 431st pilots, Lt. Stewart Greene, was on his first mission after transitioning to first pilot from co-pilot. Greene's good friend Lt. George Hendrickson, bombardier, volunteered to fly with him aboard the B-24 *My Devotion*.[18]

The F-5s and their Lightning escorts approached from the northwest, released their 300-gallon fuel drop tanks, and throttled up for the photo run. They crossed the beaches at fifty feet altitude while Japanese pilots desperately rushed to their planes. When a twin-engined Japanese bomber, code-named Betty, got airborne, one of the F-5s was forced to swerve off its photo run to avoid a head-on collision.

P-38 pilot Capt. Judge Wolfe, leading another element of ten P-38s, approached just ahead of the B-24 formation to provide the bombers escort protection. The P-38 pilots saw several Japanese aircraft trying to get airborne, trying to avoid certain destruction on the ground. Captain Wolfe and his men dove in pursuit.

Wolfe opened fire on a Betty, closing within 600 feet, and saw the Japanese plane crash into the ocean. Wolfe turned to attack a second Betty. The Japanese tail gunner scored hits on Wolfe's P-38 before the second Japanese bomber hit the water.

Lt. Everett Balkum, Wolfe's wing man, flamed another Betty as Wolfe banked to return to the B-24 formation. Lt. Henry Stampe, flying escort on the deck with the F-5s, also shot down a Betty, and 2nd Lt. John Donohoe scored on a Zero.

The B-24s crossed Iwo Jima in an arc, curving southerly at 17,000 feet through 210 to 124 degrees, bomb bay doors open. Lead bombardier 2nd Lt. Charles Swan suddenly lost sight of the target and toggled his bomb release to initiate the drop, and the other bombardiers dropped their bombs on Swan's signal.[19] Because of the blind drop, results were poor, most of the bombs exploding north and east of the target. Aboard *My Devotion*, Lieutenant Greene asked bombardier Lieutenant Hendrickson if all the bombs were away. Hendrickson replied, "Yes, let's get the hell out of here."[20] And at that instant, a phosphorous flak burst exploded forward and to the left of Greene's B-24, puncturing the cowling of number 1 engine and driving a fragment through the bombardier's compartment. The shell fragment pierced Lieutenant Hendrickson's flak helmet and penetrated his skull at the left temple.[21]

The bomb run completed, the P-38s rejoined the B-24 formation, the faster Lightnings circling to stay close. P-38 pilot Lt. Wayne Duerschmidt spotted a Zero returning to Iwo, nosed his fighter over to close the distance, and shot the Japanese plane down.

Bombardier Lieutenant Hendrickson died during the return flight. While the other planes continued to Guam, Lieutenant Greene landed at Saipan where he watched in anguish as medical corpsmen took his friend's body away.

Elements of Lt. Edwin Brashear's strike on Haha Jima and the 431st Squadron's mission to Iwo Jima were still returning after sunset on February 10 when Sgt. Herman Scearce's next mission took flight from Guam. Ten B-24s took off in staggered starts, Scearce with Churchill in a new B-24 "M", equipped with a light-weight tail turret. Behind them one of the ten, #521, *Road to Tokyo*, aborted 165 miles out and turned back to Guam because of an electrical fire.[22]

The four and a half hour flight to the target was routine, smooth, visibility twenty miles or better with scattered cumulus clouds topped out at 7000 feet. And it was cold. The men weren't on bombing missions in T-shirts any more. The cold reminded them that they were well north of the equator now, much closer to Japan.

At 12,000 feet over Iwo Jima a burst of Japanese anti-aircraft gunfire missed wide and low. Searchlights caught and held two B-24s briefly, but the bombers quickly angled down and turned away and the lights lost them. The nine Liberators over Iwo Jima that night dropped eighteen tons of General Purpose bombs on Airfield #2 and gun positions just north of the airfield.

After "bombs away," Churchill's plane shuddered and the familiar droning sound of its engines changed pitch. Every man on the crew knew immediately what the sound meant and they could feel through the metal structure of the aircraft that the plane had lost an engine. There was no panic because this was a veteran crew, but each man's muscles tensed, their hearts beat just a little faster, adrenalin flowed. There was work to be done and it had to be done *right now*.

Yankus instinctively checked the fuel levels while Churchill began the procedure for an engine restart, but the dead engine would not fire. Scearce sent a coded message to Saipan and 625 miles away on Saipan's Isely Field the ground operator recorded the message with the bomber's identification, heading, location, estimated time of arrival, and the words, ON THREE ENGINES.

"Throw out anything loose," Churchill ordered. "Get rid of the ball turret!" Churchill feathered the propeller on the dead engine. If they lost another one they would be lucky to ditch under control. The flight manual said a Liberator could fly on three engines normally, but losing every excess pound increased the chances the remaining three engines could bring them home. And not knowing why one had failed meant they couldn't be sure the same problem wasn't about to cause another engine to quit. This veteran crew wasn't going to go down wishing they had done something more to keep the plane in the air.

Yankus grabbed the fire axe from its mount in the fuselage and went aft. He chopped through the ball turret supports until it seemed to hang by a thread, then Yankus and the ball gunner kicked the turret back and forth, rocking it until it fell away. Next he chopped through the top turret seat hinges and threw it out. The crew threw waist guns and ammunition out windows, flak suits followed. Every man searched his position for anything loose, anything expendable to throw out.

Scearce got the radar turret free and dropped it away, and then pulled out radio equipment, yanked out the connections, and pitched it. He took the axe from Yankus and chopped the legs from under his radio operator's table, worked the table loose and threw it out. For four hours the crew worked and sweated and their shirts stuck cold and wet to their backs, until Captain Churchill landed at Saipan on three engines. Yankus took charge of getting the bad engine fixed, and four and a half hours later the exhausted crew flew back to Guam, last of the aircraft on the mission to return. Scearce had thirty-nine missions down and one to go.

During the moonless night of February 12, 1945, four B-24s bombed Iwo's Airfield #2, individually, about an hour between each one. Each plane dropped forty 100-pound bombs. A few searchlights switched on but didn't find an American bomber to track, and there was no gunfire from the dark island below.[23]

On the return flight, Sergeant Scearce stood at his waist window and saw another aircraft passing below at 7,000 feet. The unidentified plane had running lights on and a white flashing light on its fuselage; the

B-24's lights were off. The diverse headings of the aircraft and Scearce's line of sight formed a fast-expanding triangle over the black Pacific until the lights of the mysterious aircraft receded into a single point and finally disappeared.

When the mission ended and the debriefing concluded, Scearce returned to his crew quarters, pulled off his boots, and lay back on his cot. Eyes welled with tears, he looked straight up and whispered slowly, softly, and to no one else, "Forty." Settling to a peaceful rest, he saw the mysterious aircraft speeding away again in his mind and wondered about its crew, who they were, where they were going, and whether they had made it, too.

Epilogue

ON THE SAME DAY Sgt. Herman Scearce finished his fortieth mission, Capt. Charlie Bunn drafted the following letter:

42D BOMBARDMENT SQUADRON (H)
Office of the Radar Officer
APO 246
12 February 1945

TO WHOM IT MAY CONCERN:

Technical Sergeant Lester H. Scearce, Jr., 13033593, has been a member of this squadron for approximately two years. During the first year he was Radio and Radar Operator for the Squadron Operations Officer, and during the last year he has been Squadron Radar Operator and Radar Photographer on the Squadron Commander's crew. Throughout this period he was actively engaged in the operation of and instruction of operators on SCR 717, SCR 729, SCR 718, and SCR 695. He was Radar Operator on experimental missions in high altitude bombing with SCR 717 and AN/APQ-5 (Modified for High Altitude Bombing).

Sgt. Scearce has demonstrated exceptional ability both as a Radio Operator and a Radar Observer. His knowledge of the technical aspects and tactical use of the above equipment is unequaled in the squadron. Through his intelligence, initiative, and ability he has developed operating procedures for high altitude bombing with SCR 717 and AN/APQ-5, and Radar Scope Photography techniques which have materially increased the efficiency of this squadron.

After the squadron moved to the forward area, it was assigned a special project calling for a new tactical use of blind bombing equipment. Sgt. Scearce's initial work in Radar Photography and photo interpretation, and in the planning and execution of Radar sorties was a very valuable and vital contribution to the success of the project.

Through close association with Sgt. Scearce, I have found him to be an excellent soldier of superior intelligence, ability, and character, —always sober in his thoughts, actions, and deeds.

In my opinion, Sgt. Scearce's thorough knowledge of both radio and radar and its tactical use, his combat experience, character and ability would best serve the interests of the Armed Forces as a commissioned officer.

(Signed)

CHARLES I. BUNN

Capt., Air Corps

Radar Officer

A field commission was a big deal, and rare, and the process was simple. Scearce would appear before a board of officers, all of them men he knew, and they might ask him a few questions, just a formality, really, and he would become a second lieutenant. He would pin gold bars on his shirt, move his things from the enlisted men's quarters to the officer's area, and begin a new assignment as a radar officer in the ground echelon.

But "going home" had been the objective on the minds of crewmen from the day they finished training. It was their motivation. For some men "home" meant getting back to a wife or girlfriend. Others had family, maybe a job waiting for them. They looked forward to something, but Herman Scearce didn't have a girlfriend or wife back home, didn't have a job, and didn't have connections. "Home" didn't mean the same thing to Scearce as it did to most men. His mother still struggled to make ends meet in Danville, Virginia, and his father lived alone in Roanoke Rapids, North Carolina, neither of them in a position to welcome an ex-service man boarder. "Going home" for Herman Scearce was nothing more than getting back to the States and getting on with his life, whatever it might be.

No one knew how much longer the war would last, and becoming an officer meant staying in the combat zone. Scearce thanked his friend Charlie Bunn and turned down the field commission.

Scearce spent three weeks on Guam waiting for a flight to Hawaii, keeping busy on the flight line working on radio and radar sets. On a flight checking out repaired radar equipment, Scearce saw the American invasion fleet executing a huge turn toward Iwo Jima. The scale of the armada exceeded anything Scearce had ever seen afloat.

Scearce and his buddies on Guam followed news of the invasion. Younger airmen were amazed the Japanese were able to put up such a fight after the pounding Iwo Jima received before the Marines went ashore, but those who were around when Tarawa was invaded weren't so naive.

Scearce was transferred from the 11th Bomb Group to 30th Bomb Group Headquarters on February 24, 1945, an administrative change, the beginning of his processing out of the Army. He got a ride in a worn-out B-24 J on March 8, 1945, to Kwajalein, retracing the route the 42nd took when the squadron had flown to Guam five months before.

On the ground at Kwajalein the men were told they wouldn't be able to proceed to Hawaii, because every available aircrew was needed to search for a high-ranking officer. Gen. Millard Harmon's transport plane had been missing since February 26, and there had been no contact, no hint of trouble. Searches every day since the twenty-sixth had found no trace.

On March 8, it seemed obvious to Scearce and the other men on the crew there was no hope of finding General Harmon's plane; after all, it was going on two weeks. Experience told them the odds of finding anyone alive dropped dramatically as time passed, especially when there had been no contact to help fix a position. They could have gotten lost and gone down just about anywhere.

The crew Scearce accompanied as a passenger was ferrying a tired B-24 back to Hawaii. The plane was overdue for engine changes and had a long list of repairs needed. The pilot submitted an engineer's report of the maintenance items and the message was clear: "Here's what you'll have to do to this plane if you want us to fly search missions around Kwajalein." They were sent on their way. On March 9, they flew nine and a half hours to Johnston Island where they spent the night, reaching Oahu on the tenth. Within a couple of days, Scearce hopped a transport plane back to the States.

After the war, Scearce wrote to Leah Hitchcock, Bob Lipe's mother. Scearce told her he had known Bob, that Bob was a good guy, and that he was sorry. She wrote a response to him on Tuesday morning, December 11, 1945. The war had been over for four months. She wrote:

> I was so glad to receive your welcome letter, so glad you are again home, and do hope you are well and suffer no effect of this awful war . . .
>
> I received Bob's Air Medal. I had it sent to me as I could not see where it would mean anything to Bob for me to go to Columbus to receive it. I am still praying Bob will be home to get it.

You spoke of Lt. Dechert—his father has been in the hospital. I
hope he is better by now, as the Lieutenant was their only child. The
Buckles boy who was with the crew had a brother killed in Germany.
The Barwick boy's mother seemed to have cracked up and is in hos-
pital. For myself, I have tried very hard to be as brave as I know my
Bob would have me.

He sure was one grand son. I was able to do so little for my sons
after their father's death. They have all been such wonderful boys.
They are my everything.

We are having some cold weather here, snow and ice, roads are
slick. A lot of flu which is closing a lot of our schools.

I wish to thank you for sending the picture of Bob. That smile
of Bob's sure shows why he was everyone's friend. Sometimes we
wonder why things should happen to a boy like him, but so glad he
was a good boy and we can always think of him in pride for to know
him was a joy. I am not working now. We made tarps, mostly the 13
x 10 size but the order was canceled in August. I did not go back to
my old job. They are after me to take charge of a new department
but I don't think I will just now.

I will close this hoping for the best of everything for you, and
hoping that we will have good news of our Bob, and it will be soon.

It had already been two years. Bob Lipe's loss while flying with
George Dechert's crew was the only loss among the original crew of
Dogpatch Express.

Charlie Pratte's loss was a mystery that endured for many years. Clues to
solve the mystery existed in the record of a Marine Corps investigation
in January 1946, but it was the publication of a book by Chester Hearn

that brought the material to light for my dad and for surviving family members I reached during research for this book.

A short passage in Hearn's 2003 book *Sorties into Hell* describes the downing of a B-24 on Chichi Jima and the Marine search party that reached the crash site a year later. When I read the passage, I stopped to compare William Farrell's name to the names listed on the Missing Air Crew Report, though I knew I had recognized a name from Charlie Pratte's crew. These few paragraphs in Hearn's book solved the decades-old mystery and answered questions that many of the men who were close to Pratte's crew carried with them to their graves.

I called my father to share the discovery with him and had no idea how he might react. It had been more than sixty years, after all, and any faint hope the men might have survived disappeared long ago. I told Dad the story and I commented that the crash must have happened quickly because the plane was on a low altitude mission and it could not have fallen long. The crew must not have suffered, certainly a better fate than airmen captured, tortured, executed, and cannibalized by the Japanese on Chichi Jima.

After sharing these things with Dad, he responded to me very softly, and I thought I heard his voice tremble when he said, "That's just . . . really sad." Dad's sorrow wasn't reduced by the passage of time or his knowledge, deep down, all along that his good friend Joe Hyson had not survived the war. As we talked I heard and felt the reaction of an airman learning that his buddy had gone down, as if the news was fresh, just as if it was January 1945.

Disappearances were especially cruel to families. Bobby Lipe's mother hoped for a miracle long after the war ended. Flight Engineer John Magalassi's mother received a letter from her son postmarked after *Virginia Belle* disappeared, and she clung to it as proof her son was still alive. Later she was haunted by a group photograph of airmen, convinced one of the men was her son, though a child's arm obscured the man's face from the camera.

On December 18, 1944, pilot George Dechert's mother wrote to radio operator Ralph Walbeck's mother from her Riverton, Wyoming, home. In part, she wrote:

If they are being held prisoner by the Japs, they may be suffering a fate worse than death, and if they are on some island way out there in the Pacific, maybe they are starving, or sick, or insane. If there were only some way to know! The only hope that I have is that they are being cared for by friendly natives on some island.

I think and imagine such awful things that might have happened that sometimes I think I'll go crazy. It is so hard right now to hear everyone planning for Christmas with their families, and telling what they have done for their boys overseas . . . I know from your letter that you are dreading Christmas as much as I. I have done very little gift shopping . . . What little I did was torture for me.

So many sad homes the whole world over—as many and maybe more among the enemy as here at home. And after all Mrs. Walbeck, the Japs and German's mothers love their boys as much as we do ours.

It seems we almost have to live on hopes these days, doesn't it? Well that is just what we must do, keep on hoping and praying that wherever they are, our boys are in our Heavenly Father's care.

Also lost with George Dechert's crew was bombardier William "Gailor" Roy, on his first combat mission after recovering from a broken wrist. Roy's mother imagined for years that the ring of her doorbell was her son returned from the war. Once in a while she would open a trunk filled with Gailor's things and look through his boyhood schoolwork, his stamp collection, and his paper airplane models. She held on to these things until 1961.

Charlie Pratte's family was devastated by news that he was missing in action. His wife, Bernadette, had been excited for his return home because she knew, and his parents and friends and extended family knew, that he was very close to finishing his missions. They were so proud of him for the miraculous parachute landing on Tarawa more than a year before, and it seemed unthinkable that he could have survived that ordeal only to disappear when he was almost home. It made no sense, it wasn't fair.

Charlie Pratte's young cousin Dorothy had grown up idolizing Charlie. She wanted to do what he did, wanted to tag along with Charlie and his twin younger brothers wherever they went. She was eighteen and in school when she found out that her hero was missing.

Dorothy kept Charlie and Bernadette's pet dog in an apartment that she shared with Charlie's mother. Dorothy thought about Charlie sometimes at night in her downstairs bedroom, especially if there was a storm, because thunder frightened Charlie's dog, the terrier named Dopey. Dopey hid under Dorothy's bed whenever it stormed at night and Dorothy would try to comfort him. Dorothy wondered whether the thunder sounded anything like the guns the Japanese used to shoot at American airplanes.

Bernadette Pratte believed Charlie was coming home, and she fantasized about him emerging from the jungle or some nameless remote place and being reunited with her. Every time there was news or rumor about a soldier found in a prison camp or recovering in a hospital, she was convinced it was Charlie. She saw other men coming home and felt sure she would see hers return, too. She imagined holding him and not letting go; she could almost feel how complete and happy she would be when that day came.

Sgt. Bill Findle, a victim of combat fatigue sent home and later discharged, was the only survivor of Charlie Pratte's original crew. For many years, Findle wondered why he had made it back. In his own home he was disoriented and he struggled to speak because his disability left him with a profound stutter, yet he refused to seek treatment. His mother sat with him, reading with him for hours and hours, page after page, from a Sears catalog.

My father sent me an 11th Bomb Group Association newsletter in which a woman in West Palm Beach, Florida, asked for help finding information about her brother, Bill Mashaw, lost sixty-three years before. Mashaw was a crewmate of William Farrell, Joe Hyson, and the rest of Charlie Pratte's crew. I contacted her, and she wrote back to me, "Do you think there is any way I can find out just what happened over Chichi Jima? I can't imagine the thoughts and fear in their minds . . ."

Bill Mashaw was the flight engineer on Charlie Pratte's crew, and if he was able, odds are he was working desperately to help his pilots keep their plane airborne until the moment it struck the cliffs over Maruen Wan. As we continued our correspondence, Bill Mashaw's sister shared questions about the search for the crewmen, why they hadn't been recovered, why the search party didn't find any bones. She regretted having no chance to give her lost airman brother a decent burial and a fitting memorial.

There is a rock formation called Senjiniwa, Heart Rock, in the face of the cliffs overlooking the bay called Maruen Wan. It stands six hundred feet tall above the bay and spans several hundred feet across. It is stained dark red from iron oxide in soil washed down its face by rain, and its shape is unmistakably like a child's valentine cut from a folded piece of dark red construction paper.

Heart Rock towers over the bay very near the place where Charlie Pratte's B-24 Liberator crashed in 1945. I shared a photograph of Heart Rock with Bill Mashaw's sister, and she agreed that it is a beautiful memorial.

My father, Technical Sergeant Herman Scearce was honorably discharged June 18, 1945, at Fort Bragg, North Carolina. He returned to Roanoke Rapids and lived with his father while attending Roanoke Rapids High School. Good looking, a little older than most students, and an air combat veteran, Herman was popular with girls.

At Roanoke Rapids High, Herman met Flora Ann Davenport. Flora Ann's younger brother Steve cautioned her to be careful, telling her, "It's just your week." But the week became two, then a month, and soon Flora Ann's brother stopped voicing his warning. Herman and Flora Ann were married March 23, 1948.

Herman re-enlisted in the United States Air Force, a separate service from the Army since 1947. He kept his former rank until promotion to master sergeant in 1952. He served as radio operator on C-54 transport aircraft, flying Atlantic and North African routes. Scearce met Charles Lindbergh on one of those flights when Lindbergh went along as a VIP passenger and spent several hours on the flight deck chatting with the crew.

Later in his Air Force career, Master Sergeant Herman Scearce supervised radar maintenance on B-29 Superfortress and B-47 Stratojet aircraft with duty stations in the United States and French Morocco. Scearce was among the last airmen stationed at Harlingen Air Force Base, Texas, before the base closed in 1962. He retired from the Air

Force at that time with twenty-one years' service and returned to North Carolina with Flora Ann and their three children: my brother Jan, sister Rebecca, and me.

—=≡€—

Dad worked his second career in public service while I grew up. He was a magistrate in Craven County, North Carolina, working in Havelock and New Bern until his retirement in 2004. When I was a kid I often went to the Havelock police station where Dad had an office, and when things weren't busy, he shared stories with me.

I was fascinated by my father's World War II experiences. The men he flew and fought with grew in stature with me until they were like warriors of mythology and my imagination soared with them on their missions. Mom was always amused by Dad and me, talking about war stories and going over them "for the umpteenth time." She said I was the only one Dad shared his war experiences with, and I don't know why that is true, whether it's because I was genuinely interested, or because enough time had passed. Maybe both.

At home I looked at my dad's collection of photographs, dozens of them. There is a smiling Bobby Lipe standing in his barracks, a photo that saddened me because this handsome soldier didn't survive the war, didn't have a chance to grow up. There is a picture of Joe Deasy sitting on the forward section of a B-24, confident and cool. Another photo showed the crew gathered around an intelligence officer, debriefing after a mission, Deasy leaning in to make a point, Catanzarite looking exhausted, his hat pushed back on his head, shirt unbuttoned, and Lipe in an "Army Air Corps" T-shirt. Another photo shows my dad at the waist window of a B-24, holding a .50 caliber machine gun, trying to look serious while Jack Yankus fills the rest of the window opening, smiling hugely at the camera. I can almost hear Jack Yankus laughing, just looking at the picture.

But my favorite photo, when I was a kid, was the crew photo taken beside the B-24 *Dogpatch Express*. These were the men, and this was the aircraft, which came together as a fighting unit and went overseas in 1943. I was intrigued by the fact that *Dogpatch Express* was lost later that year. I felt sorry for the men who died with the plane, but I also thought that going down fighting was a noble end for the aircraft, certainly better than the fate awaiting thousands of Liberators scrapped when the war ended.

Looking through the old photos put my dad in a rare reflective mood, and he told me that he sometimes wondered why God allowed him to survive the war. The answer came to him, in time, as a gently dawning awareness that he had survived to become father to his three children, get to know them, and see them go into the world.

Endnotes

"Sergeant at Seventeen" notes

1. The Army Air Corps was renamed Army Air Forces in June 1941, in an administrative reorganization, but airmen typically continued to refer to the service as the Air Corps.

2. Rebecca Hancock Cameron, *Training to Fly: Military Flight Training, 1907–1945* (Washington, D.C.: Government Printing Office, 1999), 438.

3. *Jane's Fighting Aircraft of World War II* (New York: Random House, 1996), 251. Norman Polmar and Thomas B. Allen, *World War II, The Encyclopedia of the War Years 1941–1945* (New York: Random House, 1996), 109–10.

4. Cameron, *Training to Fly*, 438.

5. Charles A. Lindbergh, *The Wartime Journals of Charles A. Lindbergh* (New York: Harcourt Brace Jovanovich, 1970), 641–42. Lindbergh wrote, "The slightest wind would blow it over the water faster than the crew could swim after it; and since there is almost always a wind at sea, it is not likely the crew would ever reach their life rafts . ."

6. Joe Deasy, interview with the author, June 11, 2005.

7. Aircraft Inventory Sheet, Order # W 535-ac-4 DA for B-24D 41-24214.

8. Martin W. Bowman, *Consolidated B-24 Liberator* (Wiltshire, England: The Crowood Press, 1998), 7–8.

9. Geoffrey Perret, *Winged Victory: The Army Air Forces in World War II* (New York: Random House, 1997), 99.

10. Ibid.

11. Ibid.

12. Headquarters, 11th Ferrying Group, Army Air Forces, Air Transport Command, Secret Operations Order Number 93, February 7, 1943. All unpublished orders and documents are found in the Air Force Historical Research Agency, Maxwell Air Force Base, Alabama.

"Hawaii" notes

1. Polmar and Allen, *World War II*, 533.

2. Factory-installed retractable belly turrets were introduced in the B-24-H in June 1943. Martin W. Bowman, *Consolidated B-24 Liberator* (Wiltshire, England: The Crowood Press, 1998), 20.

3. Cameron, *Training to Fly*, 439–40.

4. Joe Deasy, interview with the author, June 11, 2005.

"First Mission" notes

1. Melei Telavi, *Tuvalu: A History* (Fiji: The Institute of Pacific Studies and Extension Services, University of the South Pacific, and the Tuvalu Ministry of Social Services, 1983), 141–42.

2. "Funafuti" briefing report, 1943.

3. John Costello, *The Pacific War* (New York: Harper Perennial, 1982), 134.

4. Jack Yankus, interview with the author, November 3, 1998.

5. "Bombing of Nauru" briefing report, January 10, 1944, 4.

6. Don Lipe, Wayne Lipe, and Willis Lipe, interviews with the author, December 5, 1998.

"Nauru" notes

1. The interphone had five positions: INTER, for hearing and talking with other men on the crew; COMP, for listening to the radio compass receiver; LIAISON, for listening to VHF plane-to-plane talk; COMMAND, for listening to medium frequency talk on the command radio equipment, usually plane-to-ground; and CALL, which was used to contact a crewman whose jack box was not on INTER. Each box also had a volume control knob. From "Gunner's Information File," *Air Forces Manual Number 20*, 1944, T-6 and T-7.

2. Laura Hillenbrand (biographer of Louis Zamperini), from correspondence with the author.

3. Major General Willis H. Hale, "Bombardment and Photo Mission on Nauru Island, 20 April 1943," report to CincPac, April 27, 1943, 2.

4. Robert C. Mikesh, *Zero: Japan's Legendary Fighter* (Osceola, WI: Motorbooks International, 1994), 123. By contrast, a round from a .50 caliber machine gun weighed about two ounces.

5. In late 1944, armor plate and bullet-resistant glass was installed behind the pilot's seat. Mikesh, *Zero: Japan's Legendary Fighter*, 91.

6. "Navigator's Information File," Headquarters, Army Air Forces, November 24, 1944, page 4-12-2.

7. Laura Hillenbrand, from correspondence with the author.

"Air Raid" notes

1. Major General Willis H. Hale, "Bombardment and Photo Mission on Nauru Island, 20 April, 1943," Report dated April 27, 1943, 1–2.

2. Ibid., 3.

3. Jack D. Haden, "Nauru: A Middle Ground During World War II," *Pacific Magazine*, April 3, 2000.

4. Gavan Daws, *Prisoners of the Japanese* (New York: William Morrow & Co, 1994), 278–79.

5. W. M. Cleveland, ed., *Grey Geese Calling* (Askov, MN: American Publishing Company, 1981), 30.

6. The Doolittle raid, which General Hale refers to as the "raid on Tokyo" in his report about the Nauru mission, used B-25 Mitchell medium bombers. Industrial targets were bombed by the Doolittle raiders, but the scale of the mission, and its intent from the beginning, was largely symbolic.

7. Telavi, *Tuvalu: A History*, 140.

8. "Funa Futi Field" [*sic*] schematic drawing by Seventh Air Force Office of the Engineer, October 9, 1943.

9. "Funafuti" secret briefing report, 1943.

10. Robert F. Dorr, "Unsung Battle," *Marine Corps Times*, June 21, 2004; Telavi, *Tuvalu: A History*, 141.

11. Charles J. Greene, "Funafuti: Springboard of the Pacific," *Leatherneck Magazine*, August 1944, 15.

12. "Funafuti" secret briefing report, July 1943, 1.

13. "Bombing Mission Facilities on Funafuti Island," Lt. Roger Holtz memorandum, July 29, 1943.

14. "Funafuti" secret briefing report, July 1943, 2.

15. Edward V. Rickenbacker, *Seven Came Through: Rickenbacker's Full Story* (Garden City, NY: Doubleday, Doran & Co., 1943), 69–71. For wartime security reasons, Rickenbacker refers to Funafuti as "Island Z." Edward V. Rickenbacker, *Rickenbacker, An Autobiography* (New York: Prentice Hall, 1967), 327–29.

16. Samuel Eliot Morison, *History of United States Naval Operations in World War II: Aleutians, Gilberts and Marshalls*, (Urbana, IL: University of Chicago Press, 2002), 83. Morison indicates the Liberators were followed home. However, this was not the first Japanese raid on Funafuti, so it is also possible the Japanese assumed it was the B-24's forward base from prior reconnaissance and on their knowledge of the B-24's range.

17. Lt. Col. W. E. Hicks, USMC, Extracts from Post Regulations, Funafuti Island, found in Air Force Historical Research Agency.

18. Fonnie Black Ladd, *The Wholesale Rescue* (Charleston, MS: Valley Farm Publications, 1986), 35–36. Ladd's book includes his citation awarding the Silver Star for his heroic efforts the night of the Japanese raid (p. 87). The citation puts the number of villagers in the church at "some forty." *Tuvalu: A History*, cites Samuel Eliot Morison, whose 7th volume of *History of United States Naval Operations in World War II* puts the number at 680, which seems an incredible number, since a secret 1943 briefing report on Funafuti puts the *entire* native population at 400. Morison's statement is not annotated. Ladd's description of leading a group out of the church and to the beach, quickly, and by himself, also raises doubt about Morison's number. The Silver Star citation mentioning forty appears to be the most reliable number.

19. From photo, author's collection. The native's name is from *Tuvalu: A History* (142) and his death in the raid that destroyed the church is also confirmed in this text. However, *Tuvalu: A History* reports the raid as occurring April 23. Herman Scearce recalls the raid that damaged the church, however, and was present only for the April 21 attack. The hole in which the *Dogpatch Express* crew huddled was near the church, and Scearce recalls this is the area where the bombs fell. Louis Zamperini, also present only for the April 21 raid, confirms the April 21 date and records the destruction of the church in his diary (from the author's correspondence with Zamperini biographer Laura Hillenbrand). Morison, *History of United States Naval Operations*, 83, cites the April 21 date. Funafuti's position west of the International Date Line could account for only one day's disparity. Finally, *The Wholesale Rescue* cites April 22 as the date of the destruction of the church, correct using Funafuti's calendar, west of the date line. Since there was a subsequent

Japanese raid on the night of April 22 (as Americans were bombing Tarawa) it is the author's conclusion that the church destruction and the native's death occurred in the April 21 raid, which immediately followed the U.S. attack on Nauru, and that the contributor to *Tuvalu: A History* attributed the events to the subsequent Japanese raid.

"Chance" notes

1. Frederick C. Mish, ed., *Langenscheidt's New College Merriam-Webster English Dictionary* (Berlin, Germany: Langenscheidt Publishers, 1996), 190.

2. Wallace R. Forman, *B-24 Nose Art Name Directory* (North Branch, MN: Specialty Press, 1996).

3. Eric M. Bergerud, *Fire in the Sky* (Boulder, CO: Westview Press, 2000) 354–55.

4. Mitsuo Fuchida and Masatake Okumiya, *Midway: The Battle that Doomed Japan* (New York: Ballantine Books, 1958), 40–45.

5. Ibid., 43.

6. Jack Greene, *The Midway Campaign* (Conshohoken, PA: Combined Books, 1995), 65–67.

7. Greene, *The Midway Campaign*, 194.

8. Fuchida and Okumiya, *Midway*, 66–73; Greene, *The Midway Campaign*, 165.

9. Daniel L. Haulman, *Hitting Home: The Air Offensive Against Japan* (Ann Arbor: University of Michigan Press, 1999), 3.

10. Dan van der Vat, *The Pacific Campaign* (New York: Simon & Schuster, 1991), 153–58.

11. Haulman, *Hitting Home*, 4.

12. Robert B. Edgerton, *Warriors of the Rising Sun: A History of the Japanese Military* (Boulder, CO: Westview Press, 1997), 273–75.

13. Leona Jackson, R.N., "I Was on Guam," *American Journal of Nursing*, Nov. 1942, 1244–46; Edgerton, *Warriors of the Rising Sun*, 274.

14. van der Vat, *The Pacific Campaign*, 157.

15. Greene, *The Midway Campaign*, 165.

16. Fuchida and Okumiya, *Midway*, 72; Greene, *The Midway Campaign*, 162.

17. Fuchida and Okumiya, *Midway*, 84.

18. Greene, *The Midway Campaign*, 195.

19. Ibid., 205; Fuchida and Okumiya, *Midway*, 138–40.

20. Fuchida and Okumiya, *Midway* 146–56.

21. Greene, *The Midway Campaign*, 214.

22. Fuchida and Okumiya, *Midway*, 214.

23. Following an attack on an unfortunate American Catalina flying boat, nineteen-year-old Japanese pilot Flight Officer Tadayoshi Koga noticed his oil pressure dropping. A Navy gunner on the American plane, or perhaps a gunner firing at the Zero from the ground, had scored a hit, and severed an oil return line. The Japanese pilot radioed the carrier *Ryujo*, saying he expected his engine to seize from loss of oil. He advised he would land on Akutan Island and destroy his plane, and he requested a submarine to pick him up. Akutan's marshy bogs look like grassy meadows from the air. Koga might have survived if he had landed with his wheels up, but he lowered them and when the wheels touched down, the plane tripped onto its back immediately. His wingmen had orders to destroy any Zero that was forced to land, but they left the plane intact, possibly because their comrade might still be alive. In fact, Koga's neck had snapped when his plane flipped over, killing him instantly. He hung in his harness for thirty days before Americans flying a search mission for another aircraft found his plane.

24. Admiral James S. Russell, "A Zero Is Found Bottom Up in a Bog" in *The Pacific War Remembered* (Annapolis, MD: U.S. Naval Institute, 1986), 110–11.

25. Bergerud, *Fire in the Sky*, 522–23; Fuchida and Okumiya, *Midway*, 207–8.

26. Bergerud, *Fire in the Sky*, 522–23.

27. John Prados, *Combined Fleet Decoded* (New York: Random House, 1995), 339–40.

28. Ibid., 340.

29. A notable exception was the Kawasaki Ki61 "Tony." The Tony had self-sealing fuel tanks and armor protection, but was plagued by reliability and maintenance problems until very late in the war. Bergerud, *Fire in the Sky*, 221–24.

"May 1943" notes

1. Diary of Louis Zamperini, from correspondence with Laura Hillenbrand.

2. Cleveland, ed., *Grey Geese Calling*, 160–61.

3. History of the 42nd Bombardment Squadron (H), 11th Bombardment Group (H), Seventh Air Force compiled April–May 1944 by Lt. Edward B. Petersen, 6.

4. Costello, *The Pacific War*, 302; Capt. Albert L. Raithel, Jr. "Patrol Aviation in the Pacific in WWII, Part 1," *Naval Aviation News*, July–August 1992, 34–35; Greene, The *Midway Campaign*, 202.

5. The officer conducting the pre-flight briefing didn't know there were Americans on Wake Island, so the bomber crews listening to his words were also unaware: when Wake Island surrendered to Japanese invaders on December 22, 1941, most of the captured American sailors and Marines were shipped to Yokohama and from there to prison camps. However, ninety-eight Americans were kept behind, slave labor to help strengthen the defenses of the island renamed Otori Shima, or Bird Island, by the Japanese. A civilian doctor was among them, having volunteered to remain with the others. Like the Japanese commander at Nauru, the Imperial Army defenders of Wake Island were concerned about an American invasion that would never come. But on Wake, the prisoners held by the Japanese were not killed following the B-24 raid. One was executed in July for stealing food. The rest survived to work for the Japanese until October when, just after a shelling by the U.S. Navy, their captors brought the Americans to a sandy ditch on the north side of the island and gunned them down, all but one. (see "Massacre on Wake Island," Naval Institute Proceedings, February 2001, 30). Some sources disagree regarding the number of Americans executed, but "Without a Hangman, Without a Rope: Navy War Crimes Trials after World War II" in *International Journal of Naval History*, April 2002 indicates 98, and 98 is consistent with a carving on a coral rock inscribed by a prisoner who escaped the mass execution, carved the rock, and was later recaptured and beheaded by Wake's Japanese commander, Rear Admiral Shigematsu Sakaibara. "The 98 Rock" is now a Wake Island landmark.

6. Bowman, *Consolidated B-24 Liberator*, 99. These aircraft carried the Royal Air Force LB-30 designation. Following the attack on Pearl Harbor, fifteen were reassigned to the Pacific.

7. Ibid., 107–8. Tinker Air Force Base is named for Gen. Clarence Tinker. Similarly, Andrews Air Force Base is named for Gen. Frank M. Andrews who lost his life in the crash of a B-24 in Iceland on May 3, 1943.

8. Gordon L. Rottman, *Japanese Pacific Island Defenses 1941–1945* (Oxford: Osprey Publishing, 2003), 39.

9. "Emergency Procedure, B-24 Airplane," Consolidated-Vultee Aircraft Corporation, 1944, 22–24.

10. Cleveland, *Grey Geese Calling*, 324.

11. Bob Livingstone, *Under the Southern Cross: The B-24 Liberator in the South Pacific* (Paducah: KY: Turner Publishing Company, 1998), 59–60.

12. Laura Hillenbrand, from correspondence with the author.

13. 42nd Bombardment Squadron operations log for May 30, 1943.

14. 42nd Bombardment Squadron operations log for June 6, 1943.

15. Tail skid and bumper assemblies were installed in aircraft beginning with serial number 41-23640. *Flight Manual for B-24 Liberator* (Appleton, WI: Aviation Publications, 1977), 71–73.

"The Squadron's Objectives" notes

1. Morison, *Aleutians, Gilberts, and Marshalls*, 82–85.

2. van der Vat, *The Pacific Campaign*, 303.

3. Cleveland, *Grey Geese Calling*, 159.

4. 42nd Bombardment Squadron operations log for June 14, 1943.

5. Lieutenant Edward B. Petersen, comp., History of the 42nd Bombardment Squadron (H), 11th Bombardment Group, Seventh Air Force, compiled April–May 1944, 13.

6. Ibid., 14.

7. Cleveland, *Grey Geese Calling*, 81–84.

8. Ibid., 81–84.

9. Ibid., 261.

10. 42nd Bombardment Squadron operations log for June 27, 1943, also Petersen, History of the 42nd Bombardment Squadron (H), 14.

11. "Danny Boy" lyrics by Frederick Weatherly, 1910. Public Domain.

12. Joe Deasy, interview with the author, June 11, 2005. "I couldn't make all our flights in the afternoon," Joe Deasy said, "The boys thought I had a lot more control over things than I really did."

13. Headquarters, 11th Ferrying Group Secret Operations Order #93, February 7, 1943.

14. "U.S. Planes Bomb Nauru," *Life* magazine, July 5, 1943, 120–25.

15. Morison, *Aleutians, Gilberts and Marshalls*, 83. Morison states that Hale led the mission "in person." Louis Zamperini confirmed that Hale had gone on the mission, but had been in a plane in the rear of the flight. Some of the men of the 42nd believed that Hale had flown with the group to Funafuti, but had not gone on the bombing mission, and it was this belief that fueled their cynicism.
16. "Killed In Action," *Life* magazine, July 5, 1943, 15–39.
17. Harold Brooks was survived by his mother, Edna M. Brooks and brother, Lyle C. Brooks. From Department of the Army, Individual Deceased Personnel File for Harold V. Brooks.
18. "Bombing of Wake Island," 42nd Bomb Squadron Operational Log, 28a-28d.
19. LaSalle Gilman, "Raid on Wake Island by U.S. Described by LaSalle Gilman," *Honolulu Adviser*, July 30, 1943, reprinted in the 42nd Bomb Squadron History.
20. Sgt. Arvid B. Ambur, "The Last Flight of Daisy Mae," *The Midway Mirror*, February 1993, 16.
21. Petersen, History of the 42nd Bombardment Squadron, 15.
22. 98th Bombardment Squadron History 16 Dec. 1941 – 1 April 1944, 21.
23. 42nd Bombardment Squadron operations log for August 6, 1943.
24. Lt. Stay's Distinguished Flying Cross citation is included as an exhibit in the 42nd Bomb Squadron History.
25. Cleveland, *Grey Geese Calling*, 163. A partial listing of the squadron's personnel and decorations awarded is also included in the 42nd Bombardment Squadron History, 21–27.
26. Cleveland, *Grey Geese Calling*, 163.
27. Brig. Gen. T. H. Landon, Commendation letter from Headquarters VII Bomber Command to 11th Bombardment Group, July 27, 1943.

"The Pacific Preferred" notes

1. Donald L. Miller, *Masters of the Air* (New York: Simon & Schuster, 2006), 188.
2. Ibid., 190–91.
3. Ibid.
4. Ibid., 192.
5. Marguerite Madison Aronowitz, *Maternity Ward* (Prescott, AZ: Pine Castle Books, 1998), 136.

6. Miller, *Masters of the Air*, 192.

7. John Ellis, *World War II: A Statistical Survey* (New York: Facts on File, 1993), 260, Table 62.

8. Brian D. O'Neill, *Half a Wing, Three Engines, and a Prayer* (New York: Mc-Graw Hill Professional, 1998), 17.

9. Miller, *Masters of the Air*, 208.

10. Budd J. Peaslee, *Heritage of Valor* (Philadelphia: J.B. Lippincott, 1963), 151–52.

11. Miller, *Masters of the Air*, 90–92.

12. Ibid.

13. Ibid.

14. Bowman, *Consolidated B-24 Liberator*, 32.

15. Miller, *Masters of the Air*, 127.

16. Ibid., 128–36.

17. Ibid., 180.

18. Bowman, *Consolidated B-24 Liberator*, 27.

19. Bergerud, *Fire in the Sky*, 279.

20. Rickenbacker, *Seven Came Through*, 18–20.

21. Odds improved dramatically late in the war, especially for B-29s flying from the Marianas to targets in Japan.

22. Bergerud, *Fire in the Sky*, 524.

23. Vincent F. Fagan, *Liberator Pilot: The Cottontails' Battle for Oil* (Blue Ridge Summit, PA: California Aero Press, 1992), 6; Wright Lee, *Not as Briefed: 445th Bombardment Group (H) Eighth Air Force: Memoirs of a B024 Navigator/Prisoner of War 1943–1945* (Spartanburg, SC: Honoribus Press, 1995), 132–34, also contains an eyewitness story of a bomber surrendering to German fighters.

24. Peaslee, *Heritage of Valor*, 178–80.

25. Bergerud, *Fire in the Sky*, 524–29.

26. 42nd Bombardment Squadron operations log for December 20, 1943, report on Taroa mission.

"Softening Tarawa" notes

1. Morison, *Aleutians, Gilberts and Marshalls*, 69–85.

2. Rottman, *Japanese Pacific Island Defenses*, 57.

3. Morison, *Aleutians, Gilberts and Marshalls*, 146–49.

4. Herman Scearce, from interviews with the author.

5. Army Air Forces chronology of 42nd Bomb Squadron missions, 19 Sep. 1943, 65.

6. 42nd Bombardment Squadron operations log for September 19, 1943, report on Tarawa mission.

7. 98th Bombardment Squadron History, Dec. 16, 1941–April 1, 1944, 32.

8. "Bombing of Tarawa Island," Headquarters VII Bomber Command, 18–19 Sept. 1945.

9. 98th Bombardment Squadron History, Dec. 16, 1941–April 1, 1944, 32.

10. 98th Bombardment Squadron "Consolidated Mission Report of Strike Against Tarawa, 19 November 1943," 3.

11. 42nd Bombardment Squadron operations log for September 19, 1943, report on Tarawa mission.

12. 98th Bombardment Squadron History, Dec. 16, 1941–April 1, 1944, 32.

13. Cleveland, *Grey Geese Calling*, 167.

14. 42nd Bombardment Squadron Missing Air Crew Report, Nov. 15, 1943.

15. Letters from Byers' father and Magalassi's mother are quoted in a memorandum of Nov. 14, 1944, attached to the Missing Air Crew Report.

16. Martin Russ, *Line of Departure: Tarawa* (New York: Doubleday, 1975), 18.

17. Report "Analysis of Jaluit Mission 15 Nov. 1943," Headquarters, VII Bomber Command, December 3, 1943.

18. Annex "A," Bomb Plot Chart, in Report "Analysis of Jaluit Mission 15 Nov. 1943," Headquarters, VII Bomber Command, December 3, 1943.

19. The aircraft received field repairs and was flown to the Hickam Air Depot, where it was salvaged. Herman Scearce, from interviews with the author.

20. "D" model Liberators had inward-opening nose wheel doors, as did B-24 J's until 1944. B-24 G and H models had outward-opening nose wheel doors as did later "J" models. Martin W. Bowman, *Consolidated B-24 Liberator* (Wiltshire, England: The Crowood Press, 1998), 21.

21. 431st Bombardment Squadron History, August 1917–March 1944, 17.

22. Scearce recalls hearing parts of the radio transmissions during the invasion. The language of these transmissions is recorded in Tarawa battle histories such as Russ' *Line of Departure: Tarawa*, 85–87, and Alexander's *Utmost Savagery: The Three Days of Tarawa*, 3.

"Forever Consequences" notes

1. Army Air Force Bombardiers Information File, March 1945, 7-2-3.
2. Army Air Force Bombardiers Information File, Aerial Bombs classification chart, 7-1-5, March, 1945.
3. Alexander, *Utmost Savagery,* 117.
4. Ibid.
5. Report "Bombing of Mille," Headquarters, Seventh Air Force, Dec. 27, 1943.
6. Missing Air Crew Report dated Dec. 2, 1943, and its enclosed witness account by Capt. Jesse Stay.
7. 42nd Bombardment Squadron operations log for December 1, 1943, report on the Mille strike.
8. Cleveland, *Grey Geese Calling,* 167. Susan Taylor, William G. Roy's niece, in correspondence with the author indicated her uncle Gailor broke his wrist in a ballgame.
9. "S.Sgt Robert Lipe, Air Corps Gunner, Reported Missing," *The Columbiana Ledger,* Dec. 17, 1943.

"Losing Altitude Fast" notes

1. "Bombing of Nauru" report of January 10, 1944, Headquarters, VII Bomber Command, 5–6. 42nd Bombardment Squadron operations log for December 4, 1943, Nauru strike.
2. Ibid.
3. Morison, *Aleutians, Gilberts and Marshalls,* 215.
4. Missing Air Crew Report, Headquarters, 42nd Bombardment Squadron, December 22, 1943.
5. Rottman, *Japanese Pacific Island Defenses,* 38–39.
6. Ibid.
7. Jesse Stay, from correspondence with the author, Feb. 28, 1999. There is also an account of the loss of *Dogpatch Express* by Jesse Stay in the historical compilation, *11th Bomb Group (H) The Grey Geese* (Turner Publishing Co., 1996), 73. Minor details of Stay's story varied over time, and where details differ, I have used the version corroborated by other sources or the earliest recorded version.
8. 431st Bombardment Squadron History, Aug. 1917–March 1944, 20.

9. 42nd Bombardment Squadron operations log for December 20, 1943, Taroa strike.

10. Missing Air Crew Report, Headquarters, 42nd Bombardment Squadron, December 21, 1943.

11. Morison, *Aleutians, Gilberts and Marshalls*, 212.

12. Cleveland, *Grey Geese Calling*, 80.

13. Cleveland, *Grey Geese Calling*, 180, quoting an article from *BRIEF*, the 7th Air Force newspaper.

14. Letter from General H. H. Arnold to General Willis Hale, War Department, Headquarters of the Army Air Forces, March 8, 1944, copy included in 42nd Bomb Squadron History.

15. Cleveland, *Grey Geese Calling*, 181.

16. Morison, *Aleutians, Gilberts and Marshalls*, 211.

17. Jesse Stay, from correspondence with the author, Feb. 28, 1999.

18. Ibid.

19. 26th Bombardment Squadron operations log for December 20, 1943.

"Back to Hawaii" notes

1. Cleveland, *Grey Geese Calling*, 39.

2. 98th Bombardment Squadron History, 39; Cleveland, *Grey Geese Calling*, 327.

3. 431st Bombardment Squadron History, Aug. 1917–March 1944, 22.

4. 42nd Bombardment Squadron operations log for September 22, 1943.

5. Cleveland, *Grey Geese Calling*, 163.

6. 431st Bombardment Squadron History, Aug. 1917-March 1944, 17.

7. 42nd Bombardment Squadron History, report of the mess hall fire dated December 16, 1943.

8. Orders of Commanding General, VII Bomber Command, Dec. 23, 1943 "Movement of 42nd Bomb Sq. (H)" attached as Exhibit E in 42nd Bombardment Squadron History, Feb. 1940–March, 1944.

9. John C. Reilly, Jr., "Organization of Naval Aviation in World War II," *Naval Aviation News*, May–June 1991, 31.

10. 431st Bombardment Squadron History, Aug. 1917–March 1944, 20.

11. 42nd Bombardment Squadron History, July 18, 1942–Aug. 10, 1943, narrative report of the squadron's move.

12. Cleveland, *Grey Geese Calling*, 129.

13. 42nd Bombardment Squadron History, July 18, 1942–Aug. 10, 1943, narrative report of the squadron's move.

14. Cleveland, *Grey Geese Calling*, 331 (98th); 69 (26th); 131–32, 167–68 (42nd); 267–68 (431st); also respective squadron histories.

15. 98th Bombardment Squadron History, 42.

16. 98th Bombardment Squadron History, 42, and 42nd Bombardment Squadron operations log for January 13–14 and March 6, 1944.

17. 431st Bombardment Squadron History, Aug. 1917–March 1944, 23.

18. 98th Bombardment Squadron History, 39.

19. Dorothy T. Pratte, Charlie Pratte's cousin, interview with the author, June 1, 2009.

20. 42nd Bombardment Squadron operations log for January 11, 1944.

21. 42nd Bombardment Squadron History, July 18, 1942–Aug. 10, 1943, narrative report of the squadron's move.

22. Cleveland, *Grey Geese Calling*, 159; Dave Turner, *11th Bomb Group (H) The Grey Geese* (Paducah, KY: Turner Publishing Co, 1996), 10–12.

23. Cleveland, *Grey Geese Calling*, 150–51.

24. Ibid.

25. 42nd Bombardment Squadron operations log for January 17, 1944.

26. 42nd Bombardment Squadron History, Feb. 1940–March, 1944, 19.

27. 42nd Bombardment Squadron operations log for January 26, 1944.

28. Morison, *Aleutians, Gilberts and Marshalls*, 212.

29. Herman Scearce, from interviews with the author.

30. *On the Beam with CASU-16*, a unit publication produced in 1944 now in the Navy Department Library, Special Collections, call number 790-05, 4–5.

31. Preflight procedures adapted from *Flight Manual for B-24 Liberator*, Consolidated Aircraft, Sept. 15, 1942, reprinted by Aviation Publications, 1977, 135–42 and from interviews with Jack Yankus and Herman Scearce, who remembers this particular preflight was done "by the book" because of the aircraft's history.

"Last Flights" notes

1. Morison, *Aleutians, Gilberts and Marshalls*, 257–72; S. L. A. Marshall, *Island Victory; The Battle of Kwajalein Atoll* (Toronto: Bison Books,

2001). Marshall's book provides a highly detailed account of the battle for Kwajalein.

2. From transcribed text of phone message to VII Bomber Command reporting on invasion, February 2, 1944, included as an exhibit in 98th Bombardment Squadron History.

3. 42nd Bombardment Squadron operations log for February 24, 1944.

4. Lt. Edward B. Petersen, comp., History of the 42nd Bombardment Squadron (H), 11th Bombardment Group, Seventh Air Force compiled April-May 1944, 12.

5. Petersen, History of the 42nd Bombardment Squadron (H), 12.

6. 42nd Bombardment Squadron (H) Addendum to Petersen, Squadron History, September 11, 1945.

7. Louis Zamperini with Helen Itria, *Devil at My Heels* (New York: E. P. Dutton and Co., 1956), 71. Details in the 1945 squadron report and the 1956 book vary regarding the day of the overflight (Zamperini indicates the third day is correct; the book indicates it was the second day) and also differ with respect to the number and placement of shots from the flare gun. All document the search overflight of the B-24. It was the 1956 book that gave Scearce his first account of the overflight.

8. After the war Zamperini happened to attend a revival meeting where a young preacher named Billy Graham spoke, and the preacher's words resonated with the former bombardier. Zamperini became a Christian and committed himself to a lifetime of service in his faith. More than sixty years after his plane went down in the Pacific, Zamperini expressed his hope that Scearce felt no regret about missing the raft during the search mission.

9. Petersen, History of the 42nd Bombardment Squadron (H), 19–20.

10. 42nd Bombardment Squadron operations log for January 23, 1944.

11. S. Sidney Ulmer and William Davis Parker, *Waist Gunner: The Diary of William Davis Parker in World War II* (Bloomington, IN: Xlibris Corp, 2000), 148.

12. Morison, *Aleutians, Gilberts and Marshalls*, 317.

13. Information about the loss of *Heavy Date*, including the record of the radio transmissions, is from the Missing Air Crew Report. The radio log was edited for clarity.

14. 42nd Bombardment Squadron operations log for April 28, 1944.

"Ask the Man Who Owns One" notes

1. 42nd Bombardment Squadron operations log for April 10, 1944.

2. 42nd Bombardment Squadron operations log for March 19, 1944.

3. 42nd Bombardment Squadron operations log for March 26, 1944.

4. Stan Cohen, *V for Victory: America's Home Front During World War II* (Blacksburg, VA: Pictorial Histories Publishing Company, 1991), 93.

5. 42nd Bombardment Squadron operations log for June 23, 1944.

6. 42nd Bombardment Squadron operations log for February 12, 1944.

"The Meaning of Boxes" notes

1. 42nd Bombardment Squadron History, May 1944, 1.

2. Ibid.

3. Ibid.

4. Ibid.

5. Headquarters, 11th Ferrying Group, Army Air Forces, Air Transport Command, Hamilton Field, California, Operations Order 93, February 7, 1943.

6. 42nd Bombardment Squadron History, August 1944, 2.

7. Samuel Eliot Morison, *History of the United States Naval Operations in World War II: New Guinea and the Marianas* (Urbana: University of Illinois Press, 2002), 9.

8. Ibid.

9. *Jane's Fighting Aircraft of World War II*, 209 (B-29) and 216 (B-24); William N. Hess, *Great American Bombers of World War II* (St. Paul, MN: MBI Publishing, 1998), 297–307.

10. van der Vat, *The Pacific Campaign*, 319.

11. Costello, *The Pacific War*, 21.

12. Morison, *New Guinea and the Marianas*, 157–58.

13. Costello, *The Pacific War*, 143.

14. "Religious Life During the Japanese Occupation," Guampedia, http://guampedia.com/religious-life-during-the-japanese-occupation, 2007, 3.

15. Costello, *The Pacific War*, 155.

16. Ibid.; Edgerton, *Warriors of the Rising Sun*, 261.

17. http://guampedia.com/religious-life-during-the-japanese-occupation.

18. Cat Major, *Myths of Guam* (Publisher Unknown, 1987), 82–85.

19. Jackson, 1244–46.

20. Ibid.

21. van der Vat, The *Pacific Campaign*, 27.

22. Jackson, 1244–46.

23. Costello, *The Pacific War,* 475; Morison, *New Guinea and the Marianas,* 160.

24. Costello, *The Pacific War,* 476. Costello points out the irony for Nagumo that he now faced three battleships that had been present at Pearl Harbor on December 7, 1941, but Costello indicates that these three ships (they were the *California, Pennsylvania, and Tennessee*) were sunk. *California's* hull plates were ruptured by explosions and the ship settled to the bottom on an even keel, its superstructure above water. *Pennsylvania* was in dry dock during the Pearl Harbor attack and was damaged when a destroyer in the same dry dock exploded. *Tennessee* was trapped along Battleship Row between its moorings and the *West Virginia,* with *Arizona* directly astern and *Maryland* ahead, the *Maryland* similarly trapped by the overturned *Oklahoma. Tennessee* was damaged by fire and heat from nearby ships, debris from explosions, and by bomb hits.

25. van der Vat, *The Pacific Campaign,* 317–18; Morison, *New Guinea and the Marianas,* 160.

26. van der Vat, *The Pacific Campaign,* 317.

27. Costello, *The Pacific War,* 476.

28. van der Vat, *The Pacific Campaign,* 320; Costello, *The Pacific War,* 477.

29. Morison, *New Guinea and the Marianas,* 197; van der Vat, *The Pacific Campaign,* 320.

30. van der Vat, *The Pacific Campaign,* 321; Costello, *The Pacific War,* 478; Morison, *New Guinea and the Marianas,* 197–208.

31. Hess, *Great American Bombers,* 323.

32. Costello, *The Pacific War,* 487; Hess, *Great American Bombers,* 323.

33. 26th Squadron History, June 1944, 3.

34. Ibid.

35. Morison, *New Guinea and the Marianas,* 197.

36. van der Vat, *The Pacific Campaign,* 320–21; Costello, *The Pacific War,* 478.

37. Morison, *New Guinea and the Marianas,* 221; *Jane's Fighting Aircraft of World War II,* 191, 193.

38. Morison, *New Guinea and the Marianas,* 221.

39. Morison, *New Guinea and the Marianas,* 260.

40. 431st Bomb Squadron Mission Report, Mission #H-270, June 19, 1944, dated June 20, 1944 attached as an exhibit in the 431st Bomb Squadron History for June, 1944.

41. 26th Squadron History, June 1944, 4.

42. Morison, *New Guinea and the Marianas*, 260–61.

43. 98th Squadron History, June 1944, 3.

44. Ibid.

45. Morison, *New Guinea and the Marianas*, 273.

46. Major O.R. Lodge, USMC Historical Monograph, "The Recapture of Guam," USMC, Historical Branch, G-3 Division, Headquarters, U.S. Marine Corps, 1954 Chapter v., "Air Support," 108–9

47. Morison, *New Guinea and the Marianas*, 319–21.

48. Ibid., 320–21.

49. Post-war interrogation of Vice Admiral Jisaburo Ozawa, United States Strategic Bombing Survey Interrogations of Japanese Officials, OPNAV-P-03-100, "The Battle of the Philippine Sea," October 16, 1945, 5.

50. Morison, *New Guinea and the Marianas*, 359.

51. Ibid., 369.

52. Ibid., 371.

53. Ibid., 338 (Saipan), 400 (Guam).

"Guam" notes

1. 42nd Bomb Squadron History, August 1944, 2.

2. Ibid.

3. 42nd Bomb Squadron History, July, 1944, 1; also 42nd Bomb Squadron operations log for July and August, 1944.

4. 42nd Bomb Squadron History, July 1944, 1.

5. Ibid.

6. Ibid., July through August, 1944.

7. Ibid., 2.

8. Herman Scearce, from interviews with the author.

9. 42nd Bomb Squadron History, August, 1944, 4; Cleveland, *Grey Geese Calling*, 133. The Squadron's Operations log for August 8, 1944, identifies the man killed as *Thomas* Bales.

10. 42nd Bomb Squadron operations log for August 2 and August 5, 1944.

11. 42nd Bomb Squadron History, August 1944, 2.

12. Ibid.

13. 42nd Bomb Squadron History, September 1944, 2.

14. Ibid.

15. Ibid.

16. Ibid.

17. Ibid.

18. Ibid.

19. 42nd Bomb Squadron History, September 1944, 3.

20. Ibid.

21. 42nd Bomb Squadron History, October 1944, 3.

22. 42nd Bomb Squadron History, September 1944, 7.

23. 42nd Bomb Squadron History, September 1944, 4.

24. Ibid.

25. ADVON 11th Bomb Group (H) Journal, October, 1944, 1. (ADVON is ADVance EchelON.)

26. 42nd Bomb Squadron History, September 1944, 5.

27. ADVON 11th Bomb Group (H) Journal, October, 1944, 2.

28. Ibid., 3.

29. 26th Bomb Squadron History Sept. 1944, 4.

30. 431st Bomb Squadron History Sept. 1944, 2; 26th Bomb Squadron History Sept. 1944, 5; 98th Bomb Squadron History Sept. 1944, 11.

31. 98th Bomb Squadron History October, 1944, 2–3. See heading "October 5th."

32. Ibid.

33. The 98th Squadron History for December 1941–April 1944, 23–24 includes a long passage titled "98th Uses Secret Weapon" describing dropping beer bottles over Japanese territory. The bottles apparently emitted a "piercing eerie shriek like the wail of a banshee," struck the ground "with a sharp report" and littered the area with broken glass. Also Cleveland, *Grey Geese Calling*, 441, lists the various ordnance the Group used. The last item is "case—empty beer bottles."

34. 98th Bomb Squadron History October, 1944, 5. See heading "The Baker Two Nine."

35. Cleveland, *Grey Geese Calling*, 345. See photo.

36. 98th Bomb Squadron History, October, 7; 431st Bomb Squadron History, October 1944, 4–5; 26th Bomb Squadron History, October 1944, 4.

37. 431st Bomb Squadron History October 1944, 5.

38. Marshall, *Island Victory*, 61, 66.

39. 98th Bomb Squadron History, May 1944, 4.

40. 98th Bomb Squadron History, August 1944, 3.

41. 98th Bomb Squadron History, September 1944, 5.

42. 98th Bomb Squadron History, November 1944, 6.

43. 431st Bomb Squadron History, October 1944, 5.

44. 42nd Bomb Squadron History, September, 1944, 5.

45. ADVON 11th Bomb Group (H) Journal, October, 1944, 2–3.

46. Ibid., 4.

47. 42nd Bomb Squadron History, September 1944, 5.

48. 42nd Bomb Squadron History, October 1944, 4.

"Back in Business" notes

1. Information about the loss of Lt. Thomas Reale's aircraft comes from a Missing Air Crew Report dated Sept. 13, 1944 (the crash occurred on the twelfth). It includes accounts from the three survivors and statements from crewmen of the other aircraft.

2. 42nd Bombardment Squadron operations log for August 5, 1944.

3. Herman Scearce, from interviews with the author.

4. 42nd Bomb Squadron History, Sept. 1944, 7.

5. Ibid.

6. ADVON Journal, 2.

7. "WRFTF" stood for "We'd Rather Fuck Than Fight" though Cleveland, *Grey Geese Calling*, 133, indicates it was "We'd Rather Fun Than Fight." The aircraft's artist was certainly savvy enough to know that "Fuck" wouldn't be allowed, so he used an acronym instead. "We'd rather fuck than fight" is a line from a ribald soldier's song called "The Foreskin Fusiliers," the lyrics commonly modified to fit any unit.

8. 42nd Bomb Squadron History, Oct. 1944, 2.

9. Ibid., 5.

10. Ibid., 2.

11. Ibid., 5.

12. Ed Rosky, Bill Findle's son-in-law, from correspondence with the author, June and July, 2009.

13. "Flak Analysis and Evasive Action," *Bombardier's Information File*, March 1945, 8-5-4.

14. 42nd Bomb Squadron History, Nov. 1944, 4.

15. From National Archives photo 342-FH-3A-39594-65053-AC. The 42nd Squadron crest is also illustrated in *Grey Geese Calling*, 247, and described on page 433.

"Halfway to Forty" notes

1. Malcolm Macfarlane, *Bing Crosby Day by Day* (Lanham, MD: Scarecrow Press, 2001), 193–94.

2. "Seventh Air Force Tribute," Johnny Burke and Jimmy Van Heusen, sung by Bing Crosby with Crosby's introductory comments, Armed Forces Radio Service broadcast, air date unknown. The original record label is also unknown, but the song was reproduced in 1986 on Broadway Intermission Records, catalog number BR-138, from the radio broadcast recording.

3. Headquarters VII Bomber Command, Mission Report 11-25, October 31, 1944.

4. Details about MIKE missions come from a comprehensive December 1944 MIKE Mission Report in 42nd Bomb Squadron records.

5. Samuel Eliot Morison, *History of United States Naval Operations in World War II: Victory in the Pacific* (Urbana: University of Illinois Press, 2002), 10.

6. 42nd Bomb Squadron History, December 1944, 6.

7. Cleveland, *Grey Geese Calling*, 181–82.

8. 42nd Bomb Squadron History, December, 1944, 6–7.

9. Costello, *The Pacific War*, 526.

10. Richard F. Newcomb, *Iwo Jima* (New York: Bantam Books, 1965), 28.

11. Newcomb, *Iwo Jima*, 34; Morison, *Victory in the Pacific*, 9–10, describes the strategic shift from the suppression of bypassed islands to concentrate on bombardment of Iwo Jima.

12. Kumiko Kakehashi, *So Sad to Fall in Battle: An Account of War Based on General Tadamichi Kuribayashi's Letters from Iwo Jima* (New York: Ballantine Books, 2007), 99.

13. John W. Lambert, *The Pineapple Air Force: Pearl Harbor to Tokyo* (St. Paul, MN: Lambert, Phalanx Publishing, 1990), 96.

14. Newcomb, *Iwo Jima*, 42; Morison, Victory *in the Pacific*, 11.

15. Stephen M. Perrone, *World War II B24 Snoopers: Low Level Anti-Shipping Night Bombers* (Los Angeles: New Jersey Sportsmen's Guides, 2001). "Snooper" was the name originally given to low-altitude nighttime radar missions against Japanese shipping flown first by twenty-two 13th Air Force B-24s in the South Pacific in 1943. The term "snooper" quickly evolved to apply to night operations using radar bombing techniques.

16. Morison, *Victory in the Pacific*, 9–12.

17. 42nd Bomb Squadron History, December 1944, 8–9.

18. Kakehashi, *So Sad to Fall in Battle*, 92.

19. Ibid., 43.

20. Newcomb, *Iwo Jima*, 42.

21. Kakehashi, *So Sad to Fall in Battle*, 84.

22. 42nd Bomb Squadron History, December 1944, 9.

"January, 1945" notes

1. Chester Hearn, *Sorties into Hell: The Hidden War on Chichi Jima* (Guilford, CT: The Lyons Press, 2003), 164–65. Hearn indicates the crash occurred "in November or December 1944," an approximation from the post-war testimony of Fumio Kudo. The crash actually occurred January 22, 1945, and is confirmed Pratte's aircraft by the identification of clothing and letters belonging to William Farrell.

2. From Missing Air Crew Report dated January 24, 1945.

3. Hearn, *Sorties into Hell*, 164–65.

4. 42nd Bomb Squadron History, February 1945, 4.

5. 42nd Bombardment Squadron (H) Office of the Commanding Officer, Extract from Form 5 of Scearce, Lester H. Jr. dated February 21, 1945 (official strike mission record).

6. From Missing Air Crew Report dated January 26, 1945.

7. Hearn, *Sorties into Hell*, 164–65.

"Endings for Some" notes

1. Kakehashi, *So Sad to Fall in Battle*, 39–40.
2. Tarfu was GI slang for "Things are really fucked up," akin to Snafu: "Situation normal, all fucked up," and Fubar: "Fucked up beyond all recognition." Presumably Fubar was worse than Snafu or Tarfu.
3. 26th Bomb Squadron History, January 1945, 5.
4. Hq 7th Bomber Command Mission Report # 11-183.
5. 26th Bomb Squadron Office of the Intelligence Officer mission report 11-199, also Missing Air Crew Report dated February 9, 1945.
6. Cleveland, *Grey Geese Calling*, 91; Missing Air Crew Report 26th Bomb Squadron, dated February 9, 1945.
7. Mission details from Headquarters VII Bomber Command Mission Report #11-198, February 14, 1945.
8. Cleveland, *Grey Geese Calling*, 158, photo.
9. U.S. Air Force Fact Sheet, 26th Space Aggressor Squadron (as the 26th was later redesignated) prepared by Judy G. Endicott, Air Force Historical Research Agency, undated; also 26th Bomb Squadron History January 1945, 2.
10. Harry Gibbons, from correspondence with Bruce Curley, nephew of *Royal Flush* crewman Frank Curley, dated March 16, 1999 and online at www.pacificwrecks.com/aircraft/b-24/44-41465/gibbons.html.
11. Flak Analysis and Evasive Action." *Bombardier's Information File*, March 1945, 8-5-1.
12. Details of the loss of *Royal Flush* from 26th Bombardment Squadron, Office of the Intelligence Officer, Mission Report # 11-202, February 11, 1945, and the Missing Air Crew Report dated February 11, 1945. The Missing Air Crew Report contains the radio log which was edited here for clarity.
13. 26th Bomb Squadron History, January 1945, 12.
14. Headquarters Seventh Air Force, General Orders Number 57, May 1, 1945.
15. www.pacificwrecks.com/aircraft/b-24/44-41465/gibbons.html.
16. 26th Bomb Squadron History January, 1945, 5, 92.
17. Lambert, *The Pineapple Air Force*, 100.
18. Cleveland, *Grey Geese Calling*, 296–98.
19. 431st Bombardment Squadron Mission Report #11-201, February 12, 1945.
20. Cleveland, *Grey Geese Calling*, 298.
21. Ibid.; 431st Bomb Squadron History, February, 1945, 3.

22. Headquarters VII Bomber Command Mission Report # 11-203, February 16, 1945.

23. Headquarters VII Bomber Command Mission Report # 11-204, February 19, 1945.

Bibliography

Archives Consulted

Air Force Historical Research Agency, Maxwell Air Force Base, Alabama

National Archives and Records Administration, College Park, Maryland

Personal Interviews

Hess, Ed. Interview by author. Chicago, IL, January 4, 1998.

Yankus, Jack. Interview by author. Tempe, Arizona, November 3, 1998.

Lipe, Don. Interview by author. Columbiana, Ohio, December 5, 1998.

Lipe, Wayne. Interview by author. Columbiana, Ohio, December 5, 1998.

Lipe, Willis. Interview by author. Columbiana, Ohio, December 5, 1998.

Deasy, Joe. Interview by author. Boston, Massachusetts, June 11, 2005.

Pratte, Dorothy T. Interview by author. Providence, Rhode Island, June 1, 2009.

Books and articles

Alexander, Joseph H. *Utmost Savagery: The Three Days of Tarawa* . New York: Ivy Books, 1995.

Ambur, Arvid. "The Last Flight of Daisy Mae." *The Midway Mirror*, February 1993.

Aronowitz, Marguerite Madison. *Maternity Ward: Final Flight of a WWII Liberator*. Prescott, AZ: Pine Castle Books, 1998.

Bergerud, Eric M. *Fire in the Sky: The Air War in the South Pacific*. Boulder, CO: Westview Press, 2001.

Bowman, Martin W. *Consolidated B-24 Liberator (Crowood Aviation S.)*. Wiltshire, England: The Crowood Press, 1998.

Cameron, Rebecca Hancock. *Training to Fly: Military Flight Training, 1907-1945*. Washington, D.C.: GPO, 1999.

Cleveland, W. M., ed. *Grey Geese Calling*. Askov, MN: American Publishing Company, 1981.

Cohen, Stan. *V for Victory: America's Home Front During World War II*. Blacksburg, VA: Pictorial Histories Publishing Company, 1991.

Columbiana Ledger. "S. Sgt. Robert Lipe, Air Corp Gunner, Reported Missing." December 17, 1943.

Costello, John. *The Pacific War: 1941–1945*. New York: Harper Perennial, 1982.

Daws, Gavin. *Prisoners of the Japanese: POWs of World War II in the Pacific*. New York: William Morrow & Company, 1994.

Dorr, Robert. "Unsung Battle." *Marine Corp Times*, June 21, 2004.

Edgerton, Robert B. *Warriors of the Rising Sun: A History of The Japanese Military*. Boulder, CO: Westview Press, 1997.

Ellis, John. *World War II: A Statistical Survey*. New York: Facts on File, 1993.

Fagan, Vincent F. *Liberator Pilot: The Cottontails' Battle for Oil*. Blue Ridge Summit, PA: California Aero Press, 1992.

Flight Manual for B-24 Liberator. Appleton, WI: Aviation Publications, 1977.

Forman, Wallace. *B-24 Nose Art Name Directory*. North Branch, MN: Specialty Press, 1996.

Fuchida, Mitsuo, and Masatake Okumiya. *Midway: The Battle that Doomed Japan*. New York: Ballantine Books, 1958.

Getz, C. W. *The Wild Blue Yonder: Songs of the Air Force*. San Mateo, CA: The Redwood Press, 1981.

Gibbons, Harry, letter to Bruce Curley. "PACIFIC WRECKS - World War II Pacific." PACIFIC WRECKS - World War II Pacific. http://pacificwrecks.com (accessed August 8, 2005).

Greene, Charles. "Funafuti: Springboard of the Pacific." *Leatherneck Magazine*, August 1944.

Greene, Jack. *Midway Campaign.* Conshohocken, PA: Combined Books, 1995.

Haden, Jack. "Nauru: A Middle Ground During World War II." *Pacific Magazine*, April 3, 2000.

Haulman, Daniel L. *Hitting Home: The Air Offensive Against Japan.* Ann Arbor: University of Michigan, 1999.

Hearn, Chester G. *Sorties into Hell.* Guilford, CT: The Lyons Press, 2003.

Hess, William N. *Great American Bombers of World War II.* St. Paul, MN: MBI Publishing, 1998.

Jackson, Leona. "I Was on Guam." *The American Journal of Nursing,* November 1942.

Jane's Fighting Aircraft of World War II. New York: Gramercy, 1994.

Kakehashi, Kumiko. *So Sad to Fall in Battle: An Account of War Based on General Tadamichi Kuribayashi's Letters from Iwo Jima.* New York: Ballantine Books, 2007.

"Killed in Action." *Life* magazine, July 5, 1943.

Ladd, Fonnie Black. *The Wholesale Rescue.* Charleston, MS: Valley Farm Publications, 1986.

Lambert, John W. *Pineapple Air Force: Pearl Harbor to Tokyo.* St. Paul, MN: Phalanx Publishing Co., 1990.

Lee, Wright. *Not As Briefed: 445th Bombardment Group (H) Eighth Air Force: Memoirs of a B-24 Navigator/Prisoner of War 1943-1945.* Spartanburg, SC: Honoribus Press, 1996.

Lindbergh, Charles A. *The Wartime Journals of Charles A. Lindbergh.* New York: Harcourt Brace Jovanovich, 1970.

Livingstone, Bob. *Under the Southern Cross: The B-24 Liberator in the South Pacific.* Paducah, KY: Turner Publishing Company, 1998.

Macfarlane, Malcolm. *Bing Crosby: Day by Day*. Lanham, MD: The Scarecrow Press, Inc., 2001.

Major, Cat. *Myths of Guam*. 2nd ed. Guam, 1988.

Manchester, William Raymond. *Goodbye, Darkness: A Memoir of the Pacific War*. Boston: Little, Brown, 1980.

Marshall, S. L. A. *Island Victory: The Battle of Kwajalein Atoll (World War II)*. Toronto: Bison Books, 2001.

Mikesh, Robert. *Zero: Japan's Legendary Fighter*. Osceola, WI: Motorbooks International Warbird History, 1994.

Miller, Donald L. *Masters of the Air: America's Bomber Boys Who Fought the Air War Against Nazi Germany*. New York: Simon & Schuster, 2007.

Mish, Fredrich C., ed. *Langenscheidt's New College Merriam-Webster: English Dictionary*. Berlin: Langenscheidt Publishers, 1996.

Morison, Samuel Eliot. *History of United States Naval Operations in World War II. Vol. 7: Aleutians, Gilberts and Marshalls June 1942–April 1944*. Urbana: University of Illinois Press, 2002.

———. *History of United States Naval Operations in World War II. Vol. 8: New Guinea and the Marianas, June 1942–April 1944*. Urbana: University of Illinois Press, 2002.

———. *History of United States Naval Operations in World War II. Vol. 14: Victory in the Pacific, 1945*. Urbana: University of Illinois Press, 2002.

Newcomb, Richard F. *Iwo Jima*. New York: Bantam Books, 1965.

Norman, Thomas B., and Allen Polmar. *World War II: The Encyclopedia of the War Years, 1941-1945*. New York: Random House, 1996.

O'Neill, Brian D. *Half a Wing, Three Engines and a Prayer*. New York: McGraw-Hill Professional, 1998.

Parker, William Davis, and S. Sidney Ulmer. *Waist Gunner*. Bloomington, IN: Xlibris Corporation, 2000.

Peaslee, Budd J. *Heritage of Valor.* Philadelphia: J. B. Lippincott Company, 1963.

Perret, Geoffrey. *Winged Victory: The Army Air Forces in World War II.* New York: Random House, 1997.

Perrone, Stephen M. *World War II B-24 Snoopers: Low Level Anti-Shipping Night Bombers.* Los Angeles: New Jersey Sportsmen's Guides, 2001.

Prados, John. *The Combined Fleet Decoded.* New York: Random House, 1995.

Raithel, Albert L. Jr. "Patrol Aviation in the Pacific in WWII Part I." *Naval Aviation News*, Jul.–Aug. 1992.

Reilly, John C. Jr. "Organization of Naval Aviation in World War II." *Naval Aviation News*, May.–Jun. 1991.

"Religious Life During the Japanese Occupation." Guampedia. www. guampedia.com (accessed July 12, 2008).

Rickenbacker, Edward V. *Rickenbacker: An Autobiography.* New York: Prentice-Hall, 1967.

———. *Seven Came Through: Rickenbacker's Full Story - Including His Message to America.* Garden City, NY: Doubleday, Doran & Company, 1943.

Rottman, Gordon. *Japanese Pacific Island Defenses 1941–45 (Fortress).* Oxford, England: Osprey Publishing, 2003.

Russ, Martin. *Line of Departure: Tarawa.* New York: Doubleday, 1975.

Russell, James S. *The Pacific War Remembered: An Oral History Collection (Bluejacket Paperback Series).* Annapolis, MD: US Naval Institute Press, 1986.

Telavi, Melei. *Tuvalu: A History.* Tuvalu: Institute of Pacific Studies and Extension Services, University of the South Pacific, and The Tuvalu Ministry of Social Services, 1983.

Turner, Dave. *11th Bomb Group (H) The Grey Geese*. Paducah, KY: Turner Publishing Company, 1996.

"U.S. Planes Bomb Nauru." *Life* magazine, July 5, 1943.

van der Vat, Dan. *Pacific Campaign: The U.S.-Japanese Naval War 1941–1945*. New York: Simon & Schuster, 1991.

Welch, Jeanie M. "Without a Hangman, Without a Rope: Navy War Crimes Trials after World War II." *International Journal of Naval History* 1 (2002): not paginated.

Zamperini, Louis. *Devil at My Heels*. With Helen Itria. New York: E. P. Dutton & Co., 1956.

Index